Christian Theology in a Pluralistic Age

Christian Theology
in a Pluralistic Age

Edited by DAVID H. JENSEN

☙PICKWICK *Publications* · Eugene, Oregon

CHRISTIAN THEOLOGY IN A PLURALISTIC AGE

Copyright © 2024 Wipf and Stock Publishers. All rights reserved. Except for brief quotations in critical publications or reviews, no part of this book may be reproduced in any manner without prior written permission from the publisher. Write: Permissions, Wipf and Stock Publishers, 199 W. 8th Ave., Suite 3, Eugene, OR 97401.

Pickwick Publications
An Imprint of Wipf and Stock Publishers
199 W. 8th Ave., Suite 3
Eugene, OR 97401
www.wipfandstock.com

PAPERBACK ISBN: 978-1-6667-8481-7
HARDCOVER ISBN: 978-1-6667-8482-4
EBOOK ISBN: 978-1-6667-8483-1

Cataloguing-in-Publication data:

Names: Jensen, David H., editor.

Title: Christian theology in a pluralistic age / edited by David H. Jensen.

Description: Eugene, OR: Pickwick Publications, 2024. | Includes bibliographical references.

Identifiers: ISBN 978-1-6667-8481-7 (print). | ISBN 978-1-6667-8482-4 (print). | ISBN 978-1-6667-8483-1 (epub).

Subjects: LSCH: Theology. | Religious pluralism. | Comparative theology. | Christianity and other religions.

Classification: BR127 C25 2024 (print). | BR127 (epub).

For John Frierson, in memoriam

Contents

List of Contributors | ix

Introduction | xi

1
Learning About, From, With, and As the Other: A Prepositional Approach to Interreligious Engagement | 3
                              JOHN J. THATAMANIL

2
Religious Hybridity as Food for Comparative Theology | 19
                              CATHERINE CORNILLE

3
"All Under Heaven" and the City of God: A Familial and Ecclesial Reflection | 39
                              HYO-DONG LEE

4
Supper with the Lord: Comparative Liturgical Theological Reflection on Eucharist and Prasada | 61
                              MARTHA MOORE-KEISH

5
"Living Together the Length of Their Days": What Jewish Hesitancy About Interfaith Marriage Might Contribute to Reformed Theology | 80
                              DAVID H. JENSEN

6
Can Religion (Really) Work for the Common Good? | 99
MICHELLE VOSS

7
"A Small Intellectual Agora": Richard Kearney's Anatheism and the Inner Space to Engage Otherness | 120
HENK VAN DEN BOSCH

8
Neo-Levinas, Contra Milbank: Moral Realism Theory | 138
WILLIAM GREENWAY

9
Rendering the Secular Sacred: Protestant Military Chaplaincy in a Pluralistic Age | 161
DEBORAH VAN DEN BOSCH-HEIJ

Contributors

CATHERINE CORNILLE
Professor, Newton College Alumnae Chair of Western Culture,
Boston College

WILLIAM GREENWAY
Professor of Philosophical Theology,
Austin Presbyterian Theological Seminary

DAVID H. JENSEN
Professor, Clarence N. and Betty B. Frierson Distinguished Chair of
Reformed Theology,
Austin Presbyterian Theological Seminary

MARTHA L. MOORE-KEISH
J. B. Green Professor of Theology,
Columbia Theological Seminary

HYO-DONG LEE
Associate Professor of Comparative Theology,
Drew Theological School, Drew University

JOHN J. THATAMANIL
Professor of Theology and World Religions,
Union Theological Seminary, New York

HENK VAN DEN BOSCH
Centre for Professional and Spiritual Formation,
Protestant Theological University, the Netherlands;
Research Fellow, Department of Systematic Theology,
University of the Free State, Bloemfontein, South Africa

Contributors

DEBORAH VAN DEN BOSCH-HEIJ
Protestant Military Chaplain,
Armed Defense Forces, the Netherlands;
Research Fellow, Department of Historical and Constructive Theology,
University of the Free State, Bloemfontein, South Africa

MICHELLE VOSS
Professor of Theology,
Emmanuel College of Victoria University, University of Toronto

Introduction

CHRISTIANITY BEGAN IN A pluralistic milieu. Jesus of Nazareth gathered disciples in a renewal of Israel's faith and traditions, one of several first-century Jewish renewal movements. It was a time of great religious ferment among the covenant people, spawning parties as diverse as Pharisees, Essenes, and Zealots. The faith of Israel in those days was hardly uniform. Jesus directed his teaching primarily to the people Israel—teachings that corresponded closely to other Jewish movements of his day, but at other times existing in tension with those movements. Jesus' disciples were aware of this correspondence and conflict as they followed the One they called Rabbi. Early on, these disciples distinguished their movement from other currents of the day. But from its inception, the Jesus movement had to exist alongside other religious traditions. Articulating the convictions of this movement, thus, involved dialogue with others. At times, the dialogue became heated. The gospels indicate that some of this conflict contributed to Jesus' death.

Within a generation, Christianity spread to the Gentile world, primarily in urban areas of the Mediterranean basin. Here the context was more intensely pluralistic: Roman imperial cults, Hellenistic mystery religions, Greek philosophical movements, and local traditions contributed to a veritable bazaar of religious and philosophical traditions. The apostle Paul was acutely aware of this context. In the book of Acts, he cites Athenian poetry that describe God as the One in whom "we live and move and have our being" (Acts 17:28) as a prolegomenon to the Gospel. As the new faith took root in Mediterranean cities, the new converts negotiated their beliefs in the company of others. How did the new faith correspond to the earlier traditions that had formed them? How did it conflict? Pluralism, in short, played an indispensable role in the development of the early church. As the nascent Christian movement interacted other religious traditions, it

Introduction

incorporated, modified, and adapted them into its own theology, creeds, and liturgy.

Over several centuries, as Christianity became more firmly entrenched in European cultures, the pluralistic milieu began to fade. To be sure, there was much internal pluralism within Christianity: desert hermits, universities celebrating theology as the queen of the sciences, monastic reform efforts, crusading militants. But as Christianity became more established, dialogue, engagement, and appreciation of other traditions gradually decreased. The experience of Jews in Europe is illustrative of this diminished pluralism. In the many areas of Christian Europe where Jewish communities thrived, the Christian church saw their existence as a threat. Time and again, Christians expelled Jews from one region, forcing their migration to another. If persecuted Jews could not be converted, they had to leave, or, in worst cases, killed. Pogroms often displayed a Christian theological vengeance.

Over time, Christianity gradually suppressed its pluralistic inception. As it grew and flourished in areas that were overwhelmingly Christian, it engaged in less conversation with other traditions, and when it did engage, the conversation tended toward polemic. Recent history, however, has reversed some of these trends. Christianity's dramatic growth in the global South has compelled it to reckon with indigenous traditions that are decidedly non-Western. Mass migration has made many areas of the "Christian" North Atlantic more religiously diverse than ever. The most dramatic growth in religious demographics in North America are the non-affiliated, often described as the "nones and dones." Wherever the Christian church exists at present, it almost always must engage with other religious traditions, or traditions of secularity and non-affiliation. If Christianity began in a pluralistic milieu, it now exists in a context of radical pluralism.

The essays in this volume grapple with the question of how to think and write Christian theology in today's pluralistic age. The authors, Roman Catholic and Protestant, from North America and Europe, from seminary, university, and chaplaincy contexts, offer timely reflections on interfaith dialogue, religious diversity, trends of secularity and religious fundamentalism, and how all these realities affect Christian faith, doctrine, and the vocation of the theologian. Part 1, "Interfaith Learning and Belonging," asks broad questions of how to address religious diversity constructively. John Thatamanil offers a helpful typology of ways of engaging our religious neighbors—about, from, with, and as others—and how that engagement

Introduction

changes us. Catherine Cornille reflects on the perils and promise of religious hybridity—being claimed by multiple religious traditions—for the discipline of comparative theology. Part 2, "Comparative Theology," offers focused examples of Christian theologians offering thick readings of another religious tradition and how those readings affect theology itself. Hyo-Dong Lee draws on Confucian political thought and its understanding of families as resources for constructing Christian ecclesiology and political theology. Martha Moore-Keish offers liturgical reflections Hindu practices of Prasada and Reformed practices of Eucharist, exploring what these rituals surrounding food say about the divine and the human. My essay examines Conservative Jewish reservations about interfaith marriages and what these reservations might contribute to a renewed theology of marriage in Reformed Christian traditions. Part 3, "Otherness, Community, and the Common Good," gathers a diverse set of essays focused primarily on the topic of human flourishing in a pluralistic age. Michelle Voss asks the hard question of whether religion can be a force for the common good, given the rise of Christian nationalism. Henk van den Bosch offers a close reading of Richard Kearney's notion of *anatheism* as a resource for a productive engagement of otherness in these conflicted times. William Greenway offers an example of ethics for a pluralistic age by delving into the philosophy of Emmanuel Levinas and the notion of *agape* as resources for Moral Realism Theory. The volume concludes with Deborah van den Bosch-Heij's essay on Protestant military chaplaincy in the Netherlands, an intriguing case study of the secular and sacred.

This book project emerged from the Frierson Conference held on the Austin Seminary campus in April 2023. Over three beautiful Texas spring days, the authors engaged each other's work in conference rooms and over meals. The conversation was collaborative, energetic, collegial, and probing. The atmosphere provided a rich context for comparative theological work that has continued in many conversations since the conference. In addition to the writers of this volume, thanks are also due to Cynthia Rigby and John Sheveland, who offered thought-provoking presentations, timely questions, and unique perspectives to the gathering. An academic symposium is only as stimulating as its participants; this conference was extraordinary in its level of engagement. For that, I thank each author for saying "yes" to the invitation to travel to Austin.

The Frierson Conference is made possible by the generous gift of a faithful family with long ties to Austin Seminary, the Friersons. Two

Introduction

generations of this family have now served on the Seminary Board of Trustees. Nurtured in the congregation of First Presbyterian Church, Shreveport, Louisiana, the four Frierson brothers, Archer, John, Tannie, and Chris, along with their spouses, Ivy, Christie, Jennifer, and Paula, endowed the chair in Reformed theology that makes these conferences possible. This is now the second book to emerge out of such gatherings. More are surely to come. As I was putting the finishing touches on this book, John Frierson died after a valiant struggle with cancer. John was a model of Christian faith, kindness, humility, and hospitality; husband, father, and grandfather; an avid LSU football fan; a cotton farmer; a deacon, elder, and trustee of First Presbyterian Church. He valued theological education. This book is dedicated in memory of him.

PART I

Interfaith Learning and Belonging

1

Learning About, From, With, and As the Other

A Prepositional Approach to Interreligious Engagement

JOHN J. THATAMANIL

THIS PEDAGOGICAL ESSAY SEEKS to frame a "prepositional approach" to interreligious engagement and learning. It offers a rubric that emerged from teaching a successful seminary class; students in that class found this rubric to be a helpful framework with which to organize the distinct types of interreligious learning taken up in this course.[1] In what follows, I keep the seminary or divinity school classroom in view as the primary context for this chapter. Nonetheless, this approach might also be applicable to a variety of contexts including but not limited to church adult education programs.

The entirety of this essay presumes both a religiously committed stance and a disposition toward religious diversity as a positive good. By committed, I mean that this essay is for those who are existentially invested

---

1. I refer here to Union Theological Seminary's core course, "Introduction to Interreligious Engagement." Although the course was initially crafted by Paul Knitter and myself, in its current form, it bears the decisive stamp of my colleague Jerusha Rhodes. Although this prepositional framing is mine, the structure I discern in the course is most definitely hers. For that reason, I dedicate this essay to Jerusha Rhodes's brilliant and compelling teaching, although she should bear no blame for any shortcomings in my framing.

in the quest for religious truth. Much of the extant literature presumes that persons who care about religious truth are insiders to a particular tradition. As much interreligious work begins from within Christian tradition, it is customary to use the word "theology" or "theologian" to name the project to be undertaken. By contrast, I recognize that a religiously invested or committed seeker may not be a part of a particular religious tradition, Christian or otherwise. Persons interested in truth seeking learning, even in seminary classrooms, increasingly come from a variety of traditions or none at all. An invested seeker might be engaged, for example, in multiple religious participation (MRP) or even multiple religious belonging (MRB) or be Spiritual But Not Religious (SBNR). The project of interreligious learning can no longer take for granted models that assume singular religious belonging within one home tradition followed by the subsequent work of "crossing over" and "coming back" home. Hence, my use of the more neutral phrase of "religiously or existentially invested seeker."

The project also assumes and so does not defend a positive stance toward religious diversity. By positive stance, I mean that I take for granted herein that religious diversity is to be recognized as promise rather than problem, which is to say that it is good that religious diversity exists; it is a promise to be received and not a problem to be solved. This paper seeks to describe the work of interreligious learning and its permutations. It does not seek to defend the worth of the very project. As such, it is compatible with any theology of religious diversity that recognizes interreligious learning as possible, necessary, and religiously desirable.[2]

At the most rudimentary level, interreligious learning typically begins by learning *about* the other. Such learning can take a variety of forms but certainly includes exposure to texts including world religions textbooks, scriptures, and other forms of mediated information. A further step in the work of interreligious engagement is the move from learning about to learning *from*. Learning from can take a variety of expressions and includes interreligious dialogue, interreligious activism, and even comparative theology. Learning from begins the process of moving from forms of knowledge production that are typically considered objective, neutral, or

---

2. For my argument that even certain varieties of exclusivism and inclusivism leave the door open to the possibility of interreligious learning, see Thatamanil, *Circling the Elephant*, 41–107. Of course, I also argue therein that I find a "relational pluralism" to be the most satisfying option for a theology of religious diversity that makes maximal room for interreligious learning.

scientific to modes of learning in which the subjective experiences and meanings of religious traditions are encountered.

The next step in the prepositional journey is learning *with*. While some forms of learning from are dialogical, not all are. The comparative theologian who works with religious texts and commentarial traditions may not be in ongoing relationship with persons from other religious traditions. This is not the case in learning with. Learning with is explicitly dialogical. A paradigmatic form of learning with—perhaps most familiar to scholars, students, and even religious communities—is scriptural reasoning (SR). In SR, Jews, Muslims, and Christians (and the circle is constantly expanding) read carefully selected scriptures from their respective traditions in robust conversation with each other. Participants learn how persons from other traditions read scriptures: not just as such reading pertains to their own scriptures but also the scriptures of others. Each is exposed to and transformed by multiple styles of reading and meaning-making.

A final step on the prepositional journey is learning *as* the other learns. Learning as entails an extraordinary intimacy and, at its best, requires permission gained from the religious other. Learning as brings the religious neighbor into the concrete rituals and contemplative practices of the other. In "learning as" one might engage in deep apprenticeship with or under the other as in learning Zazen from a Zen master or participating in the worship rituals of other traditions. Learning as is the most robust and the most fraught form of interreligious learning—robust because one is not merely *informed about* but seeks to be *transformed by* the practices of others and fraught because done without reverence, respect, and permission, learning as can fall over into appropriation and a host of other risks including existential and theological disorientation. I will argue that each of these modes of prepositional learning has its place, power, promise, and peril. None are disposable. Each is vital and curricular thinking about interreligious engagement must attend to each of these forms of prepositional learning.

LEARNING ABOUT

Learning about, however rudimentary it might seem, cannot be bypassed. Interreligious encounter and learning require having basic, reliable, accurate and trustworthy information about a variety of religious communities. Of course, very practical questions arise immediately about limits and finitude: Which traditions ought to be studied? Who gets left out? Is learning about implicated in and even compromised by the limitations of "the world religions" model? How are we to balance breadth of coverage with depth of learning? How do we account for how knowledge about the other was produced in the first place? What assumptions about the other and about "religion" are built into what is to be learned? There are also vexing questions to be faced about the status of knowledge generated by religious studies scholars who are outsiders to the traditions being studied. How, for example, should we think about knowledge about Hindus generated by non-Hindus? While a comprehensive engagement with these questions is impossible within the limits of this brief essay, we can strive to make a judicious start.

A variety of approaches and goals are articulated for how to think well about the goals of "learning about." Perhaps the most widely recognized model aims for the goal of "religious literacy." In what follows, I will not offer a survey of this now considerable literature. Instead, I wish largely to affirm religious literacy as a salutary and worthwhile first step in interreligious learning. The term itself is most commonly associated with the work of Stephen Prothero.[3] Prothero not only commends religious literacy but teaches a model with which to begin to make comparative judgments that prevents beginning students from adopting a bias toward sameness—the reflexive affirmation that religions are all the same. To prevent such facile judgments, Prothero insists that the religions are really different; indeed, he insists that positing sameness is nothing less than "dangerous, disrespectful, and untrue."[4]

My intention here is not to offer an unqualified and full-throated endorsement of Prothero's insistence on difference. Both similarity and difference can only be discerned *after* comparison and not before. Moreover, entire religions cannot be compared; comparison requires selecting respects in which traditions can be judged to be similar or different. Similar in respect to what? Different with respect to what? Comparative judgments require time and learning. But, Prothero is surely right that a "pretend pluralism" is not the right starting point. To judge that religions are worth learning about requires positing that there are real differences that make such learning necessary. If we're all the same, what is there to learn and why?

3. Prothero, *Religious Literacy*.
4. Prothero, *God Is Not One*, 2.

Learning About, From, With, and As the Other

How to appreciate real and substantial differences between traditions? Prothero commends that learners begin by recognizing that religious traditions do not even engage the same problem. He writes:

> At the heart of this project is a simple, four-part approach to the religions, which I have been using for years in the classroom and at lectures around the world. Each religion articulates: a *problem*; a *solution* to this problem, which also serves as the religious goal; a *technique* (or techniques) for moving from this problem to this solution; and an *exemplar* (or exemplars) who chart this path from problem to solution.[5]

Prothero's model offers a helpful structure for learning and even for beginning comparison. Some such structure enables students to begin learning and comparison. Students quickly realize that Prothero's model works better with some traditions than others. In this way, the work of comparison tutors students about the limitations brought to comparative work.

My similar fourfold model is borrowed from the Buddha's Four Noble Truths.[6] Generalizing and extending from Buddhist traditions, I urge my students to ask, How does a given text, thinker, or strand of a tradition (1) diagnose the human predicament; (2) offer an etiology for that predicament; (3) specify a prognosis; and (4) commend a therapy.[7] When commending my particular heuristic, I take care to insist that religious traditions are not constituted by internal agreement on these matters. One cannot speak—without a level of generalization that is sure to gloss over internal diversity—about how an entire tradition approaches these matters. Traditions are constituted as much if not more so by their *arguments* about these matters than their *agreements*.

While religious literacy ought to be as wide-ranging as time and one's own limitations permit, it is worth recognizing that many of the standard approaches, particularly in classrooms, is restricted to the "world religions" model. Among the most commonly taught traditions are Hinduism,

---

5. Prothero, *God Is Not One*, 14.

6. On my use of this model, see Thatamanil, *Immanent Divine*. In this book, I do not compare traditions but two theologians, one Hindu and one Christian, who both understand God as "being-itself."

7. To see how I use this structure to compare the thinking of the Hindu theologian Sankara with the German-American theologian Paul Tillich, see my *Immanent Divine*. As with Prothero, I, too, came to this model because it proved to be a compelling heuristic for teaching.

Buddhism, Judaism, and Islam.[8] There are many obvious limitations to this model, most notably that this framework largely ignores Indigenous traditions. The global presence of Indigenous traditions and the interaction of those traditions and communities with the so-called "world religions" can go largely unseen. Learning about will need to think about this crucial structural limitation in many of our pedagogies, particularly in a time when Indigenous traditions across the planet are experiencing both acute threat and profound resurgence.

Moreover, this model tends to vastly exaggerate the degree of difference between "religions" and the degree of similarity within them. What would thinkers within traditions have to argue about if they agreed about these matters? Many other problems plague the world religions model including the very notion that the various traditions would recognize themselves as "religions," which all too routinely presupposes that traditions accede to the religious-secular binary—a bifurcation that assumes something like a stable configuration only in European modernity. Productive learning about religious traditions—a term I much prefer to "religions"—requires teaching students about the varying degrees to which traditions and their adherents are even prepared to recognize themselves as religions, world religions or otherwise.[9]

LEARNING FROM

Recognizing that traditions do not all recognize themselves to be "religions" already signals a noteworthy if subtle transition from "learning about" to "learning from." A significant cognitive shift transpires when students begin to recognize, for example, that a great many Jews are uncomfortable with being classified as members of a "religion" called Judaism.[10] Students who are exposed to Hindus who insist that "Hinduism is not a religion but a way of life," also begin to recognize there is considerable ambiguity if not outright error in assuming that Hinduism, Buddhism, Judaism, and Christianity are specific instantiations of the same genus. An approach to learning that is limited to "learning about" may never come around to such

---

8. These were the traditions taught in my class.
9. Thatamanil, "How Not to Be a Religion."
10. See, for example, Batnitzky, *How Judaism Became a Religion*. This book shows just how very recently some Jews came to regard Judaism as a religion and how that descriptor was immediately contested.

insights. Approaches to learning about too wedded to a "world religions" model might never move to the kinds of learning that call that model into question.

Learning from can and routinely does interrupt the inherited and imposed categories routinely deployed in most standard textbook approaches to learning about. How else to check representations against those being represented? How else to grant voice and agency to those being represented? How else to ask, "Are the categories scholars deploy to depict persons from other traditions recognizable to those being depicted?" Learning from in all its modes begins to level the playing field between those who represent and those who are represented. The asymmetries of power at play in who has the authority and credentials to represent another are easily overlooked and routinely ignored so long as learning is restricted only to the single register of learning about.

Hence the need and urgency to move from taking about to learning from. Learning from begins to instantiate a measure of parity between learners, a parity that is more fully actualized when learning from becomes learning with. The boundary lines between the two latter modalities of learning are porous and fluid, but for the sake of relative clarity, let us recognize that it is both logically and factually possible to learn *from* another without learning *with* and alongside them. Consider, for example, comparative theologians who seek to learn deeply from a careful reading of the scriptures and theological texts of another tradition but who neither have time nor opportunity to read those texts with persons from another tradition. A Christian theologian might spend years learning the languages and exegetical methods of Hindu traditions and even take those texts to be truth-bearing without being in sustained interpersonal conversation with Hindus. Indeed, until the Immigration and Nationality Act of 1965 made large scale immigration from India to the US possible, US based theologians did not have ready access to Hindu communities, at least not without traveling to India. Hence, learning *from* other traditions was relatively accessible whereas learning *with* was not, at least not without considerable difficulty. Even today, students outside metropolitan areas will find it easier to access texts written by Hindus than to gain access to Hindu communities themselves.

Learning from can, in the first instance, begin with serious engagements with insider depictions of their own traditions. Whereas world religions textbooks were once written by scholars who maintained postures of neutrality and objectivity, it is now possible (although still not commonplace) to read, for example, textbooks about Hinduism written by Hindus themselves. In my own recent teaching experience, a primary textbook contained engagements between both outsider and insider perspectives on the same traditions. Pim Valkenberg's *World Religions in Dialogue: A Comparative Theological Approach* stages conversations between outsiders and insiders across a variety of traditions.[11] By engaging texts such as this one, students and their teachers make a vital shift from learning about to learning from.

Critically, texts such as this one can also introduce students to the value of both insider and outsider perspectives, particularly when outsiders in question are existentially invested readers. This valorizing of comparative theological interest, however, need not fall prey to a dismissal of critical religious studies scholarship. A commitment to learning from need in no way entail a dismissal of outsider perspectives, even perspectives from scholars who are not normatively inclined. Part of what students at both the undergraduate, graduate, and seminary levels must learn is an appreciation for a multiplicity of perspectives. Consider, for example, the disruptive institutional and national political consequences of the controversy at Hamline University generated when Muslim students protested a professor's respectful display of a fourteenth-century visual image of the Prophet Muhammad. The summary dismissal of adjunct art history professor, Erika López Prater, a clear violation of academic freedom, triggered a firestorm that eventually led to the resignation of Hamline's president. Characterizing Prater as Islamophobic—a claim that Hamline subsequently retracted—Hamline University administrators chose to prioritize Muslim student complaints over the claims of academic freedom. The trouble is that administrators did not consult any religious studies scholars of Islam prior to making their decision.

Such religious studies scholars who have knowledge of Islamic traditions in global diversity and historical depth could have informed both Hamline's Muslim students and university administrators that Muslim communities across history have held a wide range of perspectives on the question of figural depictions of Muhammad. To privilege a *particular* Muslim perspective and have it stand in for *the* Muslim perspective as such was an avoidable and regrettable error.

---

11. Valkenberg, *World Religions in Dialogue*.

Learning About, From, With, and As the Other

I rehearse this episode to signal that honoring insider perspectives and creating conditions for "learning from" religious others in no way requires marginalizing or sidelining descriptive religious studies scholarship from scholars who hold no religious commitment. Students need sophisticated multisided introductions to religious traditions and to the complexities of knowledge production including the political entanglements always at play in the generation of knowledge. A variety of perspectives matter and must be honored rather than a simplistic claim that learning from must now supersede or replace learning about. Nothing about this prepositional approach entails a reductive claim that only knowledge generated by insiders is trustworthy. Insider perspectives, as the Hamline controversy demonstrates, can have their own limitations too. Put simply, multiplicity matters.

LEARNING WITH

When "learning from" becomes interpersonal, students move into "learning with." Here, the dynamics of the learning process are distinct and marked by a greater degree of intimacy. The skills and dispositions needed to engage in such learning, therefore, are not the same and require cultivation both in the classroom and outside it. Several of the major forms of learning with include formal and informal interreligious dialogue, classroom visits by insider experts from various traditions, site visits to the religious institutions such as masjids, synagogues, temples, and churches, and scriptural reasoning among others.

As the classroom itself becomes robustly interreligious—as is the case here at Union Theological Seminary—elements of "learning with" are present in the whole of the learning process. When Jewish students are present in small group discussions of the assigned textbook readings about Judaism, non-Jewish students can begin to ask their Jewish peers questions about accuracy of representation, internal diversity within Judaism, and turn to their peers to help them prepare appropriately for site visits to the synagogue. The presence of a Buddhism and Interreligious Dialogue Program at Union also makes sustained Buddhist-Christian engagement possible both inside and outside the classroom. As this kind of interreligious pedagogical situation is relatively new, teachers are themselves necessarily new to the work of thinking through how to maximize the promise of such diversity in the classroom.[12]

12. A practice initiated by my colleague Jerusha Rhodes has promise and works well,

PART I | INTERFAITH LEARNING AND BELONGING

The most robust form of "learning with" practiced in my classroom was scriptural reasoning (SR).[13] Students were introduced and guided into the discipline of scriptural reasoning by a visiting professor from Jewish Theological Seminary, Benjamin Kamine. Students were prepared for Kamine's 3 hour classroom visit by reading some basic foundational material on what SR is, its history, and its hopes and aspirations. Readers of this chapter will know that SR brings together persons from Abrahamic traditions to read brief and focused selections from Jewish, Christian, and Islamic traditions. Often these texts are from each other's scriptures. More recently, the ambit of SR is moving beyond Abrahamic traditions. Our class included Buddhist selections as well. Students are given brief introductions to each text by insiders, but these insiders are not meant to play the role of comprehensive experts, particularly inasmuch as claims to expertise run the risk of shutting down encounter between persons and the texts. Instead, their function is to begin the work of encounter, be available to answer questions as they arise, and then to be one reader among others.

The goals of SR are multiple but include cultivating friendship across religious communities and learning to learn with and alongside each other. Texts and readers become interlaced and new readerly communities emerge, communities whose accumulated history of shared reading generate new reading practices, new practices of being interreligious community together, and a deeper appreciation of each other's scriptures and reading traditions. The building of such community is a work of mutual hospitality and can have in view a variety of ends including interreligious peace building.

For my students, no other classroom experience was met with a measure of greater delight and enthusiasm. Several students announced their intention either to form or to join other SR communities so that the practices of shared reading and learning might be sustained over time.

---

when possible: constitute interreligious discussion groups and keep those groups in place for the entire semester. Rhodes rightly believes in the promise of cultivating sustained relationships that generates trust and, in turn, increases the likelihood of deep and vulnerable conversations.

13. Because the literature on SR is now voluminous, commending any particular book or article on the subject is likely to be smack of arbitrariness. Nonetheless, one good resource is Higton, "Scriptural Reasoning." The virtue of this particular piece is that it explicitly compares scriptural reasoning along with comparative theology, two distinct modes of interreligious learning. For SR that moves well beyond the Abraham milieu and includes Confucianism, Taoism, and Buddhism, see Huawei et al., "Scriptural Reasoning."

Learning About, From, With, and As the Other

The promise of learning how to read the scriptures of others in their company and then invite those others to read one's own scriptures proved to be powerfully transformative. The freshness of seeing one's texts anew as read by others who put unanticipated questions both to the texts and its readers was experienced as invigorating. Students sensed that the sustained practice of SR made possible new forms of reading and interreligious community formation. They understood and deeply appreciated the particular joy of this modality of learning from.

LEARNING AS

Scriptural reasoning stands also at the doorway of "learning as." By watching and learning from how Jews and Muslims read their scriptures, Christians begin move from learning from to learning as. Other habits of text reading begin to become their own, and a new step in interreligious learning unfolds.

The labor of "learning as" is marked by the greatest degree of intimacy with co-learners from traditions that are not one's own because in "learning as" persons are learning to see and read the world through the specific religious disciplines and practices of others. Perhaps the most widely known form of "learning as" is the work of learning to take up the contemplative practices of others. Christians, monastics or lay, who take up Zazen under the guidance of a Zen master are engaged in "learning as." Learning as most often calls to mind such examples of contemplative "cross-training," to borrow an athletic metaphor. But the variety of forms that "learning as" can take are many and inexhaustible.

How might we define "learning as" precisely? Let us lay out some terms and work our way toward a definition. In other writing, I have insisted that to be religious is to seek "comprehensive qualitative orientation."[14] Comprehensive qualitative orientation is the work of answering the question, "What is it like to be here?" where here is understood on the broadest imaginable scale. What kind of world is this, and what is it like? Is it safe, dangerous, unstable and in constant flux, or the beautiful creation of a loving divine? The religious project—whether carried out inside religious traditions or not—is a work of tutoring desire to bring desire into right accord with the qualitative character of what there is.

---

14. Thatamanil, *Circling the Elephant*, 152–92.

Part I | Interfaith Learning and Belonging

As such, religiousness is a work of erotics. It sets out to answer the question, "What is worthy of desiring given the kind of world we inhabit?" That is to say, the work of religiousness is the work of *truing desire*. Refusing a bifurcation between knowing and desiring, to be religious is to bring one's desiring into right accord with the shape of the world as rightly discerned.

To do this work, religious traditions must offer (1) interpretations of the world and (2) practices by which bodies, individual and social, are molded so as to come into proper comportment with the world as interpreted. Traditions offer world pictures by developing (1) "interpretative schemes" using their very extended and historically deep repertoires of myths, symbols, narratives, sophisticated metaphysical accounts, and much else besides. But traditions also contain (2) "therapeutic regimes," by which persons are brought into right attunement with the world as described by a given interpretive scheme.

No tradition is an interpretive scheme. Persons within a tradition—often its intellectual elite but not exclusively—shape interpretive schemes out of the raw materials found within a tradition's vast and constantly shifting repertoire. There are considerable debates and arguments within traditions because thinkers within them do not agree about how to use their repertoires, what materials to prioritize, or what materials should even be included within a tradition's repertoire. Moreover, that repertoire is constantly undergoing historical development and transformation. To understand a tradition in a sophisticated way is to understand the patterns of interpretive scheme development within a tradition. How do thinkers within a tradition go about developing such schemes? What counts as persuasive? By what criteria?

Much interreligious learning is restricted to learning about, from, and with a tradition about its interpretive schemes. But in the work of "learning as," learners take up the therapeutic regimes of a tradition other than their own. This is the distinctive marker of learning as. Persons engaged in learning as are now learning as others learn, and this in several respects. To avoid generalizations, let us consider a specific case. A Christian who takes up Zazen is learning to see as the other sees by taking up the embodied learning practices of Zen Buddhists. The Christian's body-mind complex is being tutored to sit, attend, and be disciplined in, more or less, the same ways as the Buddhist practitioner. Of course, the "more or less" matters. If the Christian is admitted to a Zen monastery and is included in the daily rhythms of work and practice of the insider, then it will prove impossible to discern how their respective practices differ. By contrast, the Christian who listens along to a Zen practice podcast is also engaged in the work of "learning as" albeit in a considerably attenuated manner when compared to the monastery resident.

But attenuated or not, the work of learning as matters and offers access to dimensions of religious life that are otherwise inaccessible. In my recent class, students were required to take up some element of the therapeutic regimes of the tradition then under study. Thus, when studying Judaism, all students were required to practice keeping Shabbat, to some appropriate and doable degree. Given the pressures of student life, the instructional team recognized that not doing any work at all for the whole of a Shabbat period from, sundown to sundown, may prove to be impossible for some. Hence, students were encouraged to pick a substantial portion of a weekend and engage in some modified sabbath practice after having engaged in some reading about the meaning of Shabbat. Students were also required to journal (briefly) about their practice after the practice period was completed. For students, this exercise—even in its curtailed form—proved to be an illuminating and even transformative experience. Students were particularly struck by how much advance planning (and this even without the work of preparing for a Shabbat meal) is required to make deliberate rest possible. Students also noted the difference between intentional sabbath rest and the kind of distracted social media connected leisure time that many fall into which proves neither restful nor restorative. Most significantly, students were introduced to something of the quotidian rhythm of weekly Jewish life and the variety of ways in which Shabbat is observed.

Even this small example should suffice to intimate that carefully circumscribed and responsible "learning as"—particularly with competent insider guidance—can take place within the life of a single course. Meanwhile, "learning as" is increasingly becoming a feature of interreligious encounter and engagement as persons increasingly understand themselves as committed to multiple religious participation (MRP) or even multiple religious belonging (MRB).[15] In all these cases, interreligious learning makes the shift from modes of learning restricted to understanding what persons from other traditions *believe or maintain* to what persons from other traditions actually *do*. That transition marks a considerable shift from largely conceptual modes of knowing to knowing through bodily comportment.

---

15. On the meaning of these terms and their uses, see Thatamanil, "Eucharist Upstairs."

Given that a variety of traditions are not belief-centric, this shift marks a critical and long overdue turn in the work of interreligious learning.

Nonetheless, complications also abound. When does "learning as" risk falling into appropriation? Are there specific practices within a tradition that require insider status before those practices can be taught and transmitted? A wide-ranging literature is emerging to tackle these questions, and nuanced engagement with them is underway.[16] The implications of that research will take some time to metabolize, but there is every reason to believe that this research will show us that these knotty complications do not bar the way to "learning as."[17] One basic ethical parameter might entail borrowing a motto from the disability community: "Nothing about us without us." Suitably modified, we might affirm, "Take nothing from us without us," or put otherwise "Learning as must not be severed from learning with." The borrowing of practices apart from ongoing relationship with the communities in which those practices are maintained and cultivated is a risky proposition, particularly when deep asymmetries of power exist between those who borrow and those from whom practices are borrowed. Grave ethical hazards must be confronted, but they need not prove fatal to the work of "learning as."

A CONCLUDING NOTE ON TWO OTHER PREPOSITIONS: THROUGH AND FOR

Interreligious learning, both in and out of the classroom, marks a new stage in the encounter between traditions. The goal for encounter between traditions is no longer limited to mere tolerance or even peaceability—although clearly even those goals remain very much incomplete. But now, persons and communities are entertaining more fulsome possibilities for interreligious engagement. We can learn more about each other, from each other, with each other, and even learn as the other learns.

---

16. See, most especially, Bucar, *Stealing My Religion*.

17. Our classroom practice also raised critical questions. During the Islam unit, all students were required to engage in *salat*, the daily practice of Muslim prayer. While most students found the experience powerful and even transformative, questions were raised about the appropriateness of doing salat by non-Muslims who cannot possibly affirm the *shahadah*, "There is no God but God and Muhammad is the Messenger of God." And well that the question should be raised because it generated vigorous conversation about the limitations of "learning as." Why does it seem easier for Christians, say, to learn as Buddhists than as Muslims?

Learning About, From, With, and As the Other

Just what will we learn, and what will this learning make possible? Ultimately, these multiple modalities of learning, particularly learning as, hold out the possibility that persons across religious traditions might actually learn more about ultimate reality from the resources of our many traditions. This raises to view two other prepositions, namely "through" and "for." Every form of interreligious learning raises the possibility that as we learn from, with, and even as others, we might be prompted to think *through* what we learn in such depth that our antecedent religious perspectives and commitments may be revised and even transformed. When we do so, disciplines and modes of learning such as scriptural reasoning and comparative theology will begin to move into what contemporary Christian theologians call "constructive theology."

Still more, because *how* we learn not just *what* we learn is transformed, even the character of constructive theology itself might be transformed. Much Christian theology in the contemporary period understands theology as a specialized mode of academic knowledge production. But theology's analogs in other traditions do not prioritize the production of academic texts but instead cherish gnosis or wisdom. Insofar as religious learners take up the thick practices and disciplines of others, what emerges may not be standard academic theology but instead genuine interreligious wisdom, the capacity to see the world through more than one set of religious lenses and then integrate and synthesize what is seen thereby.[18] This would give new meaning to what it means to think through what we have learned.

If theological speaking and writing moves in the direction of interreligious wisdom, we can well expect that the audience and readership of such learning—who such learning is *for*—will also be transformed. Interreligious wisdom will surely be of broader appeal than to scholarly communities alone. Indeed, the very quest for interreligious wisdom might generate a new and broader community of inquiry including persons committed to multiple religious participation, the Spiritual But Not Religious, and any aspirant to wisdom within our various traditions. In an age facing multiple cascading crises, we may come to understand that interreligious wisdom is neither optional nor a luxury for the few but instead a widely desired good for all seek to mend the heart and mend the world.

---

18. For more on "interreligious wisdom," see Thatamanil, "Integrating Vision."

BIBLIOGRAPHY

Batnitzky, Leora. *How Judaism Became a Religion: An Introduction to Modern Jewish Thought*. Princeton: Princeton University Press, 2013.

Bucar, Liz. *Stealing My Religion: Not Just Any Cultural Appropriation*. Cambridge: Harvard University Press, 2022.

Higton, Mike. "Scriptural Reasoning and the Discipline of Christian Doctrine." *Modern Theology* 29.4 (2013) 120–37.

Huawei, Li, et al. "Scriptural Reasoning as a Method of Interreligious Dialogue in China." *International Review of Mission* 108.2 (2019) 415–29.

Prothero, Stephen. *God Is Not One: The Eight Rival Religions that Run the World—and Why Their Differences Matter*. New York: HarperOne, 2010.

———. *Religious Literacy: What Every American Needs to Know—And Doesn't*. New York: Harper One, 2009.

Thatamanil, John J. *Circling the Elephant: A Comparative Theology of Religious Diversity*. New York: Fordham University Press, 2020.

———. "How Not to Be a Religion: Genealogy, Identity, Wonder." In *Common Goods: Economy, Ecology, and Political Theology*, edited by Melanie Johnson-DeBaufre et al., 54–72. New York: Fordham University Press, 2015.

———. *The Immanent Divine: God, Creation, and the Human Predicament—An East-West Conversation*. Minneapolis: Fortress, 2006.

———. "Integrating Vision: Comparative Theology as the Quest for Interreligious Wisdom." In *Critical Perspectives on Interreligious Education*, edited by Najeeba Syeed and Heidi Hadsell, 100–124. Currents of Encounter 83. Leiden: Brill, 2020.

Valkenberg, Pim, ed. *World Religions in Dialogue, Enhanced Edition: A Comparative Theological Approach*. Winona, MN: Anselm Academic, 2017.

2

Religious Hybridity as Food for Comparative Theology

CATHERINE CORNILLE

THE THEOLOGIAN WHO ENGAGES other religious traditions or the reality of religious plurality inevitably often finds herself straddling the borders between religions, identifying to some extent or on some matters of belief and practice with more than one religion. The desire to study another religion generally arises from an initial fascination with certain teachings or practices, and the deepening understanding of another tradition may lead to an even greater affinity. Identification with elements from different religious traditions has come to be captured under different names: multiple religious belonging, multiple religious participation, spiritual fluidity, religious hybridity, etc. These terms indicate little more than a general appeal of more than one religion. They say little about the kind and degree of identification with more than one tradition, or about the way this is negotiated in any particular case.

The term religious hybridity is broad and may be used to cover various types and degrees of hybridity. I have made a distinction between voluntary and involuntary, permanent and temporary, and partial and full religious hybridity. The former distinguishes the types of hybridity that are given by birth in a particular culture (Chinese, Japanese) or family (where parents belong to different religions), from the kind that is freely embraced. The second distinguishes the types of hybridity that are assumed in types of crisis, when one resorts to any potential source of help until the crisis subsides, from those that form a more permanent part of one's identity.

Part I | Interfaith Learning and Belonging

The third distinguishes forms of hybridity in which one religion remains dominant and the norm for integration of elements from another tradition, from those in which there is no longer any clear or consistent normative tradition. Another kind of religious hybridity, a mixture of voluntary and involuntary, involves belonging to a particular culture, shaped by a certain religious tradition or traditions, and belonging to a religion which is not limited to a certain culture. Here too one religion may color the other, with one or the other being dominant.[1]

Just as there are different kinds and degrees of hybridity, there are different approaches to comparative theology. The main difference lies in the degree to which a comparative theologian identifies with more than one religion. Some may identify with elements from various religious traditions without predominantly identifying with any particular religion. It tends to lead to what I have called meta-confessional comparative theology,[2] or what Wesley Wildman, one of the proponents of this approach, describes it as a "postreligious theology, or nonreligious theology, that is, theology that makes intellectual sense with no specific religious tradition at its root and remains socially viable with no living tradition for support."[3] But religious hybridity may also take the form of partial identification with elements of another religious tradition while remaining committed to a particular religion. Here, one tradition thus remains dominant, and the norm for selectively integrating elements of another tradition. This partial religious hybridity characterizes the confessional approach to comparative theology.

In my own past work, I have reflected critically on the phenomenon of religious hybridity, questioning its coherence and consequences from the perspective of the inner dynamics of religious identity and belonging.[4] However, religious hybridity also offers much food for theological reflection. We will here thus focus on the various ways in which identification with more than one religion may inform and nourish comparative theology. It is clear that theology, as the systematic reflection on religious teachings, does not play the same role in different religious traditions. My own reflections will be mainly informed by my involvement in Buddhist-Christian

---

1. Albertus Bagus Laksana discusses this form of hybridity in Laksana, "Being Theological."

2. Cornille, *Meaning and Method*, 25–30.

3. Wildman, "Theology Without Walls," 247.

4. See Cornille, *Many Mansions*; "Double Religious Belonging"; "Mehrere Meister"; "Multiple Religious Belonging"; "Strategies of Negotiation"; and "Religious Hybridity and Christian Identity."

Religious Hybridity as Food for Comparative Theology

and Hindu-Christian comparative theology. But I hope they will have some relevance for the way any religion is involved in constructive engagement with other religious traditions, whether on the level of doctrine, practice, or various aspects of material culture.

THE THREAT OF RELIGIOUS HYBRIDITY

While there has been much discussion about the existence of bounded religious traditions, and about the fluidity of borders, the very term "religious hybridity" may be seen to presume the existence of religious traditions whose ideas and practices are hybridized. The term is at times also used to refer more broadly to the fact that personal identities are configured on the basis of various types of identification or affiliation, each affecting the others. Jeannine Hill Fletcher, for example, states:

> In history and today, Christian identities are always "Hybrid," that is, they are created by intersecting with other categories of identity. In any group of Christians--from local congregations to a global community--the collective will reflect a diversity. The category "Christian" itself is not homogenous. The hybrid identity of each member produces a religious community of infinite internal diversity. Theorists might say that the category "Christian" is not a solid totality but a category made up of multiplicity and fragmentation.[5]

She refers in particular to the realities of gender, profession, and generation as all forming part of one's hybrid identity. While these forms of hybridity indeed account for the internal diversity within religions, they do not in themselves present a challenge or a threat to religious traditions. It is only when elements from different religions, different traditions of faith and practice, each claiming ultimacy, are combined that religious hybridity may become a threat.

Even though every religious tradition develops through a process of integrating and reinterpreting elements from different religious traditions, the conscious or deliberate identification with elements from other religions is generally considered problematic by religious traditions[6] and denounced

---

5. Fletcher, *Monopoly*, 89.
6. When referring to "religious tradition," I use it as a shorthand to connote the official representatives of a tradition, or the normative line of thinking within a religious tradition. It is based on an internal logic of religious identity and the self-understanding

as "syncretism." Though the term syncretism may be used purely descriptively to refer to "the temporary ambiguous coexistence of elements from diverse religions and other contexts within a coherent religious pattern,"[7] it has generally acquired negative connotations within religious traditions as the illegitimate combination of irreconcilable elements.

To some extent religious hybridity does involve a certain degree of syncretism, whether considered as a purely descriptive or a normative category. As religious teachings and practices are embedded in differing and often mutually conflicting religious claims, their combination inevitably raises questions about compatibility. This may involve the compatibility of beliefs, as well as the com-possibility of practices.[8] For most religious hybrids, logical consistency is less important than practical efficacy or experiential meaningfulness. And religious hybrids also tend to often interpret the integrated elements in their own terms, thus developing their own sense of logic and consistency. However, from the perspective of religious traditions, the introduction of elements foreign to an existing system of thought and practice is thus generally regarded as a threat to the internal coherence of the system.

The experience of religious hybridity challenges the sense of wholeness and self-sufficiency of any particular religion. Most religious traditions and theological systems claim to be self-contained and to provide answers to all important religious questions and needs. While there may be evidence of development and change over time, these become absorbed and explained from within the system. The very inclination to draw from other religions suggests that certain religious or spiritual desires or needs remain unfulfilled, thus questioning religious claims to ultimate truth and comprehensiveness in matters of belief and practice.

Religious hybridity also tends to weaken religious commitment. As elements of truth and value are found outside of a particular religion, the need to accept and surrender to all the teachings of a particular religion is no longer felt. This threatens the continuity and the continued vitality of a tradition. In *Losing our Religion*, Christel Manning suggests that parents with weak or multiple religious affiliations tend to let their children sample different traditions and follow them in their choice, rather than predetermining their religious path. Insofar as the message is that no religion fulfills

---

of religions.

7. Pye, "Syncretism and Ambiguity," 93.
8. Griffiths, *Problems of Religious Diversity*, 32–36.

all religious needs and desires, there is less chance that hybrid parents, or their children will come to strongly identify with a particular religion or contribute to its vitality and continuity.[9]

Religious hybridity is thus generally based on a sense of religious autonomy and freedom in determining one's religious identity. This clashes with most religious understanding of their authority as derived from a divine source which commands complete obedience and surrender of the individual. Such surrender may at times be seen (and has been at times abused) as a way to control the lives of believers and to prevent them from exploring other religious options. But it is also in accord with the way in which religious traditions associate spiritual progress with the overcoming of one's ego and evil through a complete abandonment to a divine authority or heteronomy, and through the surrender to a particular spiritual path and discipline. Here, religious hybridity may be seen as an impediment to spiritual development.

All of this, combined with the endless diversity and unmanageability of experiences of religious hybridity may explain the reservation and the suspicion of religious traditions toward the phenomenon of religious hybridity.[10]

THE RELIGIOUS HYBRIDITY OF THE COMPARATIVE THEOLOGIAN

The choice to do theology in constructive dialogue with another religious tradition places considerable demands on a theologian. In addition to being thoroughly versed in their own theological tradition, the comparative theologian must also study the languages, history, texts, and rituals of another religious tradition. The motivation for such effort generally arises from a personal fascination with or appeal of certain elements in another religion. To be sure, the in-depth study of another religion may also come from the desire to refute its teachings and to establish the superiority of one's own tradition. And apologetics also forms an integral part of comparative theology. But as the modern discipline of comparative theology has come to distinguish itself from prior iterations of the same name through its positive

---

9. Manning, *Losing Our Religion*, 162–79.

10. For more on religious attitudes toward religious hybridity, see D'Costa and Thompson, *Buddhist-Christian Dual Belonging*; Soars and Pohran, *Hindu-Christian Dual Belonging*.

and constructive engagement with other religions, the vast majority of its current practitioners are drawn to the discipline by a passion for another religion, or at least certain aspects of another religion. As Francis Clooney puts it, the comparative theologian is a "marginal figure," on the border between traditions.[11]

It is probably not surprising that many comparative theologians are drawn in particular to the mystical traditions of other religions and to mystical thinkers and practices. The area of mysticism has long formed an easy or natural bridge between religions. It has shaped the tradition of Perennial philosophy, and the development of pluralistic approaches to religious diversity. Not only do mystics often refer to a reality and experience beyond the particular forms and expressions of any religion, but there are also undeniable resonances between the mystical paths and experiences of various traditions. Mystical traditions have also been regarded as the foundation for the possibility of religious hybridity.[12] If, from the perspective of the mystical unity of religions, all religious traditions are derived from and oriented toward the same ultimate experience, then one may identify with different aspects of various religions without inherent contradiction, and different religions may or even must learn from one another as they come to a fuller expression of that ultimate reality. Comparative theologians may thus identify with certain teachings and practices of another religion without having a sense of compromising or contradicting their commitment to their primary tradition.

For comparative theologians who remain grounded in a particular religious tradition, the experience of religious hybridity is generally voluntary, permanent, and partial. This means that they engage a particular other religious tradition, not out of necessity or circumstance, but out of choice. Though the choice of a particular other tradition may be partially dictated by the traditions one happens to be exposed to, or that happen to be taught at a particular institution, it is ultimately the theologian who chooses to study another religion. In terms of the temporary or permanent identification with another religion, comparative theologians tend toward the latter. Serious theological engagement with another religion requires lifelong study and thus a more enduring focus. In some cases, a comparative

---

11. Clooney, *Comparative Theology*, 158.

12. As Rose Drew points out, most Buddhist-Christian hybrids start from what she calls a "monocentric pluralist perspective," which claims a unified ultimate reality beyond the particularities of any religion (Drew, *Buddhist and Christian*, 53, 83).

theologian may only be interested in a particular aspect of another tradition for the purposes of shedding new light on a particular theological question or problem in her own tradition, after which such interest and attention may subside. But the very impulse for doing comparative theology generally arises out of a sense of the endless promise that the study of one religion may have for the understanding of another. Finally, the experience of religious hybridity of a confessional comparative theologian tends to be partial and framed by the experience of primary or principle belonging. This means that the questions asked and the criteria of discernment used will be derived from this primary tradition, and that the comparative theologian will be drawn mainly to those elements that are not in contradiction with the primary tradition.

In some cases, the identification of a comparative theologian with another religion may wittingly or unwittingly go so far as to lose any sense of grounding in a primary tradition. Here, theologians may go back and forth between traditions, assenting to the normativity of one in certain matters, and the normativity of another in other points of belief or practice. Though the line of separation between partial and full identification with more than one tradition is not easily drawn, we will here focus primarily on confessional comparative theology.

COMPARATIVE THEOLOGY AS REFLECTION ON EXPERIENCES OF RELIGIOUS HYBRIDITY

In a world where the teachings and practices of various traditions are readily accessible and believers are exposed to multiple alternative religious views, the experience of religious hybridity is not only the prerogative of theologians with expertise in another religion, but also of ordinary believers. Rather than uncritically embracing the teachings of one religion, believers have often become more selective, combining elements from various religious traditions to form their personal set of convictions and practices. Some individuals abandon all sense of identification with any established religion, while others still maintain a primary sense of belonging to a particular tradition. Such primary belonging often expresses itself minimally in the celebration of major life events or rites of passage in accord with the rituals of a particular tradition. But beyond this, individuals may integrate beliefs and practices derived from any religious source.

This experience of combining elements from various traditions is of course not new, as individuals throughout history have combined religious and cultural elements available to them. In the past, however, such experiences of religious hybridity were outright condemned. As Anand Amaldass points out in the case of Indian Christians: "We have a long list of banned socio-religious practices among the Christians in Goa by the Inquisition as late as the middle of the eighteenth century. These practices were banned because they contained too many Hindu elements."[13] The fact that they were banned evidently suggest that they were widely practiced.

With the greater openness toward other religious traditions, and the recognition of element of goodness and truth in them, the appeal of certain elements of belief or practice, and experiences of hybridity may not always be outright condemned. They may in fact become a source of theological inspiration and consideration. This is where comparative theology may assume the responsibility of offering a second-order reflection on the theological meaning and coherence of such experiences. It may provide a deeper understanding of the religious elements that are being combined, of the history and meaning of particular beliefs and practices and of their possible compatibility. A challenge for comparative theology is the vast diversity of forms of religious hybridity, as any individual may combine elements from any religious tradition. In principle, any form of hybridity may offer food for critical and constructive reflection. But there are certain forms that are more recurrent and that may merit particular attention of comparative theologians.

For example, in the past decades, many cradle Christians have become immersed in the practice of yoga, at times unsure (but also often unconcerned about) whether this practice is compatible with the Christian tradition, whether adopting such a practice is disrespectful of its original tradition and a form of cultural hegemony, etc. Answering these questions requires considerable knowledge of the history of yoga in its Indian context, and of its historical developments and permutations. It thus requires comparative theologians with a background in Hinduism, Buddhism, and Christianity to answer these questions. This does not mean that all comparative theologians will be in agreement, as is evident from the various positions on the question of the compatibility of Christianity and yoga. But at least a thorough scholarly and theological investigation may shed light on the reasons for the different positions.

---

13. Amaldass, "Dialogue," 24.

The volumes *Buddhist-Christian Dual Belonging: Affirmations, Objections, Explorations* (2016) and *Hindu-Christian Dual Belonging* (2022) offer a good example of the way in which dual belonging may be studied and evaluated by theologians from various religious traditions. It also illustrates that the question cannot be settled in general or in an abstract way, but that it needs to focus on the particular elements of the traditions that are being combined in the experience or practice of believers.

As religious belief and practice are closely intertwined, and as theologians are to engage the experience of faith not only from the top down, but also from the bottom up, comparative theologians might also find common ground with pastoral theologians to consider the coherence and value of certain types of religious hybridity. If nothing else, religious hybridity points to certain areas of religious thirst that may be an occasion for genuine learning from other religions.

RELIGIOUS HYBRIDITY AS A SIGN OF HUNGER

The experience of religious hybridity, whether of the comparative theologian or of the ordinary believer may have many different causes, and the particular combination of elements from particular religions may be as much a matter of serendipity as of necessity. But they often suggest a certain religious or spiritual need or hunger that may not be fulfilled in their primary religion, or else an experience of surplus that they may not have found in their own tradition. For a good number of Christians, this involves the need or desire for a more holistic approach to the faith which also includes bodily and mental disciplines to nourish the soul. On a more purely theological or philosophical level, religious hybridity often arises from the desire to find new frameworks for interpretation of Christian faith after the challenges posed to classical metaphysics. All this may lead to experiences of religious hybridity.

In addition to this, religious hybridity may also arise from a strong identification with a particular culture and with the religion or religions that have traditionally informed or shaped that culture. This is very obviously the case with hybridity in Africa, where Christians also strongly identify with traditional African religions and practices. Here, the need is often based on the desire for physical healing or at least an etiology of the disease or problem that might help coming to terms with it. Many forms of temporary religious hybridity are based on such existential needs.

PART I | INTERFAITH LEARNING AND BELONGING

How might comparative theologians address these different types of religious hunger? First, they have the responsibility and the ability to thoroughly study the other tradition or the particular point of appeal in the other religion and to understand its meaning and function in its own religious context. Then, they may need to make a first judgment as to the compatibility of the various religious teachings or practices combined. Often, teachings or practices that are embedded in different religious traditions are not automatically or naturally reconcilable as their meaning partakes in an overall religious framework that at least in some respects clashes with other religious systems. However, in some cases, there may not be any obvious incompatibility, as certain teachings or practices address varied experiences or aspects of life. Since the Shinto tradition in Japan focuses mainly on views and rituals relating to life, Buddhism offered a welcome addition as it focused mainly on rituals relating to death and the commemoration of the dead, leading to swift theological assimilations of Buddhist and Shinto divine beings, in both directions. Since theodicy forms an enduring question or problem for Christian theologians, individuals may search for other rationalizations of their suffering, some of which may not necessarily be incompatible with Christian faith.

In addition to taking stock of the experience of religious hybridity and offering an understanding of the background and meaning of the elements that are being combined, comparative theologians may also engage in more constructive reflection on the various ways in which a tradition may learn from the experience of hunger or lack by recovering elements that may fulfill that lack or by exploring new ways of integrating elements of appeal from another tradition. Of the various types of learning I discuss in my book *Meaning and Method in Comparative Theology*, recovery and appropriation most directly respond to the needs of religious hybrids. Often, religious hybrids are drawn to elements in another religion without realizing that they may also be present in their own tradition. Each religion is internally complex and rich, and Perry Schmidt-Leukel argues in his fractal interpretation of religious diversity that

> the differences that can be observed at the *interreligious* level are, to some extent, reflected at an *intrareligious* level in the internal differences discerned within the major religious traditions, and that they can be broken down at the *intrasubjective* level to different religious patterns and structures of the individual mind.[14]

14. Schmidt-Leukel, *Religious Pluralism*, 233.

This would imply that much of what may be found in other religions has thus been proposed or practiced in one's own. While some of these beliefs and practices may have been forgotten or condemned in the course of history, comparative theologians may thus delve into the history and reasons for their abandonment and consider whether they may or may not be recovered in order to address particular needs. This is how, for example, the Hesychast tradition and the Jesus prayer has been rediscovered by various Christian meditation movements, and why Christian theologians have studied groups such as the Cathars, to reflect on the reasons why their belief in reincarnation was condemned and which arguments were used. All this is based on the experiences of religious hybridity where Christians seem to be particularly drawn by practices of meditation and by belief in reincarnation. Comparative theology has also reignited interest in particular Christian figures, such as Meister Eckhart, Marguerite Porete, or Jean Pierre de Caussade, whose experiences and spiritual teachings closely resonate with those of the contemplative traditions and practices of Hinduism and Buddhism.

Finally, the strong appeal of certain teachings or practices may lead comparative theologians to consider whether they may be integrated within Christian religious life. This would thus involve a process of borrowing or appropriating teachings or practices that originated in or are particularly developed in another religion. Since no two traditions seamlessly overlap, this also generally requires a process of reinterpretation in which the meaning of those elements are adjusted and changed to fit the new religious context. This, in turn, may raise questions about the propriety of borrowing and transforming teachings and practices from other religions. These all represent questions that need to be addressed by comparative theologians.[15] Whereas some base their arguments on the original meaning of certain practices, others acknowledge continuous development and change of the teachings and practices themselves and thus the possibility of new changes.

RELIGIOUS HYBRIDITY AS A SIGN OF ABUNDANCE

The idea of religious abundance may evoke a sense of a multiplicity of sources from which religious hybrids may draw to inform one's religious beliefs and practice. Insofar as religions recognize one another as a possible

---

15. I have tried to address some of these questions in chapter 3 of Cornille, *Meaning and Method*.

source of religious truth and inspiration, other religions may indeed represent an endless well of possibility for experiences of hybridity and for comparative theological reflection.

However, the notion of abundance may also be used to reflect on the experience of hybridity from the perspective of what continues to draw or inspire hybrids in their home tradition. While the focus of religious hybridity is usually on what individuals find appealing in another tradition, it may be also interesting and theologically relevant to reflect on why religious hybrids are still at least partly attached to their home tradition, and what elements they would not want to give up despite their attraction to another religion. This may point to elements of particularity and abundance that may only appear in light of another religious tradition, and that in turn may offer food for the other religion.[16] These elements may also emerge from the experience of "holy envy" of religious others, or from individuals who do not identify with a home tradition but who are drawn to elements in the home tradition of the comparative theologian.

The task of the comparative theologian may be here to discern what these elements may be and whether there is any consistency in the elements that surface. For many, attachment to their home tradition may be mainly a matter of nostalgia, comfort, or family loyalty. But for others it may involve elements that are not found in other religions and that are deemed particularly valuable or true. Identifying those elements may thus shed new light on the particularity of a religion, and even lead to a new approach to religious particularity and uniqueness.[17] As a form of learning, it may also lead to a reaffirmation or revaluation of elements one may have taken for granted. This may also include a reinterpretation of these elements in light of the other. For example, rather than understand the uniqueness of Jesus Christ as the marker of Christian superiority, it may also come to be understood in contrast with some other religions that (too) easily recognize the divinity of humans, and as a guarantee of spiritual or religious humility.[18]

The discernment of what may be distinctive or abundant may of course differ depending on the other tradition. In experiences of Christian-Hindu religious hybridity, it is often the centrality of love and forgiveness,

---

16. This would of course have to be determined by comparative theologians of that other tradition.

17. I have thus proposed a new approach to Christian uniqueness in Cornille, "Re-con-figuring" and "Who Do You Say."

18. This is an idea that I am working out in Cornille, "Humility and Uniqueness."

as well as the willingness to suffer for others that is regarded as particular to Christianity. One of the earliest examples of a Hindu-Christian hybrid, Brahmabandhab Upadhyaya (1861–1907), was particularly attracted to the universality of Jesus' teachings as well as to the centrality of self-sacrificing love. Pointing to the examples of St. Francis and Father Damien, he stated: "Where—we ask in wonder and amazement—where in the whole history of the world can you find instances of such heroic, supernatural love outside the fold of the Christian and Catholic Church?"[19] Though deeply inspired by the Hindu tradition of Advaita Vedanta, the French Benedictine monk Henri Le Saux (Abhishiktananda) (1910–1974) also focused on the element of love and distinctive of the Christian understanding of God as well as of the communal ideal: "Christianity is the revelation that Being is Love (cf. 1 Cor 13:2; 1 John 4:16)."[20] "The mystery of the Holy trinity reveals that *Being* is essentially a koinonia of love; it is communion, a reciprocal call to *be*; it is being-together, being-with, *co-esse*; its essence is a coming-from and going-to, a giving and receiving."[21] "The Church is essentially *agape* (love) and koinonia (being-with, being-together). She is the sign and sacrament of the divine koinonia of Being. By her very nature she is communion in love, and her function in mankind is to produce a ferment of love."[22]

Though he may not have considered himself a Hindu-Christian hybrid, the famous Protestant theologian Stanley Samartha (1920–2001) drew extensively from the Hindu tradition of non-duality in reinterpreting Christianity. Nevertheless, he also recognized that "the willingness to suffer, the readiness to bear the burdens of others, to be 'obedient even unto death' (Philippians 2:8), is probably the most obvious mark of Jesus Christ and of his followers in the world."[23] After years of engagement with Hinduism, the Jesuit theologian George Soarez Prabhu (1929–1995) stated:

> The Indian reader would at once identify active concern and forgiveness as the two poles, positive and negative, of the Dharma of Jesus–of that complex blend of worldview and values, of beliefs and prescriptions which "hold together" the followers of Jesus and integrates them into a recognizable community. For if these are not exclusively Christian attitudes, the importance given to them

19. Lipner and Gispert-Sauch, *Writings of Brahmabandhab Upadhyay*, 24–26.
20. Abhishiktananda, *Christian Approach*, 136.
21. Abhishiktananda, *Christian Approach*, 135.
22. Abhishiktananda, *Christian Approach*, 137.
23. Samartha, *Other Side*, 49–50.

in the teaching of Jesus and the concrete forms they assume in the New Testament give them a specifically Christian significance.[24]

Though he did not convert to Christianity, Gandhi indeed referred to the elements of self-sacrificing love, and forgiveness as the two distinctive Christian elements from which he drew inspiration:

> Though I cannot claim to be a Christian in the sectarian sense, the example of Jesus' suffering is a factor in the composition of my underlying faith in non-violence, which rules all my actions, worldly and temporal. Jesus lived and died in vain if he did not teach us to regulate the whole of life by the eternal law of love.[25]

> Jesus Christ prayed to God from the Cross to forgive those who had crucified him. It is my constant prayer to God that He may give me the strength to intercede even for my assassin. And it should be your prayer too that your faithful servant may be given the strength to forgive.[26]

These various kinds and degrees of religious hybridity thus point to elements of particularity and abundance that may garner renewed appreciation for members of a particular tradition and inspiration for members of another tradition. This approach to religious particularity is in no way meant to argue for the overall superiority of one religion over another. What appears as distinctive in relation to one religion may differ from what appears in relation to another tradition, or text, or practice. As such, the notion of religious particularity is fluid and variable. Moreover, the surfacing of certain elements in one comparative theological exercise does not mean that they are entirely absent in the other tradition. However, the discovery of religious particularity and abundance through the exercise of comparative theology may lead to greater theological self-awareness, and more effective contribution to the broader comparative theological exercise.

CONCLUSION

Comparative theology is often regarded as a luxury, as an extraordinary approach to theology that is still somewhat marginal to the traditional

---

24. Samartha, *Other Side*, 220.

25. From a conversation on the train to Bardoli, 1939, in Gandhi, "Is Non-Violence Ineffective?"

26. Gandhi, "Advice to Muslims," 120.

and normal ways of doing theology from within the classical theological boundaries and using classical theological sources. However, just as the reality of secularization and new philosophical developments became sources for theological renewal, the encounter with other religions represents an endlessly rich resource for advancing theological reflection. If, as most Christian churches have come to believe, the Holy Spirit is also at work outside ecclesial boundaries, it is in other religions, where individuals have searched for and experienced ultimate reality, that those elements of truth and value will most likely be found.

Comparative theologians tend to be individuals who have been personally touched and inspired by elements of truth in other religions. In identifying with these elements, they may be regarded as religious hybrids, a notion that may cause some worry or anxiety on the part of religious insiders. However, the term hybridity covers many kinds and degrees, and confessional comparative theologians still identify predominantly with one religious tradition, which remains the norm for integrating elements from other religions.

It is undeniable that the popular and widespread experience of religious hybridity represents a danger to religious traditions, as hybrids tend to be less constrained by the injunctions of any particular religion and less invested in the absolute or exclusive claims of any religion. However, religious hybridity may also represent a fertile soil for new theological developments. It offers the opportunity for comparative theologians to reflect on what may be missing in their own tradition and whether those elements may be recovered from the tradition, or else adopted and adapted from the other. It may also lead to a renewed understanding of the particularity or uniqueness of one's own tradition and what it may possibly contribute to other religious traditions and to the common good. This is where religious hybridity may become food for comparative theology, and where comparative theology plays an important and essential role in the process of theological development and growth.

PART I | INTERFAITH LEARNING AND BELONGING

BIBLIOGRAPHY

Abhishiktananda, Saccidananda. *A Christian Approach to Advaitic Experience*. London: ISPCK, 1994.
Amaldass, Anand. "Dialogue Between Hindus and the St. Thomas Christians." In *Hindu-Christian Dialogue: Perspectives and Encounters*, edited by Harold Coward, 13–27. Faith Meets Faith Series. Maryknoll: Orbis, 1989.
Clooney, Francis. *Comparative Theology: Deep Learning Across Religious Borders*. Malden, MA: Wiley-Blackwell, 2010.
Cornille, Catherine. "Double Religious Belonging: Aspects and Questions." *Buddhist-Christian Studies* 23 (2003) 43–49.
———, ed. *Many Mansions? Multiple Religious Belonging and Christian Identity*. 2002. Reprint, Eugene, OR: Wipf & Stock, 2010.
———. *Meaning and Method in Comparative Theology*. Hoboken, NJ: Wiley, 2020.
———. "Mehrere Meister? Multiple Religionszugehörigkeit in Praxis und Theorie." In *Multiple Religiöse Identität: Aus Verschiedenen Religiösen Traditionen Schöpfen*, edited by Reinhod Bernhardt and Perry Schmidt-Leukel, 15–35. Beiträge zu einer Theologie der Religionen 5. Zurich: Theologischer Verlag Zurich, 2008.
———. "Multiple Religious Belonging and Interreligious Dialogue." In *Understanding Inter-Religious Relations*, edited by David Thomas et al., 324–40. Oxford: Oxford University Press.
———. "Re-con-figuring the Uniqueness or Particularity of Christianity through Interreligious Dialogue." *Bulletin of the Nanzan Institute for Religion and Culture* 46 (2022) 31–46.
———. "Religious Hybridity and Christian Identity." *Currents in Theology and Mission* 48.1 (2021) 8–13.
———. "Strategies of Negotiation in Buddhist-Christian Dual Belonging." In *Buddhist-Christian Dual Belonging: Affirmations, Objections, Explorations*, edited by Gavin D'Costa and Ross Thompson, 143–60. Burlington, VT: Ashgate, 2016.
———. "Who Do You Say that I Am: Rethinking the Particularity of Christianity through the Religious Other." *Proceedings of the Catholic Theological Society of America* 76 (2022) 23–37.
D'Costa, Gavin, and Ross Thompson, eds. *Buddhist-Christian Dual Belonging: Affirmations, Objections, Explorations*. Burlington, VT: Ashgate, 2016.
Drew, Rose. *Buddhist and Christian? An Exploration of Dual Belonging*. Routledge Critical Studies in Buddhism. London: Routledge, 2011.
Fletcher, Jeannine Hill. *Monopoly on Salvation?* New York: Continuum, 2005.
Gandhi, Mohandas K. "Advice to Muslims [October 26, 1947]." In *Gandhi's Bible*, edited by William W. Emielsen, 120. London: ISPCK, 2009.
———. "Is Non-Violence Ineffective? [January 2, 1939]." *Jewish Virtual Library*. https://www.jewishvirtuallibrary.org/lsquo-is-non-violence-ineffective-rsquo-by-gandhi-january-1939.
Griffiths, Paul. *Problems of Religious Diversity*. Exploring the Philosophy of Religion 1. Malden, MA: Blackwell, 2001.
Laksana, Albertus Bagus. "Being Theological in a Comparative Manner in Today's Indonesia." *International Journal of Asian Christianity* 3 (2020) 203–7.
Lipner, Julius, and George Gispert-Sauch, eds. *The Writings of Brahmabandhab Upadhyay*. Vol. 2. Bangalore: United Theological College, 2002.

Manning, Christel. *Losing Our Religion: How Unaffiliated Parents Are Raising Their Children*. Secular Studies. New York: New York University Press, 2015.

Pye, Michael. "Syncretism and Ambiguity." *Numen* 18.2 (1971) 83–93.

Samartha, Stanley. *The Other Side of the River*. Madras: Christian Literature Society, 1983.

Schmidt-Leukel, Perry. *Religious Pluralism and Interreligious Theology: The Gifford Lectures—An Extended Edition*. Maryknoll, NY: Orbis, 2017.

Soars, Daniel, and Nadya Pohran, eds. *Hindu-Christian Dual Belonging*. Routledge Hindu Studies Series. New York: Routledge, 2022.

Wildman, Wesley. "Theology Without Walls: The Future of Transreligious Theology." *Open Theology* 2 (2016) 242–47.

PART II

Comparative Theology

3

"All Under Heaven" and the City of God

A Familial and Ecclesial Reflection

Hyo-Dong Lee

THIS ESSAY ATTEMPTS TO contribute a fresh voice to the already massive body of Christian theological literature on the church-state relation by staging a conversation with the tradition of Confucian political thought. First, I will trace the origin of Christian ambivalence toward the political to the biblical testimonies about the attitudes of Jesus and Paul regarding the Roman Empire and to Augustine's classical distinction between the two cities governed by two forms of love. I will center my analysis around the quasi-family-like nature of the *ecclesia* and explore its political implications against the backdrop of Hannah Arendt's influential claim about the stark opposition between the respective logic of the family and the *polis* in the classical Greco-Roman world. Secondly, I will look at an intellectual, religious-cultural, and socio-political tradition that has conceived the familial-political relation very differently, namely, the Confucian tradition. I will focus on the hallmark of Confucian political thought, which is its conception of the familial sphere as both the institutional and affective foundation of the political sphere. This conception, I argue, suggests some fruitful ways of freshly rethinking the public and political implications of the *ecclesia*. Thirdly, I will return to the ecclesial reflection with which I started and sketch an outline of the *ecclesia* reimagined as a fertile ground where the familial affections of the baptized can be nurtured to form *agape* as political love. In order for this political love not to be readily perverted into the lust for domination, I contend, the *ecclesia* must be understood as the body of a crucified people whose baptisms signify their renunciation of all essentialized hierarchies of worth, honor, and power. Lastly, I will highlight the neglect by Confucian political thought of mediating communities and institutions that bridge the familial and the political, and its consequent failure to articulate and to effectively guide the task of extending the familial moral sentiments beyond the familial sphere to shape a humane political order. In order for the Confucian tradition to remedy this—both theoretical and practical—oversight by conceptualizing those crucial steppingstones within the context of modern pluralistic societies, I submit that the ideal of *ecclesia* sketched in this essay, which is structured and governed by the principles of plurality and equality, could offer a helpful paradigm.

BETWEEN THE FAMILY AND THE POLIS: THE ECCLESIA'S (UN)FAMILIAR LOVE

"What has Christ to do with Caesar"? This is one of the most enduring questions posed, not only by those who claim membership in the Christian communion, but also by those outside as well, regarding the one who was executed by the Roman Empire as an unrecognized and illegitimate king. Very early on Christians were given a clue to how to answer this question by none other than Jesus himself, when he said, "Give to Caesar the things that are Caesar's and to God the things that are God's" (Mark 12:17).[1] Apparently, being a member of the quasi-family-like community[2] of those who are supposedly called out of this "world" was not the same thing as being a loyal or disloyal subject of the august First Citizen of the empire, even if one happened to be, like the apostle Paul, a citizen of the *res publica* or commonwealth called Rome. While Paul encouraged the nascent Roman Christian community to subject themselves to the rulers and governing authorities as respectful, upright, and tax-paying subjects (Rom 13:1–7), he

---

1. All scriptural quotes are from the New Revised Standard Version.

2. The quasi-family like character of the community of Jesus' disciples can be traced to Jesus' use of the Father metaphor for God and the sibling metaphor for his disciples, which led the earliest Christian communities to adopt the family metaphors—particularly the sibling metaphor—for the relationships among their members. See Finlan, *Family Metaphor*, 1–8.

seems to have viewed the whole political order at the same time as part of the present form of this world that was passing away, in order to make way for the true commonwealth, the *basileia* or reign of Christ, and ultimately, of God (1 Cor 7:31; 15:20–25; Phil 3:20).[3]

This Christian ambivalence shown toward the public, political order found its most well-known and influential spokesperson, when Augustine, famously and allegorically, contrasted two cities: the earthly, human city (*civitas terrena*), and the heavenly city of God (*civitas dei*).[4] The earthly city was not a true commonwealth, because its organizing and animating principle was not justice as it purported, but the lust for domination—a searing, ruinous instance of humanity's disordered and misdirected loves ubiquitous in the wake of their Fall. By contrast, the heavenly city, the city of God, was truly a *res publica*, because the love of God, charity, reigned among its citizens, the blessed saints.[5] The earthly city—a cipher for the kingdoms of this world—was a pale reflection, if not parody, of the heavenly city.[6] It denoted both a divine concession to human fallenness and God's gracious gift of a modicum of justice and order to the chaotic world,[7] so that the saints, pilgrims here below and citizens above, could live with a measure of peace in-between, until the full disclosure of the heavenly city, the consummation of the *basileia tou theou*.[8] Within that in-between time and space, the two cities are interwoven and intermixed in all manners of living together, not least within the *ecclesia* of the baptized, who yearns to be the citizens of the true commonwealth above, all the while being concerned about achieving and preserving the peace of Babylon here below in which they find themselves exiled.[9]

Augustine, then, presents to us this question: if the two cities are intermingled and entangled with each other here and now, what would be, or should be, the organizing and animating principle for the family of the adopted children of God? To the extent that the baptized aspire to be

3. For the overall oppositional though at times complicated relationship between Paul (and the whole Pauline legacy) and the Roman Empire, see Wiley, "Paul," 47–61.

4. Chvala-Smith, "Augustine," 90–91.

5. O'Donovan, *Sourcebook*, 142–43 (Augustine, *City of God* 14.28).

6. O'Donovan, *Sourcebook*, 145 (Augustine, *City of God* 15.2).

7. O'Donovan, *Sourcebook*, 142, 139, 145 (Augustine, *City of God* 5.26; 4.4; 15.4).

8. O'Donovan, *Sourcebook*, 144, 163 (Augustine, *City of God* 15.1; 19.26).

9. O'Donovan, *Sourcebook*, 45–46, 163 (Augustine, *City of God* 1.35; 19.26). For the classic interpretation of the relationship of non-identity between the City of God and the Church in Augustine's thought, see Markus, *Saeculum*, 154–86.

saints, the citizens of the heavenly City, that principle is no doubt the love of God, charity or *agape*. But as long as the baptized find themselves as the concerned citizens of the various dominions of the earthly city, whether by birth or by design or by forced migration, they face a quandary, for they cannot and do not want the answer to be the lust for domination. If the baptized are gifted with the peace of Babylon, either real or yet to be realized, then the manifold earthly bonds of fellowship that make such a peace possible, starting with their consanguineous families and kins, cannot be a matter of no concern. What is it that binds them together? Or, what should bind them together?

According to the Jewish-American political philosopher Hannah Arendt, the classical Greco-Roman world sharply contrasted the family and the *polis*, that is, the domestic, private realm vis-a-vis the public realm. The family was a union based on biological and economic necessities, and ruled by a patriarch—a *paterfamilias* or *dominus*—who exercised his sovereign domination over the rest of the household, including women, children, and slaves.[10] The *polis*, by contrast, constituted a sphere of freedom and equality, albeit the freedom and equality of peers, i.e., mainly free adult male citizens who exercised no rule or sovereignty over one another.[11] The public realm was a sphere of freedom and equality, to the extent that it was a realm of plurality, where different perspectives on the common good existed, and where no common denominator of or common measurement for the different positions could be devised. Compared to the public, political sphere, the family as a realm of sovereign rule could only offer a single unifying position, very often (and most likely) that of the master of the household.[12]

What was remarkable about the emergence of Christianity, Arendt avers, is that a group of essentially "worldless"[13] people waiting for the dawn

10. Arendt, *Human Condition*, 27–30.

11. Arendt, *Human Condition*, 30–32. Regarding the ancient Greeks, Arendt uses the term "family" almost interchangeably with the term "household" and draws a sharp dichotomy between the *polis* and the *oikos* (household). See Long, "Fissure," 87–88, 92.

12. Arendt, *Human Condition*, 57.

13. The "world" has a distinct meaning in Arendt's thought, referring to the world of human artifice vis-à-vis nature or the earth. The world encompasses both the private realm (such as households) and the public realm, i.e., the "common world" which, "like every in-between, relates and separates men at the same time" and precisely in so doing offers a space of co-existence and a framework of co-flourishing (Arendt, *Human Condition*, 52). The public realm encompasses the built environment (of cities, towns, roads, and bridges), cultural artifacts (like works of art and literature), and socio-political institutions (such as constitutions and laws). Kiess, *Arendt and Theology*, 99. According

of a new age, a new world, formed a community that belonged neither to the family nor to the *polis*. The early Christian community was non-public and non-political, insofar as it defined itself as and sought to form a body, a *corpus*, whose members were related to one another like the siblings of the same family. At the same time, the early Christian community was not really family-like either, as it was founded on the bond of charity, *agape*, and was not a union based on the necessities of life. Be that as it may, to the extent that the structure of the early Christian communities mimicked the relationships among the members of the non-public and non-political family, its bond of charity not being dispassionate and disinterested enough to hold together a public realm of plural perspectives via a distantiating respect, the *ecclesia* was not likely to form a political sphere of free action, where a plurality of different actors, all equal to one another, spoke and acted for the sake of the commonwealth.[14]

Arendt's analysis of the family and the polis, whose insights carry over into her influential political thoughts on the twentieth century, and her ruminations on the early Christian communities, are both controversial and have been subject to much debate.[15] While they deserve a longer

---

to Arendt, the early Christians were "worldless" because they elevated human life to the position of immortality (i.e., eternal life) while relegating the world to the realm of fleeting impermanence, to be replaced by the eschatological kingdom to come. This contrasted with the ancient Greeks who believed that, although human life was mortal, one could achieve immortality in the form of the "worldly" honor and glory attainable in the public, political realm, namely, the *polis*. See Kiess, *Arendt and Theology*, 106.

14. Arendt, *Human Condition*, 53–54, 241–43. According to Christopher Long's illuminating analysis of Arendt's famous reading of Augustine's notion of love, because it is the mode of association endemic to the family, love, even as genuinely selfless charity, is never without passion and compassion. But because passion and compassion are incapable of generalization, exclusively attuned as they are to the beauty and suffering of particular, unique individuals, love tends to abolish the distance between individuals and is therefore "unable to provide the necessary universality and impartiality requisite for the establishment and maintenance of institutions." In other words, since love is unable to sustain the plurality inherent to the public, political realm, it is "essentially 'anti-political' and must necessarily dwell in the private realm" (Long, "Fissure," 93). As John Kiess observes, the experience of many political revolutions—particularly the French Revolution—has shown, for Arendt, that when love "goes public" in a political use of it, it often degenerates into pity, as seen in those revolutions which, in the name of an abstract humanity and with the goal of eliminating human suffering, become paternalistic and eventually totalitarian (Kiess, *Arendt and Theology*, 111–12).

15. For feminist criticisms of Arendt's oppositional framing of the private and the public, of the family and the *polis*, see Dietz, *Feminist Responses*, 17–50. For a helpful survey of the scholarly debates on Arendt's view of Christianity's "worldlessness," see

exposition, for the purposes of this paper I would like to focus on the stark opposition that Arendt introduces into the relationship between the familial and the political, between the domestic and the public. If accepted as true, such a dichotomy would create a drag on any attempt to envision the family-like ecclesial body as equally, if not more capable, of offering a space free of sovereign domination when compared to any political body. There are two reasons for my misgivings about such a strident oppositional framing of the relationship between the familial and the political. First, although the family as an institution was and still is a site of patriarchal rule across many societies, nations, and cultures, it would be an exaggeration, to say the least, to intimate that domination and exclusion constitute the essence of the familial. Secondly, if the essence of the familial could be something other than domination, then it seems that the boundaries between the familial sphere and the public, political sphere could be conceived as fluid and porous, and not necessarily as jarringly discontinuous. A brief look at an intellectual, religious-cultural, and socio-political tradition that has conceived the familial-political relation very differently, namely, the Confucian tradition, could bring the two critical points into a sharper focus.

A CONFUCIAN COUNTERPOINT: THE POLITICS OF FILIAL CHILDREN

Ever since its founder, Master Kong (*Kongzi* 孔子), posed the question "What does it mean to be human?" the Confucian tradition has always maintained that the essence of being human consists in the virtue of *ren* (仁), translated as "humanity" or "humaneness." Held by every human being as an innate potential, *ren* is a universal moral capacity for sympathetic understanding of others (*shu* 恕) that is simultaneously cultivated and articulated in and through forms of proper ritual action (*li* 禮) (*Analects* 12:1–2; 15:24).[16] As fundamentally relational beings, humans come to be truly human, as they cultivate and practice their innate empathy to one another in their ritualized social interactions that are permeated, ideally, by a spirit of mutuality and reciprocity, producing social concord and harmony.

What is noteworthy here is the fact that the Confucian tradition has regarded the domestic, familial sphere as the initial and primary site in

---

Kiess, *Arendt and Theology*, 112–18.

16. See Zhu, *Sishu zhangju*, 131, 166. For an English translation, see Huang, *Analects*, 125, 156.

which the learning to be human takes place. Being the very first and most fundamental of all human relations, the parent-children relation offers the earliest and profoundly formative space for cultivating *ren* in the form of familial affection (*qin* 親), which is expressed as compassionate care on the part of the parents and as filial piety (*xiao* 孝) on the part of the children. It is for this reason that the rite of honoring and venerating one's ancestors functions as the most significant touchstone for one's possession of *ren*, as the rite is seen as an extension of filial piety to the past generations of parents. Hence the rituals of honoring parents and ancestors form one of the foundational components in the Confucian educational program of learning to be human. True enough, the Confucian tradition developed and institutionalized systems of family rituals (*jiali* 家禮) and clan law (*zongfa* 宗法) that reflected the traditional social hierarchy and gender division, and in so doing provided a cross-cultural testimony to the ample presence of sovereign patriarchal domination in the domestic sphere.[17] Nonetheless, that historical fact does not amount to a decisive refutation of the longstanding Confucian insistence that *ren* constitutes the principle of the familial.

In addition to its elevation of the familial sphere as the wellspring and nurturing ground of its cardinal virtue, it has been a hallmark of the Confucian tradition to emphasize and foreground the organic interconnection between the familial and the political. As outlined in the classic, *Great Learning*, the path of Confucian self-cultivation runs through a series of ever-enlarging concentric circles of human relations that starts from familial relations and—expanding through the larger human community or the state—eventually comes to rest at the entire world or "all under Heaven (*tianxia* 天下)" (*Great Learning* 1.5).[18] One who is on this path simply needs to extend, to non-familial others, the familial affections that one has cultivated within the family, such as one's love of the parents and one's respect for the elder siblings; and one is to do so in ritually appropriate manners predicated on sympathetic understanding of others (*Mencius* 1A:7; 7A:15, 45).[19] One is called to keep to this path until one's

---

17. Joseon-Dynasty Korea—perhaps the most Confucianized country in East Asia historically—is a showcase for this Neo-Confucian social conservatism. See Deuchler, *Confucian Transformation*.

18. See Zhu, *Sishu zhangju*, 4–5. For an English translation, see Gardner, *Four Books*, 4–5.

19. See Zhu, *Sishu zhangju*, 207–8, 353, 363. For an English translation, see Lau, *Mencius*, 9–11, 148, 156.

Part II | Comparative Theology

humane heart of empathy, *ren*, which initially was just enough to serve one's parents, becomes large enough to care for the entire world. One who possesses such a heart is called a "superior person" (*junzi* 君子) or a sage (*shengren* 聖人). The one constant aspiration that runs through the entire tradition of Confucian political thought and practice has been a rule by such superior persons or sages—self-cultivated human beings who possess the unobstructed moral capacity to manifest and to extend the humane heart of empathy to all beings. The Confucian program of classical learning and moral-ritual cultivation has aimed at educating rulers to become "sagely inside, kingly outside" (*neisheng waiwang* 內聖外王);[20] that is, rulers who could earn, by means of their benevolence and empathetic care, the allegiance and voluntary submission not only of people but of all creatures, so that the universal commonwealth, *tianxia*, may be at peace.[21] Equally important, it has endeavored to educate and produce an elite group of morally self-cultivated "superior persons" who can ably assist the sage-rulers in the task of helping *tianxia* flourish.[22]

The organic integration of the familial and the political in the Confucian political tradition means that the familial has served not only as the institutional but also affective foundation of the political. Families have been tasked with supplying a steady stream of sons who could populate the ranks of the government, for sure; but those sons are supposed to have learned and cultivated affective dispositions that are empathetic and humane. For example, during the time of Joseon Dynasty Korea, one of the most Confucian political entities if ever there was one, unfilial sons could not hope to become government officials. When a government official was found to be unfilial, his loyalty to the state was readily subject to doubt.[23] Being unfilial to one's mother was one of the stated reasons for which even kings were

---

20. The phrase first appears in the thirty-third (*tianxia*) chapter of the Daoist text, *Zhaungzi* (*Zhuangzi, Zhuangzi jishi* 1064), although the idea may have originated earlier. See Angle, *Sagehood*, 182.

21. See *Analects* 2:1, where Kongzi describes a virtuous ruler: "He who conducts government with virtue may be likened to the North Star, which, seated in its place, is surrounded by multitudes of other stars" (Huang, *Analects*, 52).

22. For an overview of the Confucian "politics of sagehood," see Angle, *Sagehood*, 13–22, 179–90.

23. This was the reason behind the state's concern about the mourning behavior of the officialdom, such as the proper observance (or neglect) of the mourning period after the passing of one's parent. Deucher, *Confucian Transformation*, 193–94.

dethroned, though in rare cases.²⁴ In the context of the ideal of humane government that a Confucian regime like Joseon Dynasty aspired to, the question was:

> If you do not care about your own parents, how can you claim to care about the others, especially "all under heaven who are tired, exhausted, sick, siblingless, childless, widows and widowers, orphaned—those who are helpless and have no one else to appeal to"?²⁵

It is to be acknowledged that the history of Confucian societies is rife with instances of nepotism and cronyism, the telltale signs of the failure to extend familial affections beyond one's kinship network into the public and political sphere. Furthermore, the Confucian conception of the continuity between the familial and the political certainly does not escape the charge of reflecting the traditional gender division, as it largely consigned women, almost arbitrarily and without a good *Confucian* argument, to the domestic sphere as the only network of relations within which they could cultivate themselves to be true human beings.²⁶ Even so, these historically based counterarguments notwithstanding, I would like to return to the ecclesial reflection with which this paper began, and throw in a thesis: If there is any truth to the Confucian conception of the familial as the foundation of the political, or put differently, the familial as the wellspring of the political, then it could suggest some fruitful ways of freshly reimagining the public and political implications of the *ecclesia*, the quasi-family like community of those who call God Abba and one another brothers and sisters, including Christ as the firstborn and the eldest.

THE CRUCIFIED HEARTS FOR THE REPUBLIC: THE ECCLESIA REIMAGINED

There is ample indication in the Newer Testament that the *ecclesia*, the community of those who are called out from all over the place to be Jesus' followers, is like a family, starting from Jesus' own reference to the ragtag

---

24. Most famously, there is the case of Gwanghaegun (reign 1608–1623) who was deposed for having stripped his official mother, Queen Dowager Inmok, of her title and imprisoned her.

25. I am quoting the famous lines from the eleventh-century Neo-Confucian Zhang Zai's *Western Inscription*, translated in Tiwald, *Readings*, 135.

26. Rosenlee, *Confucianism*, 69–94.

band of his disciples as his mother and sisters and brothers (Matt 12:48–50; Luke 8:21; Mark 3:31–35).[27] Jesus likens discipleship to joining a family of God with its own relations and shared resources in compensation for leaving the blood relatives and kinship networks behind (Mark 10:29–30; Luke 18:29–30; Matt 19:29). The Apostle Paul describes the community of the baptized as the children of God, adopted by God as their Father through faith, and led by the Spirit to be conformed to the image of the Christ the firstborn and to become join heirs with him (Rom 8:14–17, 29; Gal 3:26; 4:4–7). No longer strangers and aliens, the baptized have become "fellow citizens with the saints and also members of the household of God" (Eph 2:19).[28]

---

27. For the abundant use of the family metaphors in the New Testament for the members of the nascent Christian movement, see Osiek, "What We Do and Don't Know," 210–11. For the early Christian communities' predominant adoption of the sibling metaphor ("brotherhood"), see Hellerman, *Ancient Church*, 216–25. Philip Eisler convincingly shows how Paul lays a foundation for his designation of his addresses as brothers by pointing out their dual status as (adopted) sons of God through their faith in Jesus the son of God on the one hand and as sons of Abraham through Christ, the seed of Abraham, on the other. Eisler, "Family Imagery," 131.

28. The "anti-familal trend" in Jesus' teaching, found in the Gospels, is a contested issue. It is clear that Jesus makes a string of remarks that sound like he is against the whole idea of the family—from, "Follow me, and let the dead bury their own dead" (Matt 8:22; cf. Luke 9:60) to "Whoever comes to me and does not hate father and mother, wife and children, brothers and sisters . . . cannot be my disciple" (Luke 14:26). But the ideas and sentiments expressed by these remarks are not as radical as they at first appear, given the abundance of contemporary teachings that subordinated mundane ties, including family ties, to higher goods, as seen in Philo and Josephus within the tradition of Jewish monotheism on the one hand and the Cynics and Stoics in the Greco-Roman philosophical traditions on the other (Barton, "Relativisation of Family," 82–98). Further, Jesus' remarks should be understood against the backdrop of the eschatological mission to which the disciples are called. Following Jesus and proclaiming the imminent kingdom of God create separation, hostility, and even social ostracism from one's natural kin and the members of one's own household (Matt 10:34–36). The seemingly "anti-familial" teaching is actually a "rhetorically powerful metaphorical way of calling for the displacement of every obstacle to true discipleship of Jesus in the light of the imminent coming of the kingdom of God," even if that means subordinating the responsibilities of family and household (Barton, "Relativisation of Family," 81). Jesus himself underscores this point when he says, ""Whoever loves father or mother *more than* me is not worthy of me, and whoever loves son or daughter *more than* me is not worthy of me" (Matt 10:37 [my emphasis])—it is the matter of giving your primary loyalty to God without rejecting your loyalty to the family. As Stephen Finlan has persuasively argued, Jesus' "pro-familial" stance is supported by his promise of the eschatological reward (for those who have been forced to leave their families) in the form of the same kinship network, but now multiplied hundredfold, affirming the intrinsic goodness of family ties and family

"All Under Heaven" and the City of God

Now, if the *ecclesia* is to be like a family, then the love, which Jesus mandated (*"agapate"*) in the New Commandment (John 13:34–35) as the organizing principle of the *ecclesia*, cannot be alien to the familial affections, those "natural" moral sentiments present in the familial bodies.[29] *Agape*—the divine love with which the Abba God loves us, and with which we as God's children are to reciprocate by loving one another—appears to be rooted in something earthly, even elemental.[30] If so, then, when the members of the ecclesial family follow God's call to step into the vale of saint-making, so that the divine love, charity, may be made complete in their bodies, they may want to observe Master Kong's followers, the Confucians, who trudge through the neighboring vale of sage-making. They may learn that cultivating *agape*, like cultivating *ren*, needs first attuning

---

affection (Matt 19:29; Luke 18:29–30; Mark 10:29–30). Jesus' attending weddings, his use of weddings in his parables, his strict prohibition of divorce and critique of the practice of substituting religious offerings for the support due one's old parents (Mark 10:4–12; 7:9–13)—all these Gospel witnesses strengthen the case for the "pro-familial" character of Jesus' teaching (Finlan, *Family Metaphor*, 62–68).

29. According to Halvor Moxnes, in first-century Palestine the average family (*familia*) was a "household" (*domus*), i.e., a group of people who were connected through kinship and who lived together forming an economic unit of subsistence and mutual support. In the Synoptic Gospels, this household serves as a model for the ideals associated with the kingdom of God, especially in terms of the traditional values based on household resource sharing and village solidarity, and as such provides an oppositional paradigm vis-à-vis the exploitative structures of the elite politico-religious authorities (Moxnes, "What Is Family?," 23–25). Hence, insofar as the community of Jesus' disciples formed an alternative kinship structure that was inspired and shaped by the force of familial metaphors, its "counter-cultural" ethos was likely influenced by the spirit of mutual affective support and solidarity characterizing familial relations. Further, although with Paul and the Pauline authors of the New Testament the household with its patriarchal structure is portrayed as an integral part of the vast patronage system of the Roman cities and not antithetical to it (25–26, 37), the familial ethos of the Roman household that worked to counterbalance the enormous power of *paterfamilias*, namely, *pietas* as "a bond of reciprocal, dutiful affection" between parents and children (Lassen, "Roman Family," 107), must be taken into account if one is to imagine the alternative family-like character of the *ecclesia* within the Greco-Roman social context. My argument is in this sense somewhat akin to Ada Maria Isasi-Diaz's groundbreaking proposal that instead of seeing the *agape* that reigns (or is supposed to reign) in the Church as a completely revolutionary innovation on the ethos of the family ruled by *paterfamilias*, one should understand it in terms of the "kindom"—the familial bond of solidarity conceived and celebrated in Latinx cultures as extending far beyond the nuclear family or even blood relatives. See Isasi-Diaz, "Kin-dom of God," 171–90.

30. Quoting from the title of Catherine Keller's essay "Elemental Love," in which she rejects the traditional Christian distinction made between *agape* and *eros* and reconstructs the former as rooted in the latter. See Keller, "Elemental Love," 63–77.

Part II | Comparative Theology

themselves to the faint promptings of their sympathetic heart, given to us all in grace as the *imago dei*, and veiled in our fallenness, yet capable of transforming "All under Heaven." The first thing that the adopted children of God need to do in order to be conformed to the image of the firstborn is to tend, carefully and diligently, to those spontaneous, visceral familial feelings of sympathy and affection, starting with our dealings with those others nearest to us, namely our parents, siblings, and children, and extending those feelings to the others further removed from us. The road to sainthood, just like the path of sage-making, can be envisioned as passing through successive encounters with ever-less-familial and therefore ever-less-familiar others who relentlessly present, to Jesus' disciples, the often arduous task of extending the empathetic heart within, even to complete strangers, those not of the fold, who are labeled heathens, aliens, and enemies. Like *ren*, *agape* as the constitutive and animating principle of the *ecclesia* can be what it is meant to be by reaching beyond the familial and familiar boundaries to become a form of public, even political, love, despite Augustine's eschatologically nuanced pessimism about the human city as the site of the lust for domination.[31]

To be sure, if the familial affections of the baptized are to serve as the sprout and wellspring of *agape* understood as political love, the paradigm of the family offered by the *ecclesia*, from within which those familial affections are to germinate and to grow, must be interrogated to ascertain that they do not function to camouflage the lust for domination. Paul, especially the so-called deutero-Pauline Paul, presents a paradigm of the ecclesial family that performs a largely non-subversive mimesis of the Greco-Roman household, even as it purports to check the worst excesses of the hierarchy

---

31. Against what he considers Arendt's misreading of Augustine's notion of love as "a passionate sentiment appropriate only to a private, domesticated sphere" (Gregory, *Politics*, 210), Eric Gregory attempts to draw out its public, political implications by arguing that, for Augustine, insofar the love of the neighbor implies loving him or her *in* God, it functions as a check against the self's prideful tendencies to regard one's neighbors as existing only for the sake of one's own ends—the tendencies that lead eventually to the self's insatiable desire to possess and to dominate them (42). In other words, Augustine teaches us that the love of God sets us free to love others as really and inexhaustibly other, and by reminding us of "the dangers (to the self and the other) of a love that prematurely rests in the neighbor, in institutional purity, or the anxieties of our own moral confidence," helps us, *pace* Arendt, to envisage "the space for the vulnerable encounters with others that is characteristics of liberal politics" (362). Gregory's project of developing a politics of love resonates with what I am attempting in this essay insofar as envisaging the public, political nature of *agape* is concerned, although his Augustinian theocentrism differs from my Mencian "moral sentimentalism."

of power within the latter.³² The famous "household code" drawn up by the author of the letter to the Colossians (3:18—4:1), demanding the obedience and submission of children, wives, and slaves to fathers, husbands, and masters, is a prime example of such an imperial mimicry.³³ When (the deutero-Pauline) Paul claims that Christ the firstborn is the "head" of the church as his body (Col 1:18; 2:19; Eph 1:22–23; 4:15–16; 5:23; cf. 1 Cor 11:3), is not our dear apostle reinforcing the sovereignty of the male head of the household, the *dominus* of the *domus*? There is much to be conceded to this challenging interrogation.

All the same, if we direct our gaze to the singularly arresting object of Paul's own gaze, the crucified Christ of his letters to the Corinthian, Galatian, and Roman communities, the bond of charity, as the organizing and animating principle of the *ecclesia*, does not seem to service the sovereign rule of any single *dominus*, lord and master. After all, baptism means that one is baptized into Christ's death, Christ's crucifixion (Rom 6:3), and brought low to be considered among the dregs of the world—weak, less honorable, less respectable, and suffering (1 Cor 1:20–29; 4:9–16). In the body of the Christ that is the *ecclesia*, the "head" as the superordinate member of the body exists only in an ironic, paradoxical sense, because it has been crucified. If the baptized have clothed themselves with Christ in such a way that it is no longer they but Christ who lives in them (Gal 2:19; 3:27), each one of them has the legitimate claim to be the head of the body. But this claim can only be made on the strength of their carrying on their bodies the mark of crucifixion, which is foolishness and a stumbling block to the world, including the Roman imperial order. If being the head—i.e., living in Christ or Christ living in one—means being crucified to the world (Gal 6:14), then there cannot be any superordinate-subordinate relation within the body of Christ in accordance with the world's system of knowledge, value, and power.³⁴ The head, then, corresponds to every Jew, Greek,

---

32. Wiley, "Paul," 50–51.

33. Fiorenza, "Coequal Discipleship," 236–37.

34. The power of this ideal can be seen in the way the early Christians tried to live this "equality" structure. The "construct of irrelevant worldly differences" was making an impact in the earliest Christian communities, as witnessed by women's significant leadership roles in Christian congregational life, the integration of Jewish and Gentile Christians in many Gentile congregations (as in the Roman church), and the real possibility for slaves to be treated as equal brothers and sisters (as seen in Philemon). See Lampe, "Language of Equality," 78–79. This likely did not mean that the worldly differences were entirely abolished initially, only to be replaced by emerging patriarchal structures of authority within the church (as claimed by E. Schüssler Fiorenza), but rather that

Part II | Comparative Theology

man, woman, master, and slave within the *ecclesia* who is at the same time no longer such, having been liberated in Christ from the hierarchy of power and honor such distinctions imply (Gal 3:28). Like God whose center is everywhere and whose circumference is nowhere,[35] the *ecclesia* is called to be a body whose *dominus* is everywhere and the boundaries of whose sovereign domain are nowhere. The plurality and equality claimed by Arendt to belong only to a public, political body could well turn out to be a hallmark of the *ecclesia* as the body of the crucified people as well.[36]

Seen as such, the *ecclesia* has a good claim to be a fertile ground where the familial affections of the baptized can be nurtured to form *agape* as political love and not readily be perverted into the lust for domination. In other words, the *ecclesia* can be an excellent site of political *ascesis*,[37] the vale of saint-making, in which the baptized train to extend their spontaneous affection for those closest to them toward those who are uncomfortably, even threateningly, different from them, so that their love may become

---

the brotherhood-like ethos of the Christian fellowship was gradually being embedded in the existing patriarchal household structures and having transformative effects on the latter. See Sandness, "Equality within Patriarchal," 151–59; cf. Lampe, "Language of Equality," 70–80. The egalitarian ethos and possibly even structure endured well into the third century, as witnessed by the pagan critic Celsus who charged Christian women and children of actively engaging in the work of evangelization often in defiance of the fathers and schoolmasters. MacDonald, "Was Celsus Right?," 157–58.

35. I am quoting the well-known saying first found in a twelfth-century text attributed to the legendary Egyptian sage Hermes Trismegistus, the *Liber XXIV Philosophorum*, as one of the twenty-four answers to the question, "What is God?" and subsequently reformulated by different figures in theology, philosophy, and science, such as Alan de Lille, Nicholas of Cusa, and Blaise Pascal. See Keeper, "World Turned Inside Out," 303–13.

36. Young Suk Kim presents a powerful reading of 1 Corinthians that offers a vision of the crucified body of Christ in "radical association with the broken bodies in the world," which "envisions a community that negates hegemony and affirms diversity." See Kim, *Christ's Body*, 31. I take the phrase "the crucified people" from the influential essay on Liberation Theology by Ignatio Ellacuría who first coined it in the context of the oppression and suffering of the Latin American poor in the last decades of the twentieth century. See Ellacuría, "Crucified People," 257–78.

37. The phrase "political ascesis" is a rephrase of Charles Mathewes's "ascesis of citizenship." According to Mathewes, Augustine's nuanced theology affirms that "public life can be a way for humans to come to participate in God. It can be understood ascetically, as a means of purifying the soul for God: the ascesis of citizenship can be understood as part of the ascesis of discipleship" (Mathewes, "Theology of Public," 21). The ascesis of citizenship, he avers, finds its ideal training ground in ecclesial communities which, whatever their failings and weaknesses, still offer hard-to-find institutional spaces for an egalitarian and pluralistic thriving of differences à la Gal 3:28 (209). I concur with his argument but would like to give it a Confucian twist.

fully public and political. Sprouting from the seed-image of the divine heart with which we are all born and forged in the crucible of the structures of domination (including the ecclesial ones) in which the liberty of God's adopted children struggles to realize itself, *agape* would no longer be an otherworldly abstraction, i.e., a symbol of Christianity's "worldlessness" and escapist longing for a perfect, heavenly communion. As a profoundly worldly and earthly love, it would take shape in the faithful and hope-filled cruciform struggles of the baptized, both within and outside of the ecclesial body, to bridge chasms of earthly differences in and through public acts of sympathy and critical solidarity.

The city of God, then, comes into being precisely where and when the baptized are made into saints by their ascetic practice of political love, as Martin Luther King Jr. and the Black church heroes of the civil rights coalition amply demonstrated. By luring, prodding, and often calling out the earthly city to become a true commonwealth without any excluded, enclosed, and exploited remainder, from the George Floyds of the world to the undocumented migrants among us,[38] the saints of the heavenly city issue an earthly, political challenge to the contemporary manifestations of the lust for domination in the current world order. With their pluriform yet *equi-valent*—that is, equal in value, not in function—*charismata*, the gifts of the Spirit (1 Cor 12:4–26), the saints, who are called from every race, gender, sex, class, nation, and language, counter the growing threat to the ideal of pluralistic democratic commonwealth posed by the global realignment and re-entrenchment of white Christian supremacy. With their ascetic, cruciform bodies, the saints resist the unbridled competition of nations and states in the unregulated market for the unlimited extraction of our planet's finite bounty. Even just a few examples like these—would they not present the city of God in the way it is supposed to be, as populated by the crucified "friends of God and prophets,"[39] called out of this world yet fully engaged in it, not simply because God has commanded them to but because of the earthly image of the divine heart of sympathy pulsating within them?

---

38. That is, the "undercommons" of the earthly city. Engaging Black critical theory, Catherine Keller has drawn our attention to the *undercommons* lurking beneath the globally dominant political economy of our time and its purported "commonwealth," namely, the dehumanized and the nonhuman ("a virtual planetary majority"), that refuse to be excluded despite the enclosure of the commons (Keller, *Political Theology*, 30–31).

39. Taken from the title of Elizabeth Johnson's classic work on the communion of saints, *Friends of God and Prophets*.

Part II | Comparative Theology

A CONFUCIAN "CHURCH"?
TOWARD A STRANGER VALE OF SAGE-MAKING

A concluding reflection is in order. As one can readily observe in its history, the Confucian tradition has tended to leap straight from the familial to the political in its endeavor to theorize the basis of a humane political order. Arguably the most prominent example of this is the same path of self-cultivation mentioned earlier—as outlined in the classic, *Great Learning*—that runs through a series of ever-enlarging concentric circles of human relations. The series of circles jumps from the family directly to the state, as if there were no intermediate communal relations worth mentioning: "Only after one cultivates one's personal character can one regulate one's family. Only after one regulates one's family can one put the state in order. And only after one has put the state in order can there be peace in the world" (*Great Learning* 1.5). This omission is surely not due to the nonexistence of such communal relations, but likely to two factors. First, within traditional agrarian societies quite often the intermediate associations consisted mostly of extended kinship networks whose structure and ethos did not diverge significantly from those of the family units.[40] The family units themselves, after all, were very often large, extended ones to begin with, encompassing many degrees of kinship and spanning generations.[41] The authors of the classical Confucian texts—including the author(s) of *Great Learning*—lived in times in which the voluntary associations of any kind, independent of either the family or the state, simply were not a prominent feature, if they existed at all.[42]

Secondly, because the Confucian tradition historically tended to view society as an organic whole, "wherein individuals and their collectives are related to each other and depend on each other in a manner similar to the relationship between the individual cells of an organism,"[43] it could not envi-

---

40. For example, organized patrilineal descent groups (lineages) were a common form of local social organization in Chinese history. Ebrey, "Family and Kinship," 1.

41. *Jia* (家), designating the property-holding group that resides together and usually translated as "family," has an extended meaning referring to patrilineal groupings of very large size and depth, especially if they hold some common assets. See Ebrey and Watson, *Introduction*, 8.

42. Nosco, "Confucian Perspective," 21. Hence, insofar as what we today understand by the term "civil society" is constituted by voluntary associations, "Classical Chinese intellectual traditions did not even have words for *civil society*, much less a theory of it" (Madsen, "Confucian Conceptions," 1).

43. Shin, *Confucianism and Democratization*, 147.

sion a society inclusive of a genuinely independent sphere of intermediary associations. As the tradition regarded the state as a vast family governed ideally by a virtuous ruler whose virtue consisted in his parent-like love of the people and capacity to care for them, the existence of independent social organizations without the general permission, guidance and supervision of the paternalistic government would amount to a challenge to its organic holism.[44] Hence, the Confucian tradition never offered a principled justification for autonomous intermediary associations, since "in this Confucian communitarian perspective, the family is the only social group with which the state is supposed to interact."[45]

The problem with this organic social holism with its implied homology among the family, the intermediate associations, and the state—and the consequent lack of serious attention given to the middle term—in the traditional Confucian theorizing of the sage-making path is that it presents too simplistic a picture of the moral struggle involved in the task of becoming a humane political subject. As one moves beyond the immediate circle of the family relations, the familial sentiments as the affective basis of one's moral and "public"—that is, other-oriented—concern become naturally attenuated. Learning to become truly human(e) thus entails a tough labor to overcome the ever-prowling self-interests that beset one in a growing sea of strangers for whom one has less and less spontaneous sympathy, thus sorely needing at minimum the inspiration of moral exemplars to make a progress.[46] Especially in the context of modern pluralistic societies, the

---

44. Nosco, "Confucian Perspectives," 28–29; Madsen, "Confucian Conceptions," 6.

45. Shin, *Confucianism and Democratization*, 147. A glaring exception is the seventeenth-century Neo-Confucian scholar Huang Zongxi, who argued for constitutional limitations on the power of the ruler and an array of mediating institutions, especially schools and learned academies that could serve as centers of educated public opinion. See Madsen, "Confucian Conceptions," 9.

46. Zhao Tingyang highlights Fei-Xiatong's critique of what is arguably the greatest weakness inherent in the classical model of ethical extension of family-state-*tianxia*, namely, that "by the time this affective basis of moral concern gets extended to strangers, there is not sufficient moral motivation left over to sustain the desired ethical outcome" (Zhao, *All Under Heaven*, 73). Zhao points to the traditional Confucian answer to the challenge: the attractive and transformative power of moral exemplars such as *junzi* or *shengren* to influence others so that their initial familial moral sentiments get a boost instead of being diluted and dissipated. This traditional answer, Zhao avers, has its own blind spot however, as "although everyone may agree in admiring certain moral exemplars, not everyone is willing to emulate them" (73). I think Zhao is onto something crucial here, which is no other than the question of (moral) "transcendence" in Confucianism that is connected to the question of its "religious" character, although I do not

reality of moral *agon*, necessitated by the imperative to cultivate *ren* in face of stark and seemingly unbridgeable differences, is as clear as ever. Yet with its relative neglect of the intermediate communal relations the classical Confucian accounts of the sage-making path fail to provide an adequate guide for the disciples of Master Kong today, as they encounter genuinely non-familial—and therefore truly non-familiar—others to whom they must learn to extend their familiar affections for the sake of peaceful co-existence and co-flourishing.[47] Too facile a transition from the familial to the political (leading even to an easy and naive identification between the two),[48] in other words, deprives Master Kong's disciples of the vitally needed map of the terrain and game plan, so to speak, as they try to cultivate their familial moral sentiments in non-familial domains to the point of acquiring the sagely capacity to imagine "the world as common property" (*tianxia weigong* 天下爲公) and to care for it as such.[49] An argument can be made that this lacuna in Confucian moral-political thought is at least partially responsible not only for the repeated failure of the Confucian states to check nepotism, cronyism, and factionalism within their internal echelons of power but also for the purported authoritarian collectivism and ethical monism of Confucian societies, for which history offers an abundant number of case studies as well.

---

have space to discuss it in this essay.

47. My point is not that, historically, those who embarked on the Confucian path of sage-making did not have to pass through intermediate communal relations and associations. Clearly moral self-cultivation had to begin with the family and needed to be sustained by the familial sentiments and rituals. However, whereas "for most people in imperial China it stayed within the (extended) family . . . the more advanced levels of moral cultivation—the kind required to set oneself on the path to becoming a 'gentleman,' capable of responsible political leadership—required a plenitude of intermediary institutions: in the words of Tu Wei-ming, 'community schools, community compacts, local temples, theater groups, clan associations, guilds, festivals, and a variety of ritual-centered activities'" (Madsen, "Confucian Conceptions," 10). My criticism is directed against the *lack of theorizing* on what was actually taking place "on the ground" inevitably and crucially in the premodern past (and is taking place with far greater challenges in the modern pluralistic social contexts of East Asia today), to the detriment of the overall coherence and effectiveness of the Confucian project.

48. See Nosco, "Confucian Perspectives," 25. It is illuminating to note that the East Asian nation-states today all use the combination of Chinese characters *guojia* 國家 (pronounced *gukga* and *kokka* in Korean and Japanese, respectively), which literally means "state-family"—a neologism created by the Japanese in the nineteenth century to translate the Western terms for "state."

49. This is the description of the ideal commonwealth (*datong* 大同) that appears in *Record of Rites*, quoted in Zhao, *All Under Heaven*, 8.

Having learned much from Master Kong's disciples about the familial as the wellspring of the political; and having reimagined the public and political implications of God's family in accordance with that newly gained wisdom, the disciples of Jesus may reciprocate here. They could offer Master Kong's disciples the following challenge and a piece of wisdom: in order to extend the heart of empathy beyond the familial relations to serve the public realm for the sake of the common good, they would need training grounds beyond the familial sphere for learning *ren*-based political participation, i.e., mediating communities and institutions like the *ecclesia* that bridge the familial and the political. Those mediating communities and institutions would first need to be built on and animated by a familial ethos to the extent that they could serve as alternative or substitute families especially for those whose ties to their families of origin, whether biological or non-biological, have been degraded, broken, or destroyed. At the same time, those alternative quasi-families, like the ideal of the *ecclesia*, must have plurality and equality as their founding and operating principles so that the familial ethos nurtured within them cannot easily be corrupted into unjust partialities and favoritisms that exclude. For this reason those communities and institutions need to have a built-in drive toward universal and intersectional inclusion—that is, not be ultimately defined by the existing boundaries of race, ethnicity, gender, sexuality, and so on, although they may have their starting point in those markers of identity.

This would not be a call for the disciples of Master Kong to found a Confucian "church" necessarily, but to remedy the tradition's neglect of the crucial stepping stones for its conception of the familial as the affective foundation of the political to be made as effective as it could be in practice. Whether by forming *ecclesia*-like, "faith-based" alternative communities beyond kinship networks or by participating in civil associations and civic organizations to infuse them with the spirit of Master Kong's teachings, the disciples may create a domain of political *ascesis*. In this training ground for sage-making, they may learn not only to suffer the presence of differences but also to live and flourish with them, so that they may acquire the disposition and skills requisite for becoming sympathetic political subjects capable of building a humane political order. If commonwealth is thus furthered both locally and globally in any degree by the efforts of both groups of disciples who have read this essay, then the purpose of the Confucian-Christian dialogue staged in it will have been served.

Part II | Comparative Theology

BIBLIOGRAPHY

Angle, Stephen C. *Sagehood: The Contemporary Significance of Neo-Confucian Philosophy.* New York: Oxford University Press, 2009.

Barton, Stephen C. "The Relativisation of Family Ties in the Jewish and Graeco-Roman Traditions." In *Constructing Early Christian Families: Family as Social Reality and Metaphor*, edited by Halvor Moxnes, 97–116. London: Routledge, 1997.

Chvala-Smith, Anthony J. "Augustine of Hippo (354–430)." In *Empire and the Christian Tradition*, edited Kwok Pui-Lan et al., 79–94. Minneapolis: Fortress, 2007.

Deuchler, Martina. *The Confucian Transformation of Korea: A Study of Society and Ideology.* Cambridge: Council on East Asian Studies, 1992.

Dietz, Mary G. "Feminist Receptions of Hannah Arendt." In *Feminist interpretations of Hannah Arendt*, edited by Bonnie Honig, 17–50. University Park: Pennsylvania State University Press, 1995.

Ebrey, Patricia Buckley. "Family and Kinship in Chinese History" *Trends in History* 3 (1985) 151–62.

Ebrey, Patricia Buckley, and James L. Watson. Introduction to *Kinship Organization in Late Imperial China, 1000–1940*, edited by Patricia Buckley Ebrey and James L. Watson, 1–15. Berkeley: University of California Press, 1986.

Ellacuría, Ignacio. "The Crucified People." In *Systematic Theology: Perspectives from Liberation Theology*, edited by Jon Sobrino and Ignacio Ellacuría, 257–78. Maryknoll, NY: Orbis, 1996.

Esler, Philip F. "Family Imagery and Christian Identity in Gal 5:13 to 6:10." In *Constructing Early Christian Families: Family as Social Reality and Metaphor*, edited by Halvor Moxnes, 121–49. London: Routledge, 1997.

Finlan, Stephen. *The Family Metaphor in Jesus' Teaching: Gospel and Ethics.* Eugene, OR: Cascade, 2009.

Gardner, Daniel K., trans. *The Four Books: The Basic Teachings the Later Confucian Traditions.* Indianapolis: Hackett, 2007.

Gregory, Eric. *Politics and the Order of Love: An Augustinian Ethic of Democratic Citizenship.* Chicago: University of Chicago Press, 2008.

Hellerman, Joseph H. *Ancient Church as Family.* Minneapolis: Fortress, 2001.

Huang, Chichung, trans. *The Analects of Confucius (Lun Yu).* New York: Oxford University Press, 1997.

Isasi-Diaz, Ada Maria. "Kin-dom of God: A Mujerista Proposal." In *In Our Own Voices: Latino/a Renditions of Theology*, edited by Benjamín Valentín, 171–90. Maryknoll, NY: Orbis, 2010.

Johnson, Elizabeth, A. *Friends of God and Prophets: A Feminist Theological Reading of the Communion of Saints.* New York: Continuum, 1998.

Keefer, Michael. "The World Turned Inside Out: Revolutions of the Infinite Sphere from Hermes to Pascal." *Renaissance and Reformation* 12.4 (1988) 303–13.

Keller, Catherine. "Elemental Love: Toward a Counter-Apocalyptic Coalition." In *9/11 and American Empire: Christians, Jews, and Muslims Speak Out*, edited by Kevin Barrett et al., vol. 2, 63–76. Northampton, MA: Olive Branch, 2007.

———. *Political Theology of the Earth: Our Planetary Emergency and the Struggle for a New Public.* New York: Columbia University Press, 2018.

Kiess, John. *Hannah Arendt and Theology.* Philosophy and Theology. London: Bloomsbury T. & T. Clark, 2016.

Kim, Young Suk. *Christ's Body in Corinth: The Politics of a Metaphor*. Paul in Critical Contexts. Minneapolis: Fortress, 2008.
Lampe, Peter. "The Language of Equality in Early Christian House Churches: A Constructivist Approach." In *Early Christian Families in Context: An Interdisciplinary Dialogue*, edited by David L. Balch and Carolyn Osiek, 73-83. Grand Rapids: Eerdmans, 2003.
Lassen, Eva Marie Lassen. "The Roman Family: Ideal and Metaphor." In *Constructing Early Christian Families: Family as Social Reality and Metaphor*, edited by Halvor Moxnes, 119-36. London: Routledge, 1997.
Lau, D. C., trans. *Mencius*. Rev. ed. New York: Penguin, 2003.
Long, Christopher Philip. "A Fissure in the Distinction: Hannah Arendt, the Family, and the Public/Private Dichotomy." *Philosophy & Social Criticism* 24.5 (1998) 85-104.
MacDonald, Margaret Y. "Was Celsus Right? The Role of Women in the Expansion of Early Christianity." In *Early Christian Families in Context: An Interdisciplinary Dialogue*, edited by David L. Balch and Carolyn Osiek, 157-84. Grand Rapids: Eerdmans, 2003.
Madsen, Richard. "Confucian Conceptions of Civil Society." In *A Confucian Political Ethics*, edited by Daniel A. Bell, 190-204. Princeton: Princeton University Press, 2008.
Marcus, R. A. *Saeculum: History and Society in the Theology of St. Augustine*. New York: Cambridge University Press, 1970.
Mathewes, Charles. *A Theology of Public Life*. Cambridge Studies in Christian Doctrine 17. New York: Cambridge University Press, 2007.
Moxnes, Halvor. "What Is Family? Problems in Constructing Early Christian Families." In *Constructing Early Christian Families: Family as Social Reality and Metaphor*, edited by Halvor Moxnes, 29-57. London: Routledge, 1997.
Nosco, Peter. "Confucian Perspectives on Civil Society and Government." In *Confucian Political Ethics*, edited by Daniel A. Bell, 20-45. Princeton: Princeton University Press, 2008.
O'Donovan, Oliver, and Joan Lockwood O'Donovan, eds. *From Irenaeus to Grotius: A Sourcebook in Christian Political Thought*. Grand Rapids: Eerdmans, 1999.
Osiek, Carolyn. "What We Do and Don't Know About Early Christian Families." In *A Companion to Families in the Greek and Roman Worlds*, edited by Beryl Rawson, 198-213. Blackwell Companions to the Ancient World: Literature and Culture. Malden, MA: Blackwell, 2011.
Rosenlee, Li-Hsiang Lisa. *Confucianism and Women: A Philosophical Interpretation*. SUNY Series in Chinese Philosophy and Culture. Albany: SUNY Press, 2006.
Rozman, Gilbert. "Center-Local Relations: Can Confucianism Boost Decentralization and Regionalism?" In *Confucianism for the Modern World*, edited by Daniel A. Bell and Chaibong Hahm, 181-200. New York: Cambridge University Press, 2003.
Sandness, Karl Olav. "Equality within Patriarchal Structures: Some New Testament Perspectives on the Christian Fellowship as a Brother- or Sisterhood and a Family." In *Constructing Early Christian Families: Family as Social Reality and Metaphor*, edited by Halvor Moxnes, 166-81. London: Routledge, 1997.
Schüssler Fiorenza, Elisabeth. "The Praxis of Coequal Discipleship." In *Paul and Empire: Religion and Power in Roman Imperial Society*, edited by Richard A. Horsley, 224-41. Harrisburg, PA: Trinity, 1997.

Part II | Comparative Theology

Shin, Dol Chul. *Confucianism and Democratization in East Asia*. Cambridge: Cambridge University Press, 2012.
Tiwald, Justin, and Bryan W. van Norden, eds. *Readings in Later Chinese Philosophy: Han to the Twentieth Century*. Cambridge: Hackett, 2014.
Wiley, Tatha. "Paul and Early Christianity." In *Empire and the Christian Tradition*, edited by Kwok Pui-Lan et al., 47–62. Minneapolis: Fortress, 2007.
Zhao, Tingyang. *All Under Heaven: The Tianxia System for a Possible World Order*. Oakland: University of California Press, 2021.
Zhu Xi. *Sishu Zhangju Jizhu [Collected Commentaries on the Four Books]*. Beijing: Zhonghua Shu Ju, 1983.
Zhuangzi. *Zhuangzi Jishi [Collected Commentaries on Zhuangzi]*. Compiled by Guo Qingfan. Edited by Wang Xiaoyu. 3 vols. Beijing: Zhonghua Shu Ju, 1961.

4

Supper with the Lord
Comparative Liturgical Theological Reflection on Eucharist and Prasada

MARTHA MOORE-KEISH

INTRODUCTION

The genesis of this project dates to the collision of two worlds that I experienced my first day of entering seminary, over thirty years ago. I had just returned from a year of study of ancient Indian history and culture at Visva-Bharati University in West Bengal, and nearly immediately upon my return I began intensive Greek at Union Presbyterian Seminary in Richmond, Virginia, with the intention of preparing for congregational ministry in the Presbyterian Church (USA). As I introduced myself, I said, "My name is Martha Moore. I just returned from a year in India studying Hinduism, and I thought I would come here and give Christianity a try." Nobody laughed. Much of the rest of my professional life has been an effort to interpret that moment.

I cannot remember the first time I was offered food at a Hindu temple, either as I left the space or after observing puja (that is, worship before the image of a deity). I also cannot remember the first time I received bread and "wine" at my own church, in remembrance of Jesus, in the Christian ritual of the Lord's Supper.[1] I cannot recall the specifics, but I do know

---

1. Though the elements are commonly referred to as bread and wine, in the American

that over time my interest in both food rituals has grown, along with my curiosity about what, if anything, they have to do with each other. After all, in both cases, the gift of food comes with the understanding that it has come in contact with divine presence, and that it communicates that presence (somehow, in a way that is amply contested in the traditions) to the one who receives it. My persistent interest in this question arises from a flash of recognition of and longing for sacred food exchange in the context of sharp dissimilarity between my own home sub-tradition and devotional Hinduism.

In this essay, I begin a comparative theological reflection on (Christian) Eucharist and (Hindu) prasada, which is the name for the food received after a Hindu puja. In order to narrow the focus, I will focus on two particular ritual texts: Ramanuja's *Nityagrantham* (a key ritual manual that addresses prasada in the Srivaishnava Pancaratra tradition), and the eucharistic section of the PC(USA) *Book of Common Worship* 2018 (the most current ritual resource in my own particular Reformed Protestant tradition). In both cases, attention to these texts will be supplemented by lived experience and with respect for the particularity of these sub-traditions within the larger diversity of Hindu and Christian traditions.

At the outset, I need to acknowledge the limits of this essay: here I focus on texts more than practices, even though my driving interest is about the interaction of theology and practice. Further, the *Nityam* is not singularly representative of the Hindu temple practices that initially caught my attention. Next steps in this research will attend more specifically to embodied practices, as well as to the range of other texts that shape and describe such practices today. This is, however, a beginning.

COMPARATIVE THEOLOGY METHODS

In the past decade, with the help of scholars such as John Thatamanil and Michelle Voss, I have discovered the field of comparative theology, which offers a path into my question, a path that honors both openness to genuine learning across religious traditions and normative commitment to a home tradition. As Francis Clooney describes it, comparative theology includes

---

Presbyterian tradition, unfermented grape juice is most commonly the element used in the cup. If fermented wine is included, which is increasingly common, an unfermented option must also be provided.

acts of faith seeking understanding which are rooted in a particular faith tradition but which, from that foundation, venture into learning from one or more other faith traditions. This learning is done for the sake of fresh theological insights that are indebted to the newly encountered tradition/s as well as the home tradition.[2]

This is exactly the kind of work I have hungered for: deep learning across religious traditions, with a clear normative bent.

In her work on method in comparative theology, Catherine Cornille describes two basic approaches within comparative theology: confessional and meta-confessional.[3] While confessional approaches identify more strongly with their home traditions, "meta-confessional" approaches work more freely across traditions in their pursuit of wisdom, sometimes identifying as "theology without walls."[4] My project is more confessional in approach, but not narrowly so. As a Reformed Protestant theologian, it is my deep conviction that God is beyond all our categories and systems, even as I continue to affirm that the incarnation of Jesus Christ has normative significance for my own understanding of both God and humanity. In earlier work, I have offered specifically Reformed theological reasons for doing comparative theology, making explicit connections between comparative and confessional theologies.[5]

This project is modeled after the tightly focused approach of Clooney, Thatamanil (especially his earlier work), and Voss, among others.[6] In order to make a beginning, I am focusing on one ritual text from each tradition, with attention to what happens in the food exchange. What is attributed to divine agency, and what to human agency? What is the relationship between individual and corporate human agency? How does this ritual interaction both shape and reveal the relationship between human and divine, and among human beings?

What do I hope to learn from this exploration? Cornille describes six common types of comparative theological learning:

2. Clooney, *Comparative Theology*, 10.
3. See chapter 1 in Cornille, *Meaning and Method*. Cornille lists four principal characteristics of confessional comparative theology: (1) clear confessional identity of the theologian; (2) choice of topics; (3) criteria of discernment (including accountability to a community of practice); and (4) stated goal of the exercise. See also chapter 5 on the relationship of confessional and meta-confessional comparative theology.
4. https://www.theologywithoutwalls.com.
5. Moore-Keish, "Divine Freedom and Human Religions."
6. Cornille, *Meaning and Method*, 14–15.

- Intensification
- Rectification
- Recovery
- Reinterpretation
- Appropriation
- Reaffirmation[7]

Of these, my work so far shows signs of both rectification and recovery: *rectification*, as better understanding of another tradition informs new understanding of my own in relation to that other; and *recovery*, as comparative theology out of commitment to the Reformed Protestant sub-tradition within Christianity (often perceived to be uninterested in or even hostile to comparative theological work) leads to greater appreciation for elements in my own tradition that may be underappreciated. Indeed, my sacramental research and writing over the decades already shows recovery of elements of my own tradition as a learning from interreligious encounter, since my ongoing interest in Eucharist arose partly because of encounter with lived Hindu devotional practice. This new project gives me an opportunity to make such recovery more explicit.

CONTEXT: HINDU PRACTICES OF GIVING AND RECEIVING PRASADA

The Sanskrit word "prasada" is often translated into English as "grace," and in its broadest usage it refers to "the free choice, or action, of a deity, or power, to favor a devotee with the means to liberation (e.g., knowledge), or liberation itself."[8] The key points here are: (a) human beings need liberation (from the cycle of rebirth); (b) divine powers are able to offer means of liberation; and (c) prasada names the action by which a deity's liberating power is offered. Prasada then rests on the assumption that human liberation depends on an external divine power.[9] By extension, it comes also to

---

7. See chapter 4 in Cornille, *Meaning and Method*.
8. Johnson, *Dictionary of Hinduism*, 242–43.
9. "This idea that the liberation of the individual depends, ultimately, not on their own actions (karma), but on a power beyond them, characterized as 'grace' (prasāda) appears in the Kaṭha (2.20f) and Śvetāśvatara Upaniṣads (3.20; 6.21), and the Bhagavadgītā (e.g., 18.56, 58), and is subsequently taken up by various theistic devotional movements.

refer to the material objects that bear the divine presence from deity to worshipers at the end of a puja (worship). Either at home or at a temple, worshipers present offerings to the deity (usually food such as fruit, sweets, or rice, though offerings may also include flowers, water, or materials used for adornment of the deity), and after the puja, once the deity is understood to have partaken of the offerings, they are then shared among those who are present.[10]

In its brief entry, Encyclopedia Britannica offers the following definition:

> Prasada (Sanskrit: "favour" or "grace") in Hinduism, food and water offered to a deity during worship (puja). It is believed that the deity partakes of and then returns the offering, thereby consecrating it. The offering is then distributed and eaten by the worshippers. The efficacy of the *prasada* comes from its having been touched by the deity.[11]

Similarly, W. J. Johnson says:

> The deity's . . . favour, or prosada (*sic*), is materially conveyed to the devotees through the distribution . . . of food . . . and other previously made offerings. Because of their proximity to the deity, such left-overs . . . are considered to be "blessed"—that is to say, imbued with the deity's power and grace. It is these qualities which are then physically transferred to the devotees, bringing about their temporary identification or merger with the god.[12]

In smaller temples, prasada may be offered freely to participants immediately following a puja, as I have experienced in the Hindu Temple of Atlanta. There, devotees may bring food to offer to the deity, or it may be brought up from the temple kitchen downstairs. Following the ritual

It probably receives its most sophisticated theological treatment in the Viśiṣṭādvaita of Rāmānuja and the works of the Śrī Vaiṣṇava theologians who follow him" (Johnson, *Dictionary of Hinduism*).

10. Johnson, *Dictionary of Hinduism*.
11. "Prasada."
12. Johnson, *Dictionary of Hinduism*, 92. See also Flueckiger, *Everyday Hinduism*. The giving of food to the image of the deity in temple and receiving of prasada is well described by Flueckiger and in Eck, *Darsan*, 33–38. The image of the deity is "the real embodiment of the deity" (Eck) and is thus to be fed and cared for. The deity becomes accessible, even dependent on the human devotees. Reflections on whether the deity "needs" to be fed tend to emphasize the appropriate behavior of hospitality by the devotee and the awakening of the senses of the devotee, not the absolute need of the deity itself.

offering, the remaining blessed food (prasada) is distributed to anyone who happens to be there.[13] At larger temples, such as the Sri Venkateswara Swami Vaari Temple in Tirupati, pilgrims may purchase prasada to take home, to eat as well as share with others.[14] Prasada may also name food that is offered to and received from a guru, since a guru is understood to be a living god. In addition, all food may be regarded as prasada if it is partaken after meditating on and mentally offering it to a deity.

Hindu theologian Anant Rambachan reflects on the transformation of ordinary bananas into prasada in his own practice of offering them at temple. He says, "It is evident that the bananas have not changed; they are not different in appearance and content. When, however, I receive the banana after the temple priest offers it to the murti, the living embodiment of God, I see it as prasada, as a gift and blessing from God. This understanding brings about a corresponding change in my state of mind that may be best described as one of cheerful serenity and joy."[15] This account demonstrates how the reception of prasada can change the affective experience of the devotee, because of the perception that it is a gift of God.

In her essay, "Prasada, the Gracious Gift, in Contemporary and Classical South Asia," Andrea Marion Pinkney focuses on the continuity of the understanding of prasada over time since the classical era. She describes prasada in contemporary Hindu ritual (in Vaishnava, Shaiva, and Shakta contexts) and in classical texts (with examples from Vaishnava and Shaiva texts, including the Skandapurana and the Visnupurana) to show the strong continuity between the two, with common focus on the blessed material object. She says,

> The notion of prasada expresses the idea that an efficacious energy of generosity and benevolence is inherently manifest in the world . . . in practice, it is accessed through ritual actions that are automatically efficacious. . . . Prasada, the gracious gift, [is] at the core of contemporary Hindu religious life as well as the Hindu Sanskritic tradition. As such, prasada . . . is a crucial factor in appreciating Hindu civilization in South Asian terms.[16]

13. https://www.hindutempleofatlanta.org. At this temple, the primary deity is Visnu as Venkateswara, in connection with the major temple in Tirupati, Andhra Pradesh (https://www.tirumala.org).

14. Tirupati features special laddus (round sweets usually made from flour, ghee, and jaggery) as their prasada. In January 2023, these large sweets sold for Rs. 50 apiece.

15. Rambachan, *Essays in Hindu Theology*, 85.

16. Pinkney, "Prasāda, the Gracious Gift," 753. See also Pinkney, "Prasāda," which

Prasada, then, offers a significant locus for theological reflection on the interaction of divine and human agents, and on the experience of "grace" received by devotees.

CONTEXT: SRIVAISHNAVA TRADITION AND RAMANUJA

One of the largest traditions within Hinduism is Srivaishnavism, or the devotion to Lord Vishnu and his consort Sri. This is a major denomination within the broad family of Vaishnavism, or devotion to Vishnu. Like other branches of Hinduism, Srivaishnavism looks to the Vedas and Upanishads as foundational texts, and the initial concept of prasada has its origin in the Kaṭha and Śvetāśvatara Upaniṣads. However, it is within Srivaishnavism that prasada has received most detailed development, particularly in the work of the eleventh-century reformer Ramanuja (1017–1137).

Ramanuja's theological approach "is referred to as Qualified Nondualism (Visistadvaita) to distinguish it from the Nondual (Advaita) theology of Sankara (ca. eighth [century] CE). Although sharing with Sankara the view that the infinite brahman is the only reality, Ramanuja contends that brahman is internally complex and diverse."[17] Because of the strong influence of Vaishnavism, and because of the influence of Ramanuja in particular in developing this tradition and its emphasis on prasada, Ramanuja offers an appropriate focus for exploring prasada in this comparative project.[18]

THE NITYAGRANTHAM

It is fortuitous that Ramanuja's own ritual text, the *Nityagrantham* or simply *Nityam*, has recently been for the first time fully and adequately translated into English by Francis Clooney.[19] Although this text does not directly reflect current practices and interpretations of temple worship, it has influenced those practices, as a key writing by a foremost Vaishnava

---

echoes insights above, in brief form. For a comprehensive exploration of the concept of prasada, see Pinkney, "Sacred Share."

17. Rambachan, *Essays in Hindu Theology*, 79.

18. Edward P. Hahnenberg has offered a similar comparative project in his exploration of the concept of "image-descent" and eucharist, in conversation with Srivaishnavism, as discussed further below. See Hahnenberg, "Arcāvatāra."

19. Clooney, "Rāmānuja's *Nityagrantham*." Hereafter cited as *Nityam*.

theologian. It thus offers a specific entry point to explore prasada in the context of Vaishnava practice and interpretation.

Clooney introduces the *Nityagrantham* in this way:

> The *Nityam* is a ritual text indebted to the Vaisnava Hindu theological-ritual tradition obscurely known as Pancaratra.... It follows many standard ritual practices of that tradition, involving the recitation of mantras, offerings of honorific objects (water, incense, flowers, etc.) to the Lord, enactments of morning ablutions, the donning of fresh garments, food offerings, as well as invocations of the many lesser beings in the Lord's heavenly court.... Distinctive to the *Nityam* are the moments of intense meditation, the meditative assertion that the Lord alone is the true agent of the worship (while the worshiper is merely the instrument), and the ideal of worship as service seeking no reward in return.[20]

The *Nityam* consists of three major parts: part 1: preparations; part 2: *yaga*: contemplative worship (the more interior acts of meditation); and part 3: *puja*: intimate worship of the Lord (the external actions, which include the bath, the meal, and the "sharing of the Lord's *prasadam* with *acarya* [the teacher] and the community."[21]

Of particular interest to this project is the section from part 3 on "The Lord's Meal."[22] Here, Ramanuja describes the food offered ("the very well-prepared food rich in ghi and curd, milk and honey, and fruits, roots, and spices, as well as sweets, plus other things most pleasing in ordinary life, and things preferred by himself such as are not contrary to the instructive scriptures") to the deity, followed by the petition: "Please accept this as very abundant, entirely complete, most pleasing, done with extreme devotion."

Following the offering of the meal to Vishnu, the *Nityam* includes three sections:

1. "Ensuring the Lord's Satisfaction" (describing the actions following the meal, including drinking, washing, venerating, offering sandals and songs of praise).

2. "Meditation on the Lord's Exclusive Agency in the Worship" (which includes the meditation "By this self whose single delight is in total dependence on Him, by its activity, steadiness, proper form controlled

---

20. *Nityam*, 346.
21. *Nityam*, 347.
22. *Nityam*, 372–73.

by Him, and by his own body, senses, and mind, the Lord alone has brought about all enjoyments, such as are honorific, tangible, and pertaining to food, etc., and such as are made of His own innate and most auspicious substances. . . . All these are for His own pleasure, for Himself along with all His retinue and insignia").[23]

3. "Offerings to the Teacher and the Community": "After asking the Lord's permission, he offers to Visvaksena a bit of the oblation offered to the Lord, and then gives all the rest of Vaisnavas, beginning with his acarya.[24] He worships Visvaksena with materials, water, etc. not distinguished as part of the sacrifice to the Lord. He gives an oblation previously offered."[25]

This last section will be particularly interesting as a point of comparison with Reformed Protestant eucharistic practice, since it is the focal point of actual food sharing. How does the *Nityam* interpret the nature of the deity's presence in/through prasada? The murti (image) is strongly (though not materially) identified with the presence of God through the understanding of arcavatara,[26] but the food offering is not. This might be a significant point of comparison with Eucharist for Reformed Protestants, who do not strongly identify the food itself with the presence of God in a localized way.[27]

---

23. *Nityam*, 374.

24. Visvaksena is identified as the "commander of the Lord's [Visnu's] army," a being analogous to an archangel in Christian understanding. Frank Clooney comments, "A teacher in Chennai told me that either the worshipper, who is alone, brings the prasad to his teacher, his home, etc.—or that this, too, is done mentally. But the wording does not explain further than what I give" (Clooney, personal communication, March 7, 2023).

25. *Nityam*, 374. Prasada is counter to usual purity rules; in South Asian culture, eating from someone else's plate is unclean in most circumstances (except mother and child). But if it is the Lord's plate, then it is pure.

26. "The imaging of the Lord seems to be very vivid and detailed, but all mental; there is no material image" (Clooney, personal communication, March 7, 2023).

27. And there is a tantalizing parallel for further exploration in both traditions' emphasis on ascent as a rationale for distinction between the presence of God and the food itself. For Vaishnavism, Clooney observes that "earlier in the text, the worshipper mentally ascends to heaven to worship the Lord there, and returns to earth, to worship here" (Clooney, personal communication, March 7, 2023) In Reformed Protestantism, the body of Jesus is understood to be "ascended," which is why it is not locally present in conjunction with the bread and wine of the Lord's Supper.

PART II | COMPARATIVE THEOLOGY

ONE EXAMPLE OF EUCHARISTIC THEOLOGY AND PRACTICE: THE PRESBYTERIAN CHURCH (USA) AND THE *BOOK OF COMMON WORSHIP* 2018

For many Christians since the first century, a basic element of regular worship has been the sharing of bread and wine "in remembrance of" Jesus the Christ, whose life, death, and resurrection appearances were punctuated by shared meals.[28] This meal goes by many names depending on the context, but in current ecumenical discourse it is most commonly called the Eucharist, from the Greek word for thanksgiving. In my own context, it is also frequently named "the Lord's Supper," as a reminder that this is a meal at which the Lord Jesus is host (not we ourselves).

As someone formed by and ordained to ministry in the Presbyterian Church (USA), I am focusing on the theology and practice of the Lord's Supper in this church body as a point of comparison with the *Nityam*. The most recent official text informing eucharistic practice in the PC(USA) is the *Book of Common Worship* (2018),[29] which was a revision of an earlier landmark 1993 volume of the same name. Though particular to this denomination, both versions of the BCW are results of the ecumenical liturgical renewal of the past sixty years, the fruit of significant biblical, historical, and theological scholarship by Catholic, Orthodox, and Protestant Christians. Thus, this eucharistic order is not unique to Presbyterian/Reformed Christians, though it has distinctive emphases.

The Lord's Supper (or Eucharist), like the "Lord's Meal" in the *Nityam*, follows other acts of worship, particularly opening prayers, readings from scripture, and interpretation of scripture in the form of a sermon delivered by a leader for the gathered community. Following this act of "proclamation," the worship moves to focus on the Supper. The basic structure of this element of worship is as follows:

- Offering: the presider invites people to make offerings, which usually include financial contributions and may also include food items. These are brought forward, and the presider offers a prayer of dedication.

---

28. In earliest centuries, eucharistic meals also sometimes included additional food items, such as cheese and olives. The Synod of Hippo in 393 restricted the eucharistic elements to bread and wine.

29. PC(USA), *Book of Common Worship*. Hereafter cited as *BCW*. There are many variations on the eucharistic service in this volume, but the most basic one is on pages 25–29.

Supper with the Lord

- Invitation to the table: the presider addresses the community gathered, calling them to the feast, and concluding with words such as, "This is the Lord's Table. Our Savior invites those who trust him to share the feast that he has prepared."[30]

- Great prayer of thanksgiving: the presider offers a prayer giving thanks to the triune God for the works of salvation, including creation and redemption, with particular attention to the life, death, and resurrection of Jesus the Christ. In response to this gift, the presider voices the assembly's own offering of themselves "to live for [Jesus Christ] in joy and praise." The prayer closes with a petition for the Holy Spirit to come upon the elements of bread and wine, "that they may be for us the body and blood of Christ and that we may be his body for the world."[31] Following a concluding doxology, the assembled people say together the "Lord's Prayer."

- The presider also offers "words of institution," which are scriptural words from Jesus' "last supper" with his disciples before his death, including "This is my body that is for you. Do this in remembrance of me."[32] It is significant that the "you" here is plural, signifying the community of disciples. These words are sometimes shared as part of the invitation to the table, and sometimes as part of the prayer itself, in connection with giving thanks for Jesus' life, death, and resurrection. Both options are provided in the BCW. Most common in lived practice, however, is the use of the words of institution following the prayer, in conjunction with the acts of breaking bread and pouring the wine/juice into the cup.

- After the breaking of the bread and pouring of the wine, the elements are shared with the people gathered. This may happen in a variety of ways: most often either by passing trays from person to person through the assembly, or by inviting people to come forward and receive the elements from servers.

- The Lord's Supper ends with a prayer after communion, which may be spoken by all those gathered or may be spoken by the presider.

---

30. *BCW*, 26.

31. *BCW*, 27. These and the preceding words of self-offering are representative examples of language that may be used at this point in the prayer.

32. 1 Cor 11:24; cf. Matt 26:26–29; Mark 14:22–25; Luke 22:14–23.

PART II | COMPARATIVE THEOLOGY

On the face of it, there are clear similarities between these two ritual texts, in the sharing of food among devotees in conjunction with encounter with the presence of the divine. This is the point of contact that I wish to explore.

EXISTING COMPARATIVE WORK

Despite the clear family resemblance between the receiving of prasada and the Lord's Supper, I have been unable to find significant research comparing the two. Klaus Klostermaier makes a passing comparative reference in *A Survey of Hinduism*, when he describes temple worship, including prasada, saying "there will hardly be any Hindu who would not go to the temple once in a while and many make it a point to honor the Lord through a daily visit and to receive *prasada as a kind of communion* and a talisman against misfortune."[33] Anna King and Graham Dwyer have each written on the specific ISKCON practice of prasada, which has its own twentieth-century adaptation of Vaishnavite food preparation and practice; in their descriptions they also acknowledge similarities between prasada and Christian sacramental acts.[34] Anant Rambachan mentions the different practices of hospitality between Hindu temple and Christian Eucharist.[35] Edward P. Hahnenberg has offered a similar comparative project in his exploration of the concept of "image-descent" (*arcavatara*) and Eucharist, in conversation with Srivaishnavism. He concludes that "while aspects of the Hindu conception resonate with a Catholic sacramental imagination, fundamental differences preclude an easy comparison. The categories of transcendence, accessibility, relationship, and revelation gleaned from this introduction offer points of entry for continued dialogue."[36] My own project follows up on

---

33. Klostermaier, *Survey of Hinduism*, 277 (my emphasis).
34. See King, "Krishna's *Prasadam*"; Dwyer, "Krishna *Prasadam*."
35. Rambachan, *Essays in Hindu Theology*, 91–92.
36. See Hahnenberg, "Arcävatära," 187. The primary differences that Hahnenberg notes are: (1) the communal emphasis in Catholic eucharist (in contrast to what seems a more individual emphasis in arcavatara); and (2) the Srivaisnava notion of *suddha sattva*, "the luminous and nonearthly 'stuff'" of the *arcävatära*," which names how the deity is present in the image, but in a way seemingly different from a Christian understanding of incarnation. As a side note, Hahnenberg's article invites further reflection on how the intra-Christian eucharistic debates also interact with Christian-Hindu comparative theology: "The Catholic chooses the words 'art', 'icon', 'sacrament', and 'eucharist' to suggest this presence, this 'tangibility', of the divine. Catholicism has always avoided a stark

this invitation to "continued dialogue," though from a Reformed Protestant rather than Catholic perspective.

The most directly relevant comparative project is a 1998 article by Paul Courtright on Eucharist and Puja, in which this scholar of Hinduism (who is also a practicing Episcopalian) offers a close comparison of Eucharist and Puja through a comparative religion lens, with attention to practice and to the role of the participant observer. Consistent with the aims of comparative theology, Courtright mentions that this exercise of "entering the ritual and experience of another religion will encourage a more nuanced Christian theologian capable of more profound Christian practice."[37]

In his article, Courtright uses the categories drawn from the Pranaprastitha puja (described in detail) to describe the Christian (specifically the Episcopalian) Eucharist celebration at Easter Vigil, asking, "How might Hindu ritual categories be applied to episodes of the Eucharist in ways that will extend the range of understanding and appreciation?"[38] He draws attention to analogies between the opening prayer of the Eucharist and the sankalpa of the Puja; the Exsultet and the desalokacaranam; the similar *bhava* of joy; the preparatory gestures of the priest and the acamana of the pujari; and the central transformative moments of both rituals.

In comparing the central act of communion and the distribution of prasada, Courtright says:

> The distribution of the elements of Communion to be eaten by the assembly resembles the distribution of *prasada*, the food which is offered to the deity and then returned, consecrated, to the assembly. Both Puja and Eucharist stress the divine Body image. In the Eucharist, the food *becomes* the Body through ritual evocation and the belief of the assembly; in the Puja, the food is a gift *from* the deity as that portion he did not consume. In between this apparent distinction is the affirmation in Puja that the *prana* of the image is also the *prana* of all beings; with the Eucharist, the food/Body is the condensation and representation of the redeemed cosmos. In both cases, to put the matter negatively, the difference between the human and the divine, between the ordinary and the extraordinary, is erased. The ritual time-space becomes a locale

---

Puritanism" (196). Such a passing comment suggests an oversimplified understanding of Puritanism, a branch of Reformed Protestantism that is far from being anti-material, though its sacramentalism is not the same as that of Catholicism.

37. Courtright, "Looking at Eucharist," 426.
38. Courtright, "Looking at Eucharist," 431.

of nondifference; hence the semantic range of language and substances extends beyond previous limits. In the ritual context, one can say that the food is the divine Body, the image is living, and both are in the presence of the assembly in ways that significantly change the *bhava* (quality) of experience. As different as these two rituals are in detail and religious and cultural contexts, they bear a striking family resemblance in terms of the work they accomplish, overcoming the experience of cosmological alienation and fear of loss.[39]

Although Courtright acknowledges clear differences between the two rituals, he is most struck by the similarity between the two, both in structure and in intention. This is a helpful beginning point, but I wish to take a further step in theological reflection on these similarities and differences.

INITIAL COMPARATIVE HUNCHES

In comparing these two food-related rituals, I will explore three themes: divine and human agency, the relationship of the deity to the food elements, and the ways in which these rituals shape relationships—both the relationship between deity and devotee, and relationships among devotees.

First, agency. The *Nityam* devotes much attention to the preparation of the performer and to the initial act of offering by the devotee, in great detail. Ramanuja offers a lengthy description of "contemplative ascent to the Lord's heaven, and return" in part 2, which give the performer a sense of the cosmic and heavenly dimensions of the daily rite.[40] He then turns to "intimate worship of the Lord" in part 3. There is first an elaborate bathing ritual, which includes water, scent, flowers, incense, flame, mouth-wash, betel nut, etc. and the words, "Lord, accept all this, my self and what is mine, as permanently in your service."[41] During the preparation of the meal, there are more offerings, of "scent and flowers, adornments, collyrium, the forehead mark, mirror, incense, flame, water for sipping, flag, umbrella, fan, vehicle, conch, mark, musical instruments and drums, etc."[42] Then, at the meal itself, the devotee offers a variety of food items to the deity

---

39. Courtright, "Looking at Eucharist," 438.
40. Clooney, personal communication, March 7, 2023.
41. *Nityam*, 369.
42. *Nityam*, 371.

Supper with the Lord

"with his bowed, his eyes wide with delight, his mind delighted."[43] Finally the devotee "offers an obeisance, and then makes an offering, saying, 'Please accept this as very abundant, entirely complete, most pleasing, done with extreme devotion.'"[44] In the *Nityam*, the devotee focuses a great deal of time and energy (and specific material resources) to the veneration of the Lord, highlighting the human agency involved.

This focus on the human agency of offering in the *Nityam* contrasts with the downplaying of human agency in the Reformed/Presbyterian Eucharist. In both cases, there is an "offering" at the beginning of the food ritual, involving the giving of material gifts. In the Presbyterian context, however, the offering of the worshiper is framed as response, not initiative. The invitation reads, "The earth is the Lord's, and all that is in it, the world, and those who live in it. Let us return to God the offerings of our life and the gifts of the earth."[45] The text explicitly affirms that all things belong to God, and we *return* to God what is already the Lord's. This point is significant in Reformed theology, which emphasizes that the Eucharist is primarily a gift that we receive, not a sacrifice that we offer. This historic Reformed insistence that this is the *Lord's* table emphasizes divine initiative, as a safeguard against any human ecclesial power.

Though this at first appears to be a significant difference, with the *Nityam* highlighting human action and the Reformed Eucharist highlighting the priority of divine agency, the picture is more complicated than first appears. In the *Nityam*, the act of offering/sacrifice by the devotee stands together with strong insistence on the priority of divine agency. In the "Meditation on the Lord's Exclusive Agency in the Worship," God alone is named as the one who acts first, and humans receive and respond. The *Nityam* reads, "By this self whose single delight is in total dependence on Him, . . . the Lord alone has brought about all enjoyments, such as are honorific, tangible, and pertaining to food, etc."[46] This recalls a line from early in the *Nityam*, which says, "The Lord alone now begins, by means of me who belongs entirely to Him, to please His own self along with his whole retinue and insignia."[47] In other words, the entire ritual practice is framed

---

43. *Nityam*, 372.
44. *Nityam*, 373.
45. *BCW*, 25.
46. *Nityam*, 374.
47. *Nityam*, 351. See also similar affirmations of "the Lord alone" as the primary actor in *Nityam*, 354 (i.v), 356 (i.vii).

with the explicit understanding that it is the Lord who is the primary actor, in and through the devotee.

At the same time, though the Reformed Supper emphasizes divine agency, there is also clear human activity expected and empowered by God. In the Great Prayer, for instance, the presider says, "Remembering your boundless love revealed to us in Jesus Christ, we break bread and share the cup, giving ourselves to you."[48] In the prayer after communion, the presider says these or similar words: "Send us forth in the power of your Spirit that we may proclaim your redeeming love to the world and continue forever in the risen life of Jesus Christ, our Lord."[49] Devotees of Jesus are recipients of gifts, indeed, but not passively so. The gifts themselves empower human agency.

What then are we to make of the interplay of divine and human agency in these two rituals? Rather than seeing these as stark contrasts, it may be fairer to see these as sharing common emphasis on "the Lord alone" as primary actor, with the actions of devotees shaped by that divine initiative.

The second theme for exploration is the *relationship of the deity to the material food* elements. This question arises not directly from the two texts being considered, but from my participation in Hindu temple rituals and Reformed Protestant (as well as other Christian) eucharistic celebrations. In both cases, food which is initially "offered" before the deity is then given to the people gathered, sparking my curiosity about what has transpired between the food items and the divine presence. In the *Nityam*, there is little said about this point. While the text provides much detail about the food offered to the Lord beforehand, culminating in "the Lord's satisfaction," the sharing of the food afterward consists of simply this: "After asking the Lord's permission, he offers to Visvaksena a bit of the oblation offered to the Lord, and then gives all the rest to Vaisnavas beginning with his acarya."[50] Clearly, the sharing of food is not the main point. To answer my question more fully, we must go beyond the *Nityam* itself. In the discussion cited earlier, W. J. Johnson indicates that the deity's favor is

> materially conveyed to the devotees through the distribution . . . of food . . . and other previously made offerings. Because of their proximity to the deity, such left-overs . . . are considered to be "blessed"—that is to say, imbued with the deity's power and grace.

---

48. *BCW*, 27.

49. *BCW*, 29.

50. *Nityam*, 374.

It is these qualities which are then physically transferred to the devotees, bringing about their temporary identification or merger with the god."[51]

But what does it mean for divine qualities to be "materially conveyed" or "physically transferred"?

Perhaps I am preoccupied by the question because of historical sixteenth-century debates about eucharistic presence in my own tradition. In the Reformed Protestant context, there is also a strong association of Christ's presence with the action of the Lord's Supper, but not in a material, physical way. The presence of Christ is explicitly not localized in the bread and wine but affirmed by the power of the Spirit (sometimes identified with Christ's ascended body, sometimes with his risen body in the ecclesial context). How does this compare with the distinction between the presence of God in the image and the more tenuous presence of God in prasada? This is a question I would like to pursue further, but one which the *Nityam* alone does not help me answer.

Finally, I am curious about the way the distribution of prasada shapes *relationships (both deity/devotee and among devotees)*. Part of the context for this question is the hunger for increased openness in much American Protestant eucharistic practice in recent decades, coupled with the apparent welcome of all to receive prasada in many Hindu temples.[52] Many American Christians who encounter Hindu practices of prasada interpret this as radically inclusive, a helpful challenge to Christian practices that sometimes "fence" the table, either explicitly or implicitly.[53] I wonder: is this a fair interpretation of the distribution of prasada, or does this map Christian presuppositions onto a Hindu practice that is a quite different phenomenon?

---

51. Johnson, *Dictionary of Hinduism*, 92.

52. On this point, I acknowledge a difference between the American and Indian Christian context. From my own observation, there has not been an explicit argument for a more "open table" in the Indian Protestant context in recent years. Churches like the Church of South India (CSI) and the Mar Thoma church do welcome visitors to receive communion (sometimes explicitly contrasting this practice with Catholic and Syrian Orthodox churches), but there has not been the same eruption of literature encouraging the welcome of those who are not baptized, which has been such a lively conversation among American Protestants in the late twentieth and early twenty-first centuries.

53. See, for instance, Barbara Brown Taylor's chapter on "Vishnu's Almonds" in Taylor, *Holy Envy*. For an early reflection on this same topic, see her 2000 article of the same name in *Christian Century*.

Part II | Comparative Theology

In the *Nityam*, it is the devotee who shares the food with the gathered community. As cited above, the text reads, "After asking the Lord's permission, he offers to Visvaksena a bit of the oblation offered to the Lord, and then gives all the rest to Vaisnavas." The prasada distributed, then, may be blessed by the Lord's presence, but it is not directly the Lord (here, Vishnu) who gives the food. The free giving of prasada to all present is at root a transaction between deity and individual devotee, which is then extended to others who may be present. This contrasts with the Reformed Protestant ritual. At the end of the invitation to the table, the presider says, "This is the Lord's Table. Our Savior invites those who trust him to share the feast that he has prepared."[54] The Lord (here, Jesus the Christ) is the one who invites people to the meal and prepares the table. It is the Lord who is the subject of the sentence, and the object of the sentence is a gathered community, not an individual. The Reformed Protestant Eucharist is more focused on the committed Christian community, and it is at core a shared meal.

One way to examine the difference between these two ritual acts is to describe them in terms of vertical (deity-devotee) and horizontal (community of devotees) dimensions. While both rituals have both dimensions, there are different emphases, which is significant in interpreting the difference in "openness" to share. In the case of the *Nityam*, the primary focus is the devotion of the devotee to the deity (the "vertical" relationship), while the sharing of food with the community (the "horizontal" relationship) comes afterward. In the *Book of Common Worship*, the communal participation is central, so that it is a gathered body (not an individual) both offering and receiving the food and drink.

Even this initial reflection suggests that Christians need to exercise caution in interpreting the free distribution of "Vishnu's almonds" as a straightforward parallel to Christian Eucharist that should therefore shape specifically Christian arguments for open table. Two preliminary conclusions follow: (1) the free distribution of prasada as glimpsed in the *Nityam* disrupts any easy assumption that mainly "vertical" food rituals are obstacles to communal bonding; and (2) practices of "hospitality" may arise from genuinely different theological convictions, and legitimate "holy envy" should not overlook these differences.

---

54. *BCW*, 26.

BIBLIOGRAPHY

Clooney, Francis X. *Comparative Theology*. Chichester, UK: Wiley Blackwell, 2010.

———. "Rāmānuja's *Nityagrantham* ('Manual of Daily Worship'): A Translation." *International Journal of Hindu Studies* 24 (2020) 345–80.

Cornille, Catherine. *Meaning and Method in Comparative Theology*. Malden, MA: Wiley Blackwell, 2019.

Courtright, Paul. "Looking at Eucharist through the Lens of Puja: An Exploration in the Comparative Study of Religion." *International Journal of Hindu Studies* 2.3 (1998) 423–40.

Dwyer, Graham. "Krishna *Prasadam*: The Transformative Power of Sanctified Food in the Krishna Consciousness Movement." *Religions of South Asia* 4.1 (2010) 89–104.

Eck, Diana. *Darsan: Seeing the Divine Image in India*. Chambersburg: Anima, 1981.

Flueckiger, Joyce Burkhalter. *Everyday Hinduism*. Malden, MA: Wiley Blackwell, 2015.

Hahnenberg, Edward P. "Arcāvatāra: Srīvaisnava Image-Descent and Roman Catholic Eucharist." *Journal of Ecumenical Studies* 37.2 (2000) 187–201.

Johnson, W. J. *A Dictionary of Hinduism*. Oxford: Oxford, 2009. https://www.oxfordreference.com/display/10.1093/oi/authority.20110803100341990.

King, Anna S. "Krishna's *Prasadam*: 'Eating Our Way Back to Godhead.'" *Material Religion* 8.4 (2012) 440–65.

Klostermaier, Klaus K. *A Survey of Hinduism*. 3rd ed. Albany: State University of New York Press, 2007.

Moore-Keish, Martha. "Divine Freedom and Human Religions: A Reformed Theologian Approaches Comparative Theology." *Theology Today* 75.3 (2018) 281–96.

Pinkney, Andrea Marion. "Prasāda, the Gracious Gift, in Contemporary and Classical South Asia." *Journal of the American Academy of Religion* 81.3 (2013) 734–56.

———. "Prasada." In *Encyclopedia of Hinduism*, edited by Denise Cush et al., 628–29. London: Routledge, 2007.

———. "The Sacred Share: Prasada in South Asia." PhD diss., Columbia University, 2008.

"Prasada." *Encyclopedia Britannica*. https://www.britannica.com/topic/prasada.

Presbyterian Church (USA). *Book of Common Worship*. Louisville: Westminster John Knox, 2018.

Rambachan, Anantanand. *Essays in Hindu Theology*. Minneapolis: Fortress, 2019.

Taylor, Barbara Brown. *Holy Envy: Finding God in the Faith of Others*. New York: HarperOne, 2019.

———. "Vishnu's Almonds." *Christian Century*, March 22, 2000. https://www.christiancentury.org/article/vishnu-s-almonds.

5

"Living Together the Length of Their Days"

What Jewish Hesitancy About Interfaith Marriage Might Contribute to Reformed Theology

DAVID H. JENSEN

DURING THE FALL SEMESTER of 2019, I visited the Ziegler School of Rabbinic Studies to learn about, and to briefly experience, the ways the school was preparing rabbis and leaders for the Conservative Jewish community in a religiously diverse—and increasingly religiously unaffiliated—society. Over several days, I experienced warm hospitality: in classrooms, in conversations with faculty and administrators, and in visits with students over lunch. One professor invited me to offer a presentation (from my own Reformed Christian perspective) in her course on Jewish rituals of the human life cycle.[1] During the time of my visit, this class was discussing Jewish liturgies of marriage and the question of interfaith marriage. Thus, I

---

1. My visit to the Ziegler School would not have been possible without the generous invitation of Rabbi Cheryl Peretz, Associate Dean, who organized my schedule, provided ample conversation space, and took much time out of her busy schedule to ensure that my time at Ziegler was productive. It was in her class that I offered the presentation on marriage. I remain grateful for Rabbi Peretz's time and for the ways that the people of Ziegler continue to have an impact on my theological work. I am also grateful to Rabbi Neil Blumofe of Austin, who helped facilitate the visit and accompanied me to Ziegler.

"Living Together the Length of Their Days"

presented an overview of Christian theologies of marriage and the ways in which my Presbyterian tradition considered interfaith marriages relatively uncontroversial, concluding with the current guidelines my denomination provided for officiating at interfaith weddings. The students in the class, it seemed, were most surprised by how little my denomination debated the question of interfaith marriages. I knew, of course, that the issue of interfaith marriages was controversial within Conservative Judaism. But the students' expectation that my own tradition might have at least *some* contention over the issue led me to ask questions about that tradition, in comparison to Judaism. How could two traditions that had reached very similar conclusions to embrace same-gender marriages remain so far apart on the question of interfaith marriage?[2] What did their respective theologies of marriage claim and what stories did their liturgies of marriage narrate? Might these differences account for this ongoing divergence between Christians and Jews? And how, I wondered, might hesitancy about interfaith marriage in Judaism inform the ways Reformed Christians told their own stories of marriage?[3]

This essay is a result of that classroom encounter and the questions it evoked. In what follows, I probe some of the roots of Jewish reluctance and a comparative Protestant eagerness to embrace interfaith marriage by focusing on two traditions: Conservative Judaism, which might be understood as a mediating tradition between Reform and Orthodox branches; and, the Presbyterian Church (USA), a US branch of the broader Reformed Christian family. I will consider some biblical and Talmudic underpinnings of their distinctive marriage practices, the theologies that surround their respective liturgies, and offer some suggestions for what Jewish hesitancy toward interfaith marriage might contribute to a Reformed Christian understanding of marriage. The intent, in other words, is to interrogate a Protestant understanding of marriage by exploring a question that is largely settled within the tradition and how that settlement might be disrupted,

---

2. See Mehta and Krutsch, "Changing Jewish Family," for a helpful analysis of shifting attitudes within progressive Judaism.

3. Within the broad stream of progressive Judaism, there is diversity in understanding intermarriage: Reform Judaism recognizes interfaith marriages and allows rabbis to officiate at such services (while simultaneously avoiding *encouragement* of such marriages); Conservative Judaism effectively discourages such marriages (unless the non-Jewish partner converts) and forbids rabbis from officiating at them (though rabbis may be present at these marriages as guests).

however slightly, through serious engagement with Jewish reservations about interfaith marriage.

PRONOUNCEMENTS AND PASTORAL DILEMMAS

In 1995, the Leadership Council of Conservative Judaism published a statement that continues to influence ongoing debate:

> In the past, intermarriage ... was viewed psychologically as an act of rebellion, a rejection of Judaism. Jews who intermarried were essentially excommunicated. But now, intermarriage is often the result of living in an open society.... If our children end up marrying non-Jews, we should not reject them. We should continue to give our love and by that retain a measure of influence in their lives, Jewishly and otherwise. Life consists of constant growth and our adult children may yet reach a stage when Judaism has new meaning for them. However, the marriage between a Jew and non-Jew is not a celebration for the Jewish community. We therefore reach out to the couple with the hope that the non-Jewish partner will move closer to Judaism and ultimately choose to convert.[4]

The statement wrestles with the community's past, the realities of life as a religious minority in a pluralistic society, and the ways in which the community might extend the blessings of its common life to families where one spouse is not from the tradition. One marker of this ongoing grappling with tradition is the Conservative movement's 2017 decision to allow non-Jewish spouses to become members of synagogues. This was followed by the movement's vote in 2018 to allow rabbis to attend interfaith weddings as guests.

The rationale for this nuanced position stems not primarily from reservations about the couple's relationship and commitment, but instead about the ongoing life of the Jewish community. The argument, in other words, is more about *a people* than a couple. These reservations about interfaith marriage, when glimpsed sociologically as well as theologically, are understandable. Though an increasing number of children of interfaith marriages identify as Jewish, these numbers pale in comparison to endogamous marriages: 94 percent of children of endogamous marriages self-identify as Jewish, while only 47 percent of children of interfaith

---

4. LCCJ, "Conservative View."

marriages so identify.[5] Compounding these statistics is the fact that interfaith marriages among Jews represent 61 percent of total marriages.[6] Jewish couples in the North America tend to have fewer children than couples from other religious traditions, approximately 1.7 children per couple.[7] Such arguments about the ongoing vitality (and even existence) of a Jewish community have gained even greater traction post-Holocaust. Put simply, for there to be continuity of Jewish tradition, there need to be Jews. Because interfaith marriages tend toward more tenuous identification with the Jewish community, debates about such marriages can take on existential urgency. This element of Jewish hesitancy, at the very least, needs to be seriously considered by Christians who are also committed to the survival of the Jewish people.

Reservations about interfaith marriages, however, go beyond the sociological and the endurance of Jewish tradition. Theological concerns include the likelihood that interfaith rites invariably dilute the distinctives of *both* traditions. Noble attempts to combine elements of Christian and Jewish liturgies of marriage may run the risk of theological incoherence. The distinctive rites say different things about marriage and even when these rites bear commonalities, the distinctives can get lost in the amalgam. One critic of these attempts notes that interfaith ceremonies tend toward "a meld of impossible ingredients which betray both Jewish and Christian understandings of true marriage."[8] One example of this inconsistency, from a Jewish perspective, would be Christian sacramental understandings of marriage that emphasize the nuptial metaphor of the relationship between Christ and the church.[9] For rabbis to participate in a service that foregrounds (or even backgrounds) this metaphor might risk theological dishonesty or even a betrayal of one's tradition.

Regardless of theological, sociological, or historical argument, however, interfaith marriages will continue to occur, as they have arisen across time in nearly every religious community. The current Conservative stance

---

5. Keene, "Intermarriage."
6. Cohen, "More Conservative Rabbis Struggle."
7. Dorff, *In Search of the Good Life*, 186.
8. Wolf, "Indelicate Silence," 236.
9. Wolf, "Indelicate Silence," 239. This metaphor, however, tends to be more prevalent in Christian traditions that understand marriage as a sacrament, e.g., Roman Catholicism and Anglicanism. One question I explore later is to what extent this metaphor is operative in Reformed understandings of marriage. In my reading, other metaphors, such as covenant, come to the fore in Reformed Christianity.

puts rabbis in delicate positions, where pastoral concerns are juxtaposed with theological traditions and existential concerns for survival. In 2012, the Conservative Rabbinical Assembly posed the dilemma succinctly: "How can I show you that I care for you even when I have to say no [to your request to officiate at our wedding]?"[10]

The issue is not likely to disappear. Some rabbis have left the Conservative movement over it. Some members of Conservative congregations have transferred to Reform synagogues because of it. Some predict that it will remain *the* issue for the Conservative movement in the next decade.[11] Others within the movement hope for increased acceptance of intermarriage. Jacob Blumenthal, CEO of the Rabbinical Assembly notes:

> Intermarriage is an opportunity not a curse. . . . We need to stop seeing intermarriage as a failure or betrayal [and start] seeing that these people are engaged in loving relationships. We need to support them and engage them in loving ways of Jewish life.[12]

Some have even argued that intermarriage might even result in the *growth* of Jewish communities rather than their diminishment, since such marriages bring non-Jews into the fold. Such hopes, however, run counter to recent historical data, where interfaith marriages often lead to more tenuous ties to Jewish communities.

AN EASY EMBRACE WITH LITTLE GUIDANCE

The Presbyterian Church (USA), by contrast, does not understand interfaith marriages as a significant topic of debate. Even if objections to them have occurred throughout its history, the matter seems mostly settled. At the risk of oversimplification, the current outlook is something like this: people fall in love; churches should not restrict the categories of people whom one may fall in love with; it is good for people who fall in love to make promises to each other; and, the church ought to celebrate these ties in rites of marriage. Marriage, in this respect, is a marker of human freedom: one way that persons created in God's image respond to the living God is to make promises to one another. For many in this tradition, restrictions

---

10. Quoted in Dorff, *Modern Conservative*, 286.

11. Rumors of an impending shift on the movement's stance on intermarriage have generated controversy. See Rosenfeld, "Misinformed."

12. McGinty, "Conservative Judaism's New Narrative."

or reservations about interfaith marriages are akin to the dehumanizing ways in which society and the churches have policed human relationships in the past, such as restrictions on interracial marriage and laws prohibiting same-sex marriage that have only recently been overturned. It may even be the case that the loosening of ecclesial reservations against interfaith marriages led to more hospitable stances concerning interracial and same-sex marriages in subsequent decades. Interfaith marriages, in this regard, were the first to avoid ecclesial or civil objection.[13]

Nonetheless, the endurance of interfaith marriages has not led to coherent theologies or guidance for couples or clergy. The current *Book of Common Worship* of the Presbyterian Church (USA) is a good example. Amid its thousand-plus pages of prayers, orders for worship and rites, running the life cycle from birth to death are a scant few sentences about interfaith weddings. In one paragraph, the guidance is that "couples should consult with clergy from their respective faith traditions to learn what possibilities exist for an interfaith wedding ceremony," and that "clergy from both faiths will take part in the planning." Both traditions are to be represented with equal reverence. Three options for such services are then suggested: (1) a blending of language and traditions from both faiths, where both partners can participate "with integrity"; (2) a service that alternates between rituals from each tradition; or (3) the creation of two separate ceremonies reflective of each tradition.[14] This guidance has integrity: it seeks to honor the claims of both traditions, to avoid any hint of supercession, and to recognize the couple's ties to broader communities. But the guidance is incredibly brief. In effect, it leaves both clergy and couple free to improvise. This may be its greatest strength: combining religious traditions—both in a ceremony and in a shared life—is something that must constantly be improvised: how to mark holy days; how to pray together; how to worship; how to nurture children in one faith or both. These are topics where most religious traditions lack reservoirs of experience. Improvisation, as a mark of freedom, may be the wisest course. But the brevity of such guidance in the PC(USA) may give the mistaken impression that negotiating interfaith marriage rites is comparatively easy.

13. This is a contestable claim. In the United States in particular, racism and antisemitism are bound together in a toxic mix. Racist laws against "miscegenation" and laws and practices that led to second- or third-class status for Jews appear hand in glove. Yet popular objections to interfaith marriages (as long as the marriages were between white people) seem to have diminished at a faster rate than objections to interracial marriages.

14. PC(USA), *Book of Common Worship*, 689.

PART II | COMPARATIVE THEOLOGY

SCRIPTURAL AND TALMUDIC FOUNDATIONS: THE BURDEN AND BLESSING OF INTERFAITH MARRIAGES

One way of accounting for the differences between Jewish hesitancy and comparative Protestant nonchalance about interfaith marriages is to trace competing trajectories in their scriptures and authoritative writings. Though these trajectories are hardly monolithic, some broad patterns emerge. The Hebrew Bible and the Talmud understand marriage as a blessing, effectively encourage endogamous marriage, and—with some notable exceptions—warn against exogamous marriage. By contrast the New Testament offers an ambivalent endorsement of marriage amid apocalyptic expectation. This ambivalence, intriguingly, assumes intermarriage as one avenue for the transmission of Christian faith.

The Genesis creation stories posit two rationales for marriage: The first creation story situates the creation of male and female in the context of reproduction ("Be fruitful and multiply," Gen 1:28); the second presents marriage as a partnership and antidote to isolation ("It is not good that the man should be alone," Gen 2:18). Both rationales are significant, suggesting that marriage cannot be reduced to a single purpose. Instead, marriage is "for" several things, including the blessings of companionship and offspring. Marriage is considered the norm for human life in much of Judaism. The Babylonian Talmud, for example, contains a memorable endorsement of marriage: "Any man who has no wife lives without joy, without blessing, without goodness."[15] In partnership and progeny, marriage enhances community, redounding to the bounty God gives the world.

As this communal rationale for marriage unfolds in the Hebrew Bible, the delineation between Israel and the nations sharpens. Isaac instructs Jacob not to marry a Canaanite woman (Gen 28:1); the Deuteronomist notes a prohibition against marrying Canaanites, a prohibition that is sometimes cited as rationale against all forms of intermarriage (Deut 7:3–4); Joshua's farewell address warns against intermarriage—likening it to a trap—and connects endogamy to God's continued protection of the Israelites (Josh 23:12–13). And, in perhaps the most vociferous rejection of exogamy in scripture, Ezra instructs those Israelite men who have married foreign wives in exile, to divorce: "So now let us make a covenant with our God to send away all these wives and their children" (Ezra 10:3). Here, intermarriage

---

15. *Babylonian Talmud*, 1:418.

is seen as a compromise of God's covenant with Israel, even as a sign of idolatry. This theme is amplified in the Babylonian Talmud: "He who is intimate with a heathen woman is as though he had entered into marriage relationship with an idol."[16] In some cases, one must break the idol and false covenant to begin anew.

These warnings against intermarriage, however, are complicated by significant counterexamples. Solomon, heralded as the wisest of Israel's kings, who builds a temple to the Lord, marries Pharaoh's daughter in a strategic alliance that bolsters his reign (1 Kgs 3:1). This marriage, though not immediately condemned, is closely connected to Solomon's shortcomings. Later in the Deuteronomistic narrative, Solomon's many foreign wives are connected to Solomon's following other gods, including Astarte of the Sidonians and Milcom of the Ammonites. The final narrative judgment is harsh: "So Solomon did what was evil in the sight of the Lord" (1 Kgs 11:6). Here, intermarriage invites idolatry and a betrayal of covenant.

The most intriguing example of intermarriage in Hebrew scripture, however, is contained in the book of Ruth. Though elements of the story are well-known and oft-recited (particularly at Christian weddings), some of the details require narrative imagination. Naomi's family settles in Moab after a famine in the land surrounding Bethlehem. Her sons marry Moabite women. Whether these arrangements mean that Naomi's extended family now follows Moabite customs and worship is left to the imagination. Perhaps they did; perhaps they didn't. But Ruth's promise to Naomi after the death of the family patriarch and his two sons is unambiguous: she will follow Naomi back to Bethlehem, worship the God of Israel, and be with her people (1:16). Ruth's subsequent marriage to Boaz cements her position in a noble lineage: her firstborn is the grandfather of King David (4:17). Here intermarriage is neither condemned nor questioned. Indeed, on a prominent branch of an august family tree is a foreigner who adopts the customs and worship of Israel as her own.

The New Testament, by contrast, reads somewhat differently. Its endorsement of marriage can seem rather lukewarm while, at the same time, it assumes intermarriage as good for the transmission of the gospel. The New Testament's attitude toward marriage, particularly Paul's, is colored by apocalyptic expectation. Paul emphasizes that the church lives in a transitional time and that believers' responsibility to prepare for Christ's return means that they should refrain from new, binding arrangements that

---

16. *Babylonian Talmud*, 3:544.

dramatically alter the course of their current lives. Those who are married should remain married. Those who are single should remain single unless they are unable to restrain their passion, in which case, they are urged to marry: "For it is better to marry than to be aflame with passion" (1 Cor 7:9). Here marriage is a concession for those who cannot remain unmarried—a less preferable option than a single life that is Paul's chief recommendation (v. 8). Later strands of the New Testament, shorn of some of the apocalypticism of earlier portions, assume marriage as part of the created order. But these strands mostly offer accounts of proper relations between spouses. The household codes, for example, tend to duplicate similar exhortations found in the wider Greco-Roman world (see Col 3:18–4:1; Titus 2:1–10; 1 Pet 2:13–3:7). Perhaps the most significant endorsement of marriage occurs in the form of analogy tied directly to the Genesis creation stories. The author of Ephesians cites the "one flesh" image of Genesis 2 not only as a metaphor for marriage, but for the "great mystery" of Christ's relation to the church (5:31–2). The image is complicated: on the one hand emphasizing subjection of wives to husbands and church to Christ; and, on the other, mutual subjection (vv. 21–24). Freighted with patriarchy, but perhaps containing germs for dismantling it, the image has led in countless directions in subsequent centuries.

Conspicuously absent from these New Testament passages are arguments against intermarriage. Again, Paul is instructive. In the same passage that offers a lukewarm endorsement of marriage is a warning against separating from an unbelieving spouse: "For the unbelieving husband is made holy through his wife, and the unbelieving wife is made holy through her husband. Otherwise, your children would be unclean, but as it is, they are holy" (1 Cor 7:14). What Paul means here in terms of "making holy" is subject to debate: is it the uniting of flesh in marriage that renders holy? The transmission of faith to the next generation? Whatever the meaning, difference of faith is not an obstacle to marriage. Indeed, intermarriage may be one of the ways Christian faith grows.[17]

On this last point, the Ruth narrative offers an intriguing parallel: the interfaith marriages most enthusiastically endorsed in both traditions are

---

17. If evangelization is understood as one of the foundational arguments *for* interfaith marriage within Christianity, Jewish arguments against interfaith marriage make even more sense. From the outset, it seems, such marriages were a means of growing Christian faith and supplanting other forms of faith. Given this history, coupled with the legacy of Christian violence against Jews, contemporary Jews are rightly suspicious of glib claims of the "good" of intermarriage, particularly Jewish-Christian marriage.

marriages that lead to *conversion*.[18] But the New Testament does not specify conversion as a *prerequisite* to intermarriage. In both traditions, the meanings of marriage are bound up with concerns for transmitting faith/culture, even if one tradition grants more concessions to intermarriage than the other. A brief examination of the nuptial theologies of each tradition will further illuminate these different emphases.

MARRIAGE THEOLOGIES AND LITURGIES IN BOTH TRADITIONS

Theologies of marriage in Judaism and Reformed Christianity are richly multifaceted and impossible to summarize in an essay of this length. In this section, I simply highlight some prominent themes within these traditions, especially as they contribute to an understanding of interfaith marriages.

Judaism situates marriage within a wider framework of human relationships, such as friendships and kinship. Marriage, however, is different from many family relationships because humans *choose* to enter marriage. In this regard, marriage shares much in common with friendship. But marriage is a special kind of choice, in that those who embark on it make ritual promises to each another. Jewish marriages include a *ketubah*, a contract between two persons that outline mutual responsibilities and obligations in accord with Torah, which often includes this, or similar, language:

> Be consecrated to me as my wife according to the laws and traditions of Moses and Israel. I will love, honor, and cherish you; I will protect and support you; and I will faithfully care for your needs, as prescribed by Jewish law and tradition.[19]

This legal document does not focus primarily on a romantic story or emotional language. In fact, much of the *ketubah* focuses on the everyday tasks that sustain a shared life, such as cooking, cleaning, and finances. In this respect, it stands in contrast to individualized, romantic assumptions that surround marriage in modern Western societies. Despite the rich resonances of love-language within Judaism (one need only consider the Song of Songs, for example), the *ketubah* emphasizes that mutual obligations and responsibilities even take precedence over love. One consequence is a

---

18. I recognize the anachronistic use of the term "conversion," especially when applied to Ruth.

19. Neusner, *Introduction to Judaism*, 24.

"down to earth" understanding of marriage as commitment sustained over time. While romantic understandings of marriage can hover thousands of feet off the ground in their appeals to "matches made in heaven" that are all play and no work, the *ketubah* witnesses to the broader society that marriages require labor, patience, and mutual forbearance, even if they are labors of love.

Whereas many Christian understandings of marriage invoke the language of "covenant" to describe marriage, Jewish understandings generally shy away from it. Covenant describes the promises that God makes to Israel. And though marriage is one of the ways people respond to a covenant-making God, marriage itself is not, strictly speaking, covenantal.[20] Nonetheless, traditional Judaism situates marriage within the broader fabric of God's promises to Israel and all creation. Indeed, Jewish marital theologies offer a ritual recapitulation of those promises in their wedding liturgies, where the couple's promises to each other offer glimpses of a cosmic grace.

Traditional Jewish weddings typically take place outdoors under a huppah, a canopy that symbolizes the covering of heaven. This practice emphasizes the couple's embeddedness in a universe of blessing. Marriage does not remove a couple from the world, however temporarily; rather, it situates them squarely within it. Jacob Neusner notes that the huppah "invokes creation, the making of a new Eden" where "the couple [is] changed into the paradigm of humanity."[21] Marriage is a ritual re-enactment of the coming together of Adam and Eve, the resolution of the cry that it is not good to be alone. An obvious difference from many Christian weddings (which traditionally have taken place in church sanctuaries) is the Jewish wedding's location in the natural world rather than a worship space constructed by human hands. Indeed, the chief human construction (the huppah) symbolizes the natural world. Perhaps this is a reminder that marriage belongs to the whole world, even if the promises of Jewish weddings are particular to its tradition.

The traditional seven blessings of Jewish weddings also offer a window to this ritual re-enactment of God's promises. They include both general blessings applicable to all peoples (blessings for God who has created

---

20. See Gelfand, "Love, Marriage," for a helpful discussion of the distinction between *bein adam l'makom* (between people and God) and *bein adam l'havero* (between people and other people) as well as concise reflections on the *ketubah*.

21. Neusner, *Introduction to Judaism*, 23.

everything for God's glory; blessings for God's creation of the fruit of the vine; and blessings for the creation of humanity) as well as blessings more specific to Judaism (such as blessing for the gladdening of Zion through the return of God's people). Neusner notes that these blessings say nothing of the private couple. Instead, they situate the personal promises two people make within the scope of God's creation of a people. In this sense,

> Love and beloved are transformed from national to mythical figures. . . . Natural events of human life [such as a marriage] are by myth heightened into re-enactment of Israel's life as a people. What gives this love true meaning is acting out the myth of creation, revelation, and redemption, here and now, embodied in that love. Sacred and secular are united in profane, physical love.[22]

Jewish marriage theologies and ritual thus connect the personal (the love and commitment of two people to one another) to the communal (Israel) and cosmic. The couple, in other words, does not stand alone.

Reformed Christianity, too, has varied emphases in its rituals and theologies of marriage. Though the tradition is difficult to summarize, one place to begin is the relationship between marriage and sacrament. Whereas Catholicism understands marriage as a visible word that expresses the promises of grace in and through Jesus Christ, the Reformers understood marriage primarily as an ordinance: an institution established by God to benefit God's people. Though many Reformed wedding liturgies invoke Christ's relationship to the church in the couple's commitment to one another, they need not center such language. Like the Jewish understandings of marriage surveyed above, John Calvin claims that marriage is instituted by God so that humanity "may not lead a solitary life."[23] Marriage is one example of the blessing of community. Though Christ blesses marriages, marriage is not a sacrament in the tradition, a designation reserved only for the Eucharist and baptism.

Other strains of classical Reformed theology emphasize the mutuality of marriage and how it enhances human life. The Westminster Confession of Faith is here representative:

> Christian marriage is . . . for the happiness and welfare of mankind, into which spiritual and physical union one man and one woman enter, establishing a mutual esteem and love, bearing with each other's infirmities and weaknesses, comforting each other in

---

22. Neusner, *Introduction to Judaism*, 29.
23. Calvin, *Institutes*, 405.

trouble, providing in honesty and industry for each other and for their household, praying for each other, and living together the length of their days as heirs to the grace of life.[24]

Like traditional Jewish markers of marriage, Reformed Christianity emphasizes companionship and mutual commitment as a primary good of marriage.

Unlike Jewish understandings of marriage, however, Reformed Christianity frequently employs the language of covenant. In many respects, this language provides the overarching metaphor for marriage: God covenants with a people who respond by making covenant with each other. Marriage is the prime example of these human covenants. Though the covenants we make may break and marriages fail, the church recognizes that God's promise to "be with" echoes in marriage rites where spouses pledge to be with one another in sickness and in health, in prosperity and in want, the length of their lives.

A final mark of Reformed theologies of marriage, therefore, stresses reconciliation. Marriages point to the eschatological hope of God's healing and redemption of the world in Jesus Christ. This has been an especially prevalent emphasis in contemporary Reformed theology. The Presbyterian Church (USA)'s *Book of Common Worship* is a good example, which contains this prayer in its marriage liturgy: "Make their life together a sign of Christ's love to this sinful and broken world, that unity may overcome estrangement, forgiveness heal guilt, and joy conquer despair."[25] Marriage, in Reformed theology, is thus anticipatory. No marriage can bear all things, heal all things, or reconcile all things. But when people marry one another, they bear witness to the God who is reconciling the world in Jesus Christ.

Reformed marriage theologies have a general foundation that is not restricted to Christianity. It considers marriage a blessing for all people, not tied directly to a sacramental presence of the risen Christ. But at the same time, its understanding of marriage as an anticipatory act is bound up with a strong sense of Christ's reconciliation of all creation. Its comparative embrace of interfaith marriage thus seems more connected to its foundation rather than its eschatological hope.

---

24. PC(USA), *Book of Confessions*, 152–53.
25. PC(USA), *Book of Common Worship*, 696.

"Living Together the Length of Their Days"
HOW JEWISH HESITANCY MIGHT INFORM CHRISTIAN PRACTICE

The question of interfaith marriage is as old as Jewish and Christian traditions themselves. As North American society becomes more religiously pluralistic, interfaith marriages might become more frequent topics of discussion and debate; conversely, these debates might dissipate as such marriages become increasingly common. Christian theology, however, would do well to attend to the hesitancy that Conservative Judaism has demonstrated toward these marriages. Such hesitancy is not in the name of policing relationships, an area where the church has historically proven deeply flawed, often with devastating consequences. Hesitancy, instead, can help Christian communities better express their own theologies of marriage, what marriage is for, and how it is connected to the community's life.

Contemporary Jewish hesitancy over interfaith marriages has little to do with the couple and much to do with the community. As we have seen, a Jewish wedding envelops the couple in the ongoing story of God's creation and election of Israel. The couple become icons of this story, who in their physical love for one another are sustained by God's providential guidance of the Jewish people. In marriage rites the boundaries between couple and community, mundane and sacred, become porous. Jewish marital theology does not isolate a couple on an island of seclusion, or seal them off in a private realm; it celebrates their love, promises, and mutual obligations to each other as dimensions of the Jewish people's ongoing life. A marriage tells a couple's story within that larger narrative. Without the larger narrative, the theological meaning of marriage disappears. Thus, a key question within Judaism is how that story is told: How will an interfaith marriage narrate God's love affair with Israel? How will it express the couple's incorporation within that story?

These are questions that Christian theologies of marriage ought to address as well. For, common to both traditions is a stress on the community that surrounds the couple. Marriage rites in both traditions tell a story—of commitment, of promise, of community, of redemption. The story these rites tell is larger than the couple. In Jewish weddings, gathered members offer blessings for the couple, covering them in prayer, surrounded by others who will help sustain them. In many Christian weddings, the gathered congregation also offers promises and prayers of support. At the heart of both traditions is the acknowledgement that the couple does not stand in these promises alone. This recognition puts both Christian and Jewish theologies of marriage in contrast with contemporary North American sentiments that understand marriage as a private rite. Instead, these theologies of marriage note that the community, too, has a say—not so much in saying "no" to a couple, but in articulating how it will say "yes" to them. A Christian theology of interfaith marriage, therefore, ought to be elastic enough to ask the question of how the Jewish-Christian couple will be incorporated into the story of Israel and the ongoing life of the Jewish people in addition to their incorporation into the story of the church. If adequate attention to both stories is not possible, this may be reason enough for clergy to decline participation in an interfaith wedding.

Another point of comparison is the understanding of redemption and reconciliation within each tradition. As the wedding couple in Judaism become personifications of Israel's journey to redemption, they express some of the hope of the messianic age. Reformed Christianity, similarly, understands marriage as an anticipation of Christ's reconciliation of all creation. Though the agent of redemption/reconciliation is different in each tradition, the longing for overcoming estrangement is common to both. Interfaith marriages, in this sense, can be examples of how estranged communities find healing and hope together, in a shared life. These marriages put flesh on theological hopes, not by erasing one story in the name of the other, but by honoring and living out both stories. In the mundane activities of sharing family histories, preparing for holy days, maintaining a home, preparing meals, and caring for children, these couples bear witness to the possibilities that wounds can be healed (though not forgotten), love can overcome hatred, and community can emerge out of fracture. Rites that guide interfaith marriages ought to also express this hope in ways that can be claimed by both traditions. How is the marriage caught up in God's redemption of Israel? How is it an expression of the church's eschatological hope?

Answering these questions is difficult, though not impossible. A Christian theology of marriage that honors Jewish reservations is hard to imagine and perhaps even more difficult to embody. Nonetheless, I do not share the worry that interfaith wedding services risk incoherence or the betrayal of one or both traditions. Indeed, the proof may be the experiences of interfaith couples themselves, who are claimed by *both* traditions. One of the most powerful examples of this possibility is witnessed in the example of Susan Katz Miller, a Jew who married a Christian and has raised their children in both traditions. Writing about her experience as an interfaith parent, Katz Miller emphasizes embodiment and the physical more than the theological and spiritual. Reflecting on the children of interfaith families who take part Purim and Holy Week rituals, rooted deeply in both traditions, she notes:

> The point is not a theological reconciliation of Jewish and Christian doctrine, or of the often fraught, fractious, and even tragic entwined histories of Judaism and Christianity. Rather, [parents] were deeply moved by the physical actions of their children, performing ancient rituals, and laying claim to their identities through embodiment, voice, and ritual gestures.[26]

The everyday tasks of marriage and family interlaced with the stories and rituals of each tradition make all the difference. The "theology" of interfaith marriage, in this sense, gets worked out on the ground, in the ebb and flow of ordinary routines. In eating, singing, dancing, and loving together, these families offer significant counter-witnesses to an increasingly polarized society. In these marriages,

> the personal becomes political as the embodiment of religious complexity becomes an external statement to the surrounding society. That statement—"We're loving across boundaries, whether you approve or not"—may cause anxiety for traditional institutions, while simultaneously causing exhilaration for those who are doing the eating, singing, dancing, and loving.[27]

These families' stories, the ways that they seek to honor their communities' traditions in marriage and a shared life, offer poignant evidence for reconciliation and healing between Christians and Jews. Telling their unique stories, within the stories of their respective traditions, is exactly the point.[28]

---

26. Miller, "Eat, Sing, Love," 375–76.
27. Miller, "Eat, Sing, Love," 380. See also Miller, *Being Both*.
28. For additional analysis of Jewish-Christian marriages and families, see Mehta, *Beyond Chrismukkuh*.

PART II | COMPARATIVE THEOLOGY

BIBLIOGRAPHY

The Babylonian Talmud: Seder Nashim. Translated by Rabbi Dr. I. Epstein. Vols. 1, 3. London: Soncino, 1935–1936.

Calvin, John. *Institutes of the Christian Religion*. Translated by Ford Lewis Battles. Philadelphia: Westminster, 1960.

Cohen, Debra Nussbaum. "More Conservative Rabbis Struggle with Interfaith Marriage—and Some Are Flouting It." *Forward*, May 10, 2022. https://forward.com/news/501853/conservative-rabbis-interfaith-marriage-ban-preside-officiate-uscj-blumenthal.

Dorff, Elliot N. *In Search of the Good Life*. Library of Contemporary Jewish Philosophers 5. Leiden: Brill, 2014.

———. *Modern Conservative Judaism*. Lincoln: Jewish Publication Society, 2018.

Gelfand, Shoshana Boyd. "Love, Marriage, Commitment." In *Walking with Life*, edited by Bradley Shavit Artson and Deborah Silver. Los Angeles: Ziegler School of Rabbinic Studies, 2009.

Keene, Louis. "Intermarriage Increasingly Yields to Jewish Children, Pew Study Shows." *Forward*, May 12, 2021. https://forward.com/news/469480/intermarriage-pew-jewish-children.

Leadership Council Of Conservative Judaism (LCCJ). "Conservative View on Intermarriage." *Mazor Guides*, March 7, 1995. http://www.mazorguide.com/living/denominations/conservative-intermarriage.htm.

McGinty, Keren R. "Conservative Judaism's New Narrative on Jewish Intermarriage." *eJewish Philanthropy*, February 23, 2022. https://ejewishphilanthropy.com/conservative-judaisms-new-narrative-on-jewish-intermarriage.

Mehta, Samira K. *Beyond Chrismukkuh: The Christian-Jewish Interfaith Family in the United States*. Chapel Hill: University of North Carolina Press, 2018.

Mehta, Samira K., and Brett Krutsch "The Changing Jewish Family: Jewish Communal Responses to Interfaith and Same-Sex Marriage." *American Jewish History* 104.4 (2020) 553–77.

Miller, Susan Katz. *Being Both: Embracing Two Religions in One Interfaith Family*. Boston: Beacon, 2014.

———. "Eat, Sing, Love: How Interfaith Families Model Interfaith Engagement." *Cross Currents* 68.3 (2018) 372–82.

Neusner, Jacob. *An Introduction to Judaism: A Textbook and Reader*. Louisville: Westminster John Knox, 1991.

Presbyterian Church (USA). *Book of Common Worship*. Louisville: Westminster John Knox, 2018.

———. *Book of Confessions*. Louisville: Presbyterian Church (USA), 1996.

Rosenfeld, Arno. "'Misinformed' Intermarriage Rumors Distress Some Conservative Rabbis." *STL Jewish Light*, January 11, 2023. https://stljewishlight.org/top-story/misinformed-intermarriage-rumors-distress-some-conservative-rabbis.

Wolf, Arnold Jacob. "An Indelicate Silence." *Judaism: A Quarterly Journal of Jewish Life and Thought* 51.2 (2002).

PART III

Otherness, Community, and the Common Good

6

Can Religion (Really) Work for the Common Good?[1]

MICHELLE VOSS

EXCITING CHANGES IN THE American university and civic landscapes are coming about, in part, thanks to the efforts of Interfaith America (formerly Interfaith Youth Core), and its founder, Eboo Patel. Patel and Interfaith America help colleges and universities to lean into the religious, spiritual, and moral diversity in their communities using time-tested practices of interfaith engagement. Co-curricular means such as dialogues, service projects, and grant-supported curricular programs in interfaith leadership are helping the next generation of college and university graduates to build relationships across lines of diversity.

A guiding assumption of the interfaith movement is that, if harnessed in particular ways, religious traditions can be a force for the common good. Martin Marty laid foundations for this work in his book, *Politics, Religion, and the Common Good: Advancing a Distinctly American Conversation About Religion's Role in Our Shared Life* (2000). He begins with the thesis that "public religion can be dangerous; it should be handled with care" (chapter 1), but he spends the remainder of the book expanding on the

---

1. I owe a debt of gratitude to my colleagues Marianne Moyaert, Tom Reynolds, and Katherine Shaner, who have helped me develop the content and organization of this article, as well as to Mercer University, which invited me to deliver the Harry Vaughan Smith Lectures (February 21, 2023), and to the Frierson Conference at Austin Presbyterian Theological Seminary (April 13–15, 2023).

PART III | OTHERNESS, COMMUNITY, AND THE COMMON GOOD

thesis of the second chapter, that "public religion can and does contribute to the common good."[2]

The title of this chapter represents a real existential and vocational question for me. Can religion really be a force for the common good? Like many deep and troubling questions, this one came to me through the mouth of a child. I was a guest at Shabbat dinner, and my Jewish friends had a question. My friend April had recently shared a storybook about the Crusades with her young daughter. The daughter exclaimed that this horrific story of religious warfare couldn't *possibly* be true, and said skeptically, "Mom, you just don't want me to like Christians!" "OK," said April, "let's ask Michelle."

So, over dinner, I found myself confirming that the Crusades *were* just that terrible, and that, unfortunately, people have done and continue to do terrible things in the name of religion. The children at this Canadian dinner table were aware of the Christian churches' involvement in running the residential school system in Canada. After the Truth and Reconciliation Commission's recommendations in 2015, this history and its ongoing effects are part of the public school curriculum. The Canadian government took Indigenous children from their families and placed them in church-run facilities that disallowed their language and culture and frequently subjected them to abuse. The so-called schools were more like prisons or labor camps. Why would anyone want to be a Christian, given that Christians do things like this, not to mention its associations with slavery, sex abuse scandals, the Shoah, and antidemocratic movements? Why would anyone choose to identify as religious, given the widespread association of violence with religion in general?[3]

I spoke of my love for Jesus, who stood up to those who hurt and abused others, and whose radical vision of a society based in love and justice continues to motivate me and many other Christians. In contrast to the secularism of Canadian public life, I explained, in the US, especially the US South, Christianity is still a powerful motivator, both for good and ill. US Christians expect faith to be part of the public sphere, and this has come to include people of all faiths, working together for the common good.

I explained that for over twenty years of my professional life, my work in theological education in the US South was deeply shaped by the Civil Rights Movement. The legacy of the Rev. Dr. Martin Luther King Jr. was

---

2. Marty, *Politics, Religion, and the Common Good*.
3. Sullivan et al., *Politics of Religious Freedom*, 4–5.

omnipresent in Atlanta, where I studied, and Memphis, where I held my first academic position. Later, I taught at a theological school in Winston-Salem, North Carolina, during the height of the Rev. Dr. William Barber's Moral Mondays Movement and the Poor People's campaign. The Black church was the engine behind all of this. How exciting to tap into the radical roots of the Jesus movement as a professor, to shape the ministers who would shape future US Christians! What an inspiring, what an important thing to which to devote one's life. Of course, religious communities can be a force for the common good, and I want to be part of that, both in the US and in Canada.

I could see that my monologue was getting nowhere with these kids, so I made light of it. "I hope I'm right about this," I concluded. "Because I've only dedicated my life to it." April laughed. "You should do stand-up!" What amused my friend was my naïvete. She wasn't being mean, but my earnest story couldn't have contrasted more strongly with that moment in history. The US Supreme Court had just handed down a series of rulings that catered to the Christian right. They had curtailed women's and transgender rights, and in the previous decade they had contributed to the severe erosion of voting rights. To this crowd, faith in the public sphere only seemed to signal the triumph of a patriarchal, homophobic, petrocapitalist, White Christian supremacist order.

I received my professional formation in the post-9/11 era. I was on my way from my Christian Ethics course at Candler School of Theology to my Sanskrit reading tutorial across campus when someone told me that an airplane had flown into the World Trade Center. What I imagined, along the lines of a small propeller plane going off course, was nothing like the devastation I saw on TV when I got there. I was with South Asian colleagues when the second tower fell, and when, shortly thereafter, Osama bin Laden's face was first broadcast to a nation in shock. They let out a collective groan: they, more than I, had a strong premonition of what this could mean for anyone who looked like him—who looked like *them*. Indeed, the retribution started almost immediately, with attacks on Muslims, turban-wearing Sikhs, and people of Arab and South Asian descent.[4]

This was an era in which we were confident that education was the answer. If only we understood one another's religions and cultures, if only

---

4. Not until 2015 was this pattern of violence formally identified as hate crimes or identified with White Christian supremacist nationalism. See Kaur, *See No Stranger*, 235–37.

we were aware of the complexities of global politics, colonization, resource extraction and allocation, then we could come to just solutions. Theological education had an important role to play. But now, it's a post-truth society. In this cynical time, do we really form and change minds or just reinforce existing ideologies? Was it naïve of us to lean into religious diversity as a force for the common good?

I will approach this question as a multi-layered conversation. This essay first observes how the religious/secular divide, which relegates religion to the private sphere, attempts to address the problem of religious violence. It then considers why, today, people in the interfaith movement say that the secular solution is inadequate and doesn't avoid violence as well as secularism's proponents had hoped. Although the interfaith vision of building bridges and working together for the common good inspires many people, especially after 9/11, we must also observe what a second generation of critical interfaith activists have found missing from this approach, and how the coercive dimensions of secularism are sometimes replicated in its emphasis on the "common." This essay concludes by asking how interfaith leaders can work for the common good while prioritizing solidarity with those affected by both everyday and extraordinary forms of religious violence.

"THE RELIGIOUS" IN THE PUBLIC SPHERE

Although there are more models and types of secularism than I can survey in this essay, the kids at the table that night gravitated to the kind that draws a hard line: people should keep any religious convictions to themselves and away from public life and institutions.[5] My own child told me, "I don't need religion for social justice." I have worked with undergraduate students in the Canadian context who take this a step further, asserting that abuses in institutions like the residential schools happened *because* religion was

---

5. Charles Taylor's monumental study, *A Secular Age*, has theorized three models of secularity. Here, we are discussing the first, *secularity* 1, which imagines the absence of God from public life together. *Secularity* 2 describes societies like many parts of Canada and Europe. Such places may once have been governed by overtly religious ideals, but now smaller numbers engage religious practices and belief, and the normativity of the once-dominant tradition is contested and may continue to operate in a more muted way. As I discuss below, the current interfaith movement envisions something akin to Taylor's *secularity* 3, in which Christianity "is one possibility among others," and there is a genuine, robust "plurality of options" (Taylor, *Secular Age*, 3). See also Patel, *Interfaith Leadership*, 7.

involved. If only society had been secular and enlightened (like "we" are now), none of that would have happened.

This is quite a common response in the modern period: religion is a problem, and for it not to turn violent, we must push it to the private sphere. Representing this view, the political philosopher John Rawls considered religious diversity as a serious challenge for the functioning of democracy. As he put it, a religion posits a "comprehensive doctrine," a total worldview, which may be at odds with the comprehensive doctrine he saw as underlying liberal democracies. Couldn't loyalty to the authority of the pope in Rome supersede a Roman Catholic person's allegiance to the US president or constitution? If people of a particular religious persuasion were to gain power, would they be able to impose their religiously-based ideals on others through the mechanisms of government? Eboo Patel points out that this means that "Citizens, especially those acting in political roles, are free to practice their faith at home, but they ought not bring it into the public sphere. They should not, for example, offer religious reasons for their political positions," but instead frame their views "in terms of what Rawls calls 'public reason,' which is rooted in the social contract of a liberal democracy and is by definition devoid of religious language."[6]

We hear this argument again today in relation to mainstreaming of right-wing views of American history and society that have aligned themselves with evangelical forms of Christianity.[7] Now that the American evangelical bloc has entered a seemingly inescapable alliance with people who overtly proclaim White supremacy, must we now conclude that Rawls was right, that religious groups' self-interest undermines democracy, and that public life should follow reason, common sense, and secular values?

The kids at the dinner table seemed to think so, but there are also many who see this kind of secular solution as a bit of a problem. The next section briefly unpacks three reasons that were embedded in my impromptu response to them. First, religious, spiritual, and moral standpoints are part of people's identities that cannot be so easily set aside. Second, secularism itself is not neutral. "Secular" is often code for keeping religion those in

---

6. Patel, *Interfaith Leadership*, 8–9.

7. I am using the term "evangelical" in the sense it has taken on in the contemporary American political conversation rather than its New Testament Greek meaning or its historical links to the European Reformations. Ironically, the seeds for the rise of this alliance between evangelical Christianity and right-wing anti-democratic views in America were planted in the 1980s with a strategic effort to imitate the successes of the civil rights movement. See Mamdani, *Good Muslim, Bad Muslim*, 44.

power don't like out of public spaces, while supporting, for example, public Christian prayers at the mid-field line at high school football games. But even when it applies to the religions of dominant groups, secularism entails values and even a worldview that functions religiously. Third, religious communities generate social capital that has improved public life in America, from community service to civil rights to vigorous debates over morality and freedom.

Before we briefly explore each of these reasons, I want to flag a response that I will not pursue: that we should exonerate religion for violence because factors other than the religious are to blame.[8] In the age of Truth and Reconciliation, such reductionist apologetics ring hollow. This diversion also does not address the visceral dimension of the children's skepticism.[9] Religion as a category does not exist separately from social, cultural, psychological, economic, or political forces. In order to take the children's question seriously, we must avoid religious self-justification and acknowledge that religious communities do employ sacred texts, worldviews, and ideals in ways that can be culpable and complicit in generating violence.[10]

AN INTERFAITH ANSWER TO THE SECULAR SOLUTION

A strict relegation of "religion" to the private sphere is not the only solution to the responsibility of religious institutions for violence. In contrast with a secularity that bans faith from the public sphere, many interfaith leaders in North America now envision a model of secularity like Charles Taylor's, in which any tradition "is one possibility among others," and there is a genuine, robust "plurality of options."[11] They advocate a public movement that builds bridges across lines of religious difference by embracing religion as

---

8. One such response occurs in William Cavanagh's analysis of the persistent "myth of religious violence," which employs the so-called wars of religion in Europe as justification for secularism. Such narratives often rely on definitions of religion that exclude the political, economic, and social dimensions—definitions that do not hold up in the current study of religion and that do not reflect serious historical scholarship on that period. See Cavanaugh, *Myth*, 155.

9. On the role of the visceral in a pluralistic society, see Connolly, *Why I Am Not a Secularist*, 36.

10. Clarke, *Competing Fundamentalisms*, 152–56.

11. This describes Charles Taylor's *secularity* 3 (Taylor, *Secular Age*, 3).

part of the identities people bring to their pubic lives, by acknowledging that secularism itself is not neutral, and by harnessing the social capital created within religious and spiritual communities to promote peace. Let's look briefly at each of these points.

Religious Factors are Part of Identity

Patel cites religious philosophers like Nicholas Wolterstorff, who observe that people's religious convictions cannot be put on and taken off like articles of clothing when we go out in public. For a person of integrity, the social and political are as much implicated by one's convictions as matters of worship. In other words, people are whole selves, and we bring our whole selves with us when we go to work, when we form civic organizations, and when we vote. Context might help to determine *how explicit* we are about our spiritual orientations in this or that place, but we don't cease to be whole people when we move in and out of these spaces.[12]

Bringing our whole selves to our public interactions often means acknowledging that we are formed not by a single religion but by *multiple* views of reality, or what Rachel Mikva calls "lifestances."[13] Pegging someone as Catholic or Hindu does not predict everything about their values and behaviors. People's convictions may relate to more than one religious tradition, as well as to influences that are secular, humanist, eclectic, or based on a political party's platform or favorite media personality—more likely, some combination of all of the above. Our lives have more than one center, and that reality informs what we bring to our common spaces.[14]

Everyone stands somewhere, whether we call our values and dispositions religious, spiritual, moral, or secular. If we all have one or more operative lenses on reality, rather than insisting on the *absence* of religion and a secular public sphere, it is best to be explicit about this and make a compelling case about how these lifestances might shape our common life, institutions, and norms.

---

12. Patel, *Interfaith Leadership*, 9.
13. Mikva, "Reflections," 102.
14. See Thatamanil, *Circling the Elephant*, 187–90.

PART III | OTHERNESS, COMMUNITY, AND THE COMMON GOOD

Secularism is not Neutral

The second reason that a hard secularism falls short is that modernity and secularism, too, are chock full of values and assumptions that function as doctrines in their own right. Faith in scientific method, capitalism, humanism, and social justice function in ways that orient us toward reality.[15] These lifestances participate in what John Thatamanil calls "the religious." He observes, "*putatively secular institutions and activities continue to perform religious work.* . . . The religious is not a separate province or domain of life."[16] "The religious" is all around us, whether we think this *should* be the case, or not.

As "religious" in this way, secularism and modernity are not neutral ground. Secular modernity has presented itself as the cure for violence from the time of the European wars of religion through the 9/11 era. Treating religion as the toxic root of what ails us may seem like an easy way out,[17] but let us not forget that much violence has been done in the name of the secular and the nation state. Colonization and wars to bring "freedom," "democracy," and "modern values" have wrought destruction and have contributed to the formation of violent groups asserting religious identities against secular modernity.[18]

Social Capital Contributes to the Common Good

This third argument against a strictly secular public space is the cornerstone of Interfaith America's work on campuses. Patel draws on the work of sociologist Robert Putnam to theorize how religious communities create social

---

15. See Lewis, "Social Justice."

16. Thatamanil, *Circling the Elephant*, 172. Thatamanil is not claiming that every individual belongs to "a religion." Not only does "the religious" function inside and outside organized religions, but it is also not singular. He coins the technical term "comprehensive qualitative orientation" to develop these insights further. See Thatamanil, *Circling the Elephant*, 158–64.

17. Mamdani observes how popular it became for politicians and pundits to explain 9/11 by attempting to describe Islam as a "culture." To point to Islam as a mentality that is averse to freedom or inherently violent conveniently diverts from hard discussions of history, politics, colonialism, and economics (Mamdani, *Good Muslim, Bad Muslim*, 20). I observe something similar with the general category of "religion" in secularist approaches that treat all religions as "cultures" that are inherently responsible for abuses and atrocities.

18. See chapters 2 and 4 in Cavanaugh, *Myth*.

capital that can organize people and direct energy toward the common good. Putnam distinguishes between two kinds of social capital necessary in a diverse society. "Bonded" social capital refers to connections within identity groups. An example would be a church that gathers regularly for worship, potlucks, and Bible study. From the bond generated by these in-group activities, members can be mobilized, for example to volunteer once a month on building projects with Habitat for Humanity. "Bridged" social capital is when diverse religious communities come together and channel their collective capital "toward a positive civic purpose."[19]

Of course, tightly bonded in-groups can also be mobilized *against* other groups in times of tension. The interfaith movement has developed, in part, as a solution to the tensions and violence attributed to religious difference. Communities can interact in proactive, positive ways; and they can then call upon the bridged social capital they have accumulated in times of tension to reduce prejudice, identity-based conflict, and violence.[20]

Martin Marty argues that religious groups are uniquely qualified to play a public role in advancing the common good. Already operating in public spaces, these groups are full of motivated and committed participants, provide overlooked resources for combatting apathy and dealing positively with others, regularly give voice to the marginalized, and offer opportunities to revitalize public conversations and renew our collective life together.[21] For the interfaith movement, then, it is not a question of whether religion shows up in public, but how being religious, spiritual, or moral together can contribute to the common good.

INTERFAITH FOR THE COMMON GOOD

In *Interfaith Leadership: A Primer,* Patel builds his case through a series of definitions: *religion* is that which concerns "fundamental things"; *diversity* is a situation of "people with different identities and deep disagreements interacting with great frequency and intensity"; and *democracy* is a way of

19. Patel, *Interfaith Leadership,* 98–99; cf. Putnam, *Bowling Alone.*

20. Among the civic goods of interfaith work, Patel includes: "(1) Increasing understanding and reducing prejudice . . . (2) strengthening social cohesion and reducing the chances for identity-based conflict . . . (3) bridging social capital and addressing social problems . . . (4) fostering the continuity of identity communities and reducing isolation . . . [and] (5) creating binding narratives for diverse societies" (Patel, *Interfaith Leadership,* 98–99).

21. Marty, *Politics, Religion, and the Common Good,* 21–22.

PART III | OTHERNESS, COMMUNITY, AND THE COMMON GOOD

organizing society that offers "the freedom to advance our deepest personal convictions in public life." While disagreements are inevitable, in "a healthy religiously diverse democracy," people can "disagree . . . without violence and . . . are still able to work together."[22] Within such a context, an *interfaith leader* "is someone who can create the spaces, organize the social processes, and craft the conversations such that people who orient around religion differently can have a common life together."[23]

Certain shared practices and values are necessary to build that common life. With philosopher Jeffrey Stout, Patel affirms:

> People have a right to express themselves . . . but they should express themselves with the hope of being intelligible and convincing to one another, and they should direct significant energy to the health of the whole. Such practices strengthen what Stout calls "the civic nation."[24]

In the civic nation, people bring their convictions under the umbrella of shared values such as free speech and the right of association. Shared institutions, laws, and budgets all result from processes in which people gather, converse, persuade one another, amplify shared ideas, and make change.[25] On the level of day-to-day life, people in the civic nation engage around common interests such as sports leagues, neighborhood associations, and parent-teacher associations. Participating in the civic nation means listening to one another sympathetically, offering intelligible accounts of ourselves, and cooperating in political arrangements that treat one another with justice and dignity.[26]

To forge the human connection necessary for working together, Patel advises that interfaith conversations focus on two things: our stories, and what we hold in common. Storytelling humanizes us, relating us at the level of fundamental emotions, needs, and relationships. Patel employs stories to locate his motivations in his Muslim values and to invite others to share similar sources of motivation from their own traditions. For example, as an interfaith conversation starter, Interfaith America suggests asking participants in a shared service project to share something from their tradition

---

22. Patel, *Interfaith Leadership*, 10–11.
23. Patel, *Interfaith Leadership*, 11.
24. Patel, *Interfaith Leadership*, 10.
25. Patel, *Interfaith Leadership*, 7.
26. Patel, *Interfaith Leadership*, 10.

Can Religion (Really) Work for the Common Good?

or moral perspective that inspires them to engage in acts of service.[27] It is hard to argue with a person's experiences. Knowing where someone is coming from can go a long way toward understanding their differences; but stories also hold much of what is common to the human experience: family, joy, sorrow, change. We can harness our common needs for safety, health, education, and wellbeing to imagine and work for the world that we would like to inhabit together.

While Interfaith America works to bring together people who orient around religion *differently*, the drive is toward connection and commonality. In its early years, its treatment of difference was largely appreciative; indeed, "appreciative knowledge" is one of the tools in an interfaith leader's toolkit.[28] The sage leader would steer clear of hot-button issues, such as women's rights, sexual orientation and gender identity, or longstanding and religiously implicated conflicts such as those between Palestine and Israel, or India and Pakistan, because these issues can be divisive rather than build bridges across difference. An Interfaith America video about "good questions" advises the questions such as "What's the story of your name?" are better ice breakers than "What is your view on Israel and Palestine?"[29] Patel quips, "When people ask you why you are avoiding the elephant in the room, tell them it's because there are other animals in the zoo."[30] Our lives are so rich and complex, and there is so much to draw us together, that the guiding wisdom is to start building our relationships there, rather than with events that put everyone in a defensive posture—at least when diverse groups are just getting to know one another.

These liberal democratic ideals sustained many efforts at interfaith cooperation in the first decade after 9/11. However, over the past decade, several pieces of Patel's interfaith leadership syllogism seem to have fallen apart. White Christian nationalism has taken an overtly leading role in American public life. Democracy is no longer deliberative in the ways he describes. The algorithms of social media and niche news networks ensure that people don't interact across lines of difference as envisioned. In a world of "alternative facts," it is becoming more difficult to arrive at an understanding of the common good. In an Interfaith America podcast, Harvard Pluralism Project founder Diana Eck observes, "The rise of White

27. Interfaith America, "Shared Values."
28. Patel, *Interfaith Leadership*, 111–19.
29. Interfaith America, "Building Relationships."
30. Patel, *Interfaith Leadership*, 105.

Christian nationalism is probably the most difficult diversity issue that we face today, because it is the sort of calling card of people who don't like the diversity that the new immigration has brought."[31] Patel's response to Eck redoubles his commitment to the ideal of building a "better paradigm" together: "I'm an optimist.... Not only do I see the glass as half full, but I'm constantly trying to find ways to fill it all the way up."[32] In his analysis, "racism, antisemitism, Islamophobia, and misogyny" stand as "barriers" to interfaith cooperation but do not fundamentally alter the model.[33] He would rather be a builder than a critic.[34]

In a 2022 panel discussion at a summit for university-age interfaith leaders, Patel frames the question of how acknowledge the reality of these barriers "without fully internalizing it . . . making that define who you are, [for example,] not being more defined by Islamophobia than you are inspired by Islam." Panelist Nisha Anand's response echoes his optimism and his emphasis on the common:

> You actually win a whole lot of points if you can point fingers at other people and place blame. . . . And that's not going to bring us together. To me, and who I am as an optimist, that's not going to move the country forward. And so I choose to take a stance where I think about not trying to win points, not trying to be right, necessarily, but instead do right. . . . "It's not just the diversity you like." . . . You have to invite all the diversity. The stuff you don't know, . . . I think that finding that place of agreement, first and foremost, is really important. There is always something we share. That shared humanity is so strong. And in terms of barriers, it's also starting with that common pain. Common pain will always lead to common purpose. And I think from common purpose, you can find those common projects. We can work together. We can find something to do together. And for me, that doing is everything . . . making [this country] a place where you don't have to bump those barriers every single time you engage.[35]

---

31. Patel and Eck, "Can People Who Worship," 33:30–45.

32. Patel and Eck, "Can People Who Worship," 33:55–35:00.

33. Patel and Anand, "How Do Our Beliefs Inspire," 45:10–25. See also Patel, *We Need to Build*.

34. Patel chronicles his early intense engagement with critical race theory and his journey to build Interfaith America in chapters 1–2 of Patel, *We Need to Build*.

35. Patel and Anand, "How Do Our Beliefs Inspire," 45:40—49:00.

As an activist, Anand strategically chooses the common as a starting point as she works for policy change. Common humanity, purpose, and projects remain the focus at the same time as Interfaith America remains oriented to people who orient around religion *differently*. For example, Patel's speech before the above-mentioned panel develops the model of the potluck dinner as an alternative to the melting pot vision of America. Potlucks are successful if everyone brings their own dish, if people share the stories of their dish, and if diners discover that their dishes complement each other in surprising ways. Potlucks work because of, not despite, differences.

Patel and his colleagues know that, ultimately, excessive focus on commonality encourages people to look away from injustices. It allows people from the hegemonic group to look away from violence, both in the events that make the news and the violence in our everyday structures and practices. If we want to create a better world, we need to lean into the tough conversations to address the issues that impact us differently. This requires listening, learning, and perspective taking. Many of us will have powerful motivations from our traditions to stand on the side of those whose basic humanity is being denied, on whatever basis. People of faith can work together against injustice, whether the injustices are being done from religious or purportedly secular points of view.

FROM THE COMMON GOOD TO INTERFAITH SOLIDARITY

I am inspired by Patel's interfaith vision. The human connection created through sharing stories and finding joint interests is an important part of my teaching in a multireligious theological school. Though commonality can be an important connector, however, I challenge whether the "common" should be the primary aim of interfaith work. My academic discipline of comparative theology is generally wary of paradigms of comparative religion that expect to see patterns of sameness across the traditions designated as religions, which employ a selective Western lens for what counts as religion and often treats differences as deviations from essential norms.

I am also aware that, as a White Christian theologian, I require additional antidotes to universalizing tendencies because I have imbibed a concoction of Christian monotheism and a White settler mentality that predisposes me to think that what is true for my group is true for all.[36] In addition to the physical violence that has been inflicted in the name of liberal democratic norms, often in the name of freedom of/from religion, softer forms of pressure exert pressure to conform to those same ideals. For example, in an ironic turn, the US State Department and other governments around the world now leverage religion itself to encourage liberal modes of conduct by funding interfaith initiatives (including some of Interfaith America's programs).[37] It is important for a critical approach to interfaith work to recognize that Whiteness and Christian universalism operate, in part, through assumptions about what is or should be common.

The interfaith movement's norms often require people from minoritized traditions to conform and fit in for the sake of what is called the common good. Tracy Sayuki Tiemeier argues, "Until every facet of interreligious studies shifts so that it attends to the most vulnerable persons and populations, it cannot be a field that works for the 'common' or 'public' good."[38] Khyati Joshi similarly opines, "There is a tendency, particularly in tense times, to fall back on comforting fluff about our common humanity . . . Ideas like that are nice to bring people together, but do not deal with reality and with the more complicated truth: we are not the same."[39] Because interfaith encounters do not happen on an equal playing field, participants must interrogate structural inequities and ask what interfaith solidarity looks like.

Joshi's important book, *White Christian Privilege*, outlines how thoroughly the interfaith landscape conforms to White Christian norms. To be in solidarity with one another, Joshi recommends shifting away from

---

36. Influences on my thinking here include Jennings, *After Whiteness*; Schneider, *Beyond Monotheism*; and New Testament scholar Angela S. Parker, who offers the acronym AIR—accept that you don't know everything, interrogate your identities, read Womanist authors—as a guide for the kind of moves I make in this section. See Parker, *If God Still Breathes*, 98–99.

37. Interfaith Youth Core/Interfaith America partnered with the US government on President Obama's Interfaith Campus and Community Service Challenge and has received funding from the United States Department of State's Bureau of Democracy, Human Rights & Labor—Office of International Religious Freedom (see "Interfaith Youth Core"; Patel, *We Need to Build*, 28). The dynamics are different in other contexts, where Christianity may not be the dominant tradition, and notions of what makes for good religion or religious freedom differ. See Sullivan et al., *Politics of Religious Freedom*; Omer, "Decolonizing Religion."

38. Tiemeier, "For Whom," 154.

39. Joshi, *White Christian Privilege*, 220.

Christian language, questions, foci, foundational assumptions, and paradigms.[40] For example, Christians impose Christian *language* on other traditions when they wonder which church a person attends or what scripture they read. In addition, debates often foreground Christian *questions*:

> When policy makers are discussing, for example, "Should we stop serving pork in prisons to accommodate Muslim inmates?" or "Should Sikhs be allowed to serve in the military with *kesh* (unshorn hair) and *dastaar* (turban)?" they are really debating whether Christians should grant civil liberties to non-Christians. . . . The very question of whether the Christian majority should "let" religious minorities practice their faith assumes White Christian supremacy as normative.[41]

Similarly, interfaith participants can widen their *focus* from, for example, what the dominant group should do to show solidarity after an attack on another community "to challenge the ideologies that make such attacks possible and even popular."[42] Shifting the *foundational assumptions* also challenges the interfaith emphasis on sameness. While "In the aftermath of 9/11, . . . many Muslims emphasized that theirs is an Abrahamic faith, like Christianity, and talked about Islam's recognition of Jesus as a prophet," these connections catered to dominant Christians' prejudices by obscuring the distinctiveness of Islam as well as historical and political factors that could have led to deeper understanding of the forces at play.[43] Finally, changing the *paradigm* refers to the ways that Christian norms shape interfaith behavior, such as saying "Happy Holidays" only in December, assuming that sacred texts hold the same status in all traditions, emphasizing beliefs over practices, or making monotheism the norm.[44]

The prevailing interfaith paradigm's emphasis on finding common ground perpetuates microaggressions against potential dialogue partners. The forms of structural violence identified above are related to ideas about

---

40. Joshi, *White Christian Privilege*, 213.
41. Joshi, *White Christian Privilege*, 216.
42. Joshi, *White Christian Privilege*, 218.
43. Joshi, *White Christian Privilege*, 220; cf. Kazi, *Islamophobia*.
44. Joshi, *White Christian Privilege*, 224. Joshi connects these features of the interfaith landscape, which some might dismiss or call microaggressions, to the macro-level history of the shifting and exclusionary ways Whiteness and Christianity were held up as legal requirements for citizenship, and still undergird a certain American commonsense that underlies Muslim bans and profiling in security policies. See also Hill Fletcher, *White Supremacy*.

PART III | OTHERNESS, COMMUNITY, AND THE COMMON GOOD

religion that formed amid the violence of secular modernity. What counts as "good religion" in modern liberal democracies looks a lot like European Christian Protestantism: for example, that individual belief, interiority, textual authority, and monotheistic coherence are what matter religiously. These conceptions of good religion support the focus on what is common in interfaith encounter, including ostensibly neutral appeals to reason and the common good.[45] Because Islam has been painted as the main exemplar of a religion that is too outward, too suspect in its loyalties, and too much unlike liberal norms, Muslims are often in put in the position of having to prove that they have assimilated to US norms of what counts as good religion; and Sikhs and other minoritized traditions end up needing to defend themselves against anti-Islamic stereotypes. The internment of Japanese Americans during World War II was another shameful outcome of suspicion of divided loyalties in people who do not conform to dominant modes of religiosity. We also saw these racialized logics in the charge that President Barack Obama was a "secret Muslim" and in legislators who tried to implement anti-Shariʻa bans: both embodied a fear of Muslim allegiance to Islamic legal reasoning, which in turn is assumed at all times and places to be at odds with liberal ideals.

Failure to understand the structural differences within the interfaith movement can lead to failures in solidarity when it is most needed. Interfaith engagement presents the *option* for White Christians to learn about the food, clothing, and festivals of their neighbors. They can participate if they feel like it, but minoritized persons have often found themselves needing to engage in interfaith activities as a matter of survival. Tiemeier writes, "Faced with prejudice and ignorance, Asian religious leaders do not have much choice. They must become dialoguers if they hope to lessen violence and racism against their communities."[46] This has been the case throughout the long history of Asian immigration to North America, and it continues to be true today. For example, a week after 9/11, when a family friend, a Sikh man named Balbir Singh Sodhi, was killed outside his gas station in Mesa, AZ, Valarie Kaur started telling his story and stories like his. After the mass shooting at the gurdwara in Oak Creek, Wisconsin, on August 5, 2012, she though that the nation would finally pay attention. But in contrast

---

45. Marianne Moyaert traces the construction of good religion back to patterns in Christian scripture and through the ensuing millennia. See Moyaert, *Christian Imaginations*.

46. Tiemeier, "Asian Participation," 4.

to the brief media treatment of Oak Creek, the White children killed at Sandy Hook several months later captured the nation's imagination. While minoritized communities must participate in civic conversation as a matter of survival but often go unnoticed, majority communities have the luxury of paying attention, or not.[47]

INTERFAITH ACTIVISM

Emphasis on the common can lead interfaith participants to pay attention to others only insofar as they are "like us." It can lead to complacency about structural violence. Joshi calls for "Interfaith 2.0," which "shifts interfaith work from 'we are here to support each other' to 'we are working together to create a social justice paradigm.'"[48] Because we do not inherit a level playing field, some leaders, like Kaur and Muslim interfaith agitator Najeeba Syeed, have turned to interfaith activism and engagement through the legal system rather than primarily to dialogue and common service. When her professor encouraged her to go to law school, Kaur reflected that her Sikh ancestors

> did not have a sophisticated matrix of legal and political avenues to defend civil and human rights, nor international law to mediate conflicts between nations. We have these avenues today. We no longer need literal weapons like our ancestors. But we could still learn from how they marshaled the fighting impulse on the battlefield. My professor saw me out there holding nothing but a megaphone. *You are a woman of color*, she had said. *If you want to fight, you need armor.*[49]

The corporate, philanthropic, and government-supported interfaith movements' emphases on peacebuilding and volunteerism do not go far enough for interfaith activists.[50] Interfaith activists still vigorously engage across religious and spiritual lines as they align their efforts on issues of justice. They literally lined up together to form a human barrier between

---

47. Kaur, *See No Stranger*, 229.
48. Joshi, *White Christian Privilege*, 219.
49. Kaur, *See No Stranger*, 93.
50. For example, Edward Curtis narrates how he "increasingly had to set aside my most cherished social justice commitments [pro-Palestinian activism] in order to . . . have the privilege of participating in this kind of interfaith work" (Curtis, "How I Left," 9:00–13:10).

police and protesters in Ferguson, Missouri, after Michael Brown was killed.[51] They gather outside of detention centers to protest family separation and other unjust practices at the border.[52] They reimagine society and work to end to racial profiling by city law enforcement, close the detention centers at Guantanamo Bay, and abolish the prison-industrial complex.[53]

A social justice approach is changing the way that interfaith efforts are framed on campus and beyond.[54] Leaders need to ask themselves some hard questions. When we call upon religion as a force for the common good, do we only mean certain expressions of religion? Do we insist on peacemaking at the expense of equity, justice, and civil rights? Must minoritized communities discipline themselves according to White Protestant American Christian norms? Are they expected to rally behind military operations in parts of the world where their religions predominate?[55] Do we depoliticize our differences by insisting that religious minorities practice what makes them distinctive only in private? Are education, prosperity, and contribution to the market economy required as tickets to the interfaith table? And if the push for the common erases differences, especially differences of power, is it realistic to expect genuine community to form around it?

CONCLUSION: FAITH IN THE PUBLIC SPHERE

I shared the story of April and the kids with one of my Jewish students, Sarit, and explained that I was working on an essay about how spiritual, religious, and moral motivations can promote interfaith solidarity in the context of White supremacy. Sarit had an interesting further point: How might the context of White supremacy be contributing to this sense that my friends and family were expressing, that religion should retreat from the public sphere? Isn't it a function of White supremacy to think that we

---

51. Francis, *Ferguson and Faith*.
52. Syeed, "Birthing."
53. See chapter 6 in Kaur, *See No Stranger*.

54. Patel's 2022 book, *We Need to Build*, reflects the shift Interfaith America has undergone during the heightened tensions of the Trump years, when it has become impossible to ignore the "elephants in the room." This book, which became available to me only in the late stages of these reflections, can in some ways be read as a rejoinder and response to this line of critique and development.

55. Kazi, *Islamophobia*, 59–60, 95–96.

don't need spiritual practices? Doesn't racialized capitalism tell us that we should be self-sufficient? We call on our religious and spiritual communities because we are *not* enough. White supremacy will not save White folks, just as proximity to Whiteness has never been enough to save people who are Black, Indigenous, and people of color. As we continued our conversation, we highlighted ways that despite well-earned cynicism, people in our communities *are* digging deep into their spiritual heritages, acting from those values and motivations, and reaching out across lines of difference. April herself is doing this, as a powerful and effective writer and activist on racialized antisemitism.[56] Each must find their own stance within a complicated landscape.

Because so much harm has been done in the name of Christianity, Christians must be part of the work of today's interfaith reparation. However, so long as White Christians like me move in contexts in which Whiteness and Christianity are dominant, we will always be tempted toward habituated imperialist ways of "sharing" our vision with others. Rather than following Christian examples who have colonized others in Jesus' name, we must be guided by the Spirit of the one who proclaimed hope amid colonization and oppression, and by those communities on the margins of empire who have been guided by the same Spirit. I see this Spirit active in interfaith efforts that engage not only in private, charity-based work, but that also connect people around their experiences of social and economic systems. In my city, these networks have activated to provide sanctuary for refugees, march against racialized police violence, and petition the city for the rights of people experiencing homelessness and other human rights issues.[57]

I am inspired into interfaith solidarity by the example of Jesus of Nazareth. His ministry took place amid imperial occupation, vast economic equality, and social division. He was someone who could see the people at the margins. By seeing them, by attending to what was happening in front of him, he challenged the larger systems. Interfaith leadership does that. Rather than projecting our fears, guilts, and inadequacies at unassailable entities beyond our reach like religious violence, "Islamic terrorism," or White supremacy, we can begin by attending to this family in need of sanctuary, this unjust practice, that neighborhood lacking warm shelters, and so on. This kind of attentiveness, openness, and hope in multireligious spaces enable communities to push beyond what is common to enter into solidarity across lines of difference.

56. See her writings at https://www.aprilrosenblum.com/essays.
57. See, e.g., Gilmour, "Public Witness."

PART III | OTHERNESS, COMMUNITY, AND THE COMMON GOOD

BIBLIOGRAPHY

Cavanaugh, William T. *The Myth of Religious Violence: Secular Ideology and the Roots of Modern Conflict*. Oxford: Oxford University Press, 2009.

Clarke, Sathianathan. *Competing Fundamentalisms: Violent Extremism in Christianity, Islam, and Hinduism*. Louisville: Westminster John Knox, 2017.

Connolly, William E. *Why I Am Not a Secularist*. Minneapolis: University of Minnesota Press, 1999.

Curtis, Edward. "How I Left the Interfaith Movement and Found Interfaith Solidarity." Lecture at Luther College, February 24, 2021. https://www.youtube.com/watch?v=y3BqxWYN4gY.

Gilmour, Alexa. "Public Witness in the Local Urban Congregation." In *For the Sake of the Common Good: Essays in Honour of Lois Wilson*, edited by Kate Merriman and Bertha Yetman, 100–111. Montreal: McGill-Queen's University, 2022.

Hill Fletcher, Jeannine. *The Sin of White Supremacy: Christianity, Racism, and Religious Diversity in America*. Maryknoll, NY: Orbis, 2017.

Interfaith America. "Building Relationships through Dialogue." August 9, 2016. https://youtu.be/Fx04b14hVP0.

———. "Shared Values Facilitation Guide." *Interfaith America*. https://www.interfaithamerica.org/resources/shared-values-facilitation-guide.

Jennings, Willie James. *After Whiteness: An Education in Belonging*. Grand Rapids: Eerdmans, 2020.

Joshi, Khyati Y. *White Christian Privilege: The Illusion of Religious Equality in America*. New York: New York University Press, 2020.

Kaur, Valarie. *See No Stranger: A Memoir and Manifesto of Revolutionary Love*. New York: One World, 2020.

Kazi, Nazia. *Islamophobia, Race, and Global Politics*. Lanham, MD: Rowman & Littlefield, 2019.

Mamdani, Mahmood. *Good Muslim, Bad Muslim: America, the Cold War, and the Roots of Terror*. New York: Three Leaves/Doubleday, 2004.

Lewis, Helen. "How Social Justice Became a New Religion." *Atlantic*, August 18, 2022. https://www.theatlantic.com/ideas/archive/2022/08/social-justice-new-religion/671172.

Marty, Martin E., with Jonathan Moore. *Politics, Religion, and the Common Good: Advancing a Distinctly American Conversation About Religion's Role in Our Shared Life*. San Francisco: Jossey-Bass, 2000.

Mikva, Rachel S. "Reflections in the Waves: What Interreligious Studies Can Learn from Women's Movements in the US." In *Critical Reflections on Interreligious Education: Experiments in Empathy*, edited by Najeeba Syeed and Heidi Hadsell, 98–124. Currents of Encounter 63. Leiden: Brill, 2000.

Moyaert, Marianne. *Christian Imaginations of the Religious Other: A History of Religionization*. Hoboken, NJ: Wiley-Blackwell, 2023.

Omer, Atalia. "Decolonizing Religion and the Practice of Peace: Two Case Studies from the Postcolonial World." *Critical Research on Religion* 8.3 (2020) 273–96.

Parker, Angela N. *If God Still Breathes, Why Can't I? Black Lives Matter and Biblical Authority*. Grand Rapids: Eerdmans, 2021.

Patel, Eboo. *Interfaith Leadership: A Primer*. Boston: Beacon, 2016.

———. *We Need to Build: Field Notes for Diverse Democracy*. Boston: Beacon, 2022.

Patel, Eboo, and Nisha Anand. "How Do Our Beliefs Inspire Us to Build a Diverse Democracy?" *Interfaith America with Eboo Patel* (Podcast), April 11, 2023.

Patel, Eboo, and Diana Eck. "Can People Who Worship Differently Find Common Ground?" *Interfaith America with Eboo Patel* (Podcast), December 13, 2022.

Putnam, Robert. *Bowling Alone: The Collapse and Revival of American Community*. New York: Simon & Schuster, 2000.

Schneider, Laurel C. *Beyond Monotheism: A Theology of Multiplicity*. New York: Routledge, 2008.

Sullivan, Winnifred Fallers, et al., eds. *Politics of Religious Freedom*. Chicago: University of Chicago Press, 2015.

Syeed, Najeeba. "Birthing Interfaith Rituals of Resistance to Disrupt State Violence." Keynote Address, Ninth Annual Starr King Symposium, February 2, 2021. https://www.youtube.com/watch?v=WTqc76md8Wg.

Taylor, Charles. *A Secular Age*. Cambridge: Harvard, 2007.

Thatamanil, John J. *Circling the Elephant: A Comparative Theology of Religious Diversity*. New York: Fordham University Press, 2020.

Tiemeier, Tracy Sayuki. "For Whom, and to What End? Possibilities and Implications of Privileging Intersectionality in Interreligious Studies." In *The Georgetown Companion to Interreligious Studies*, edited by Lucinda Mosher, 147–56. Washington, DC: Georgetown University Press, 2022.

———. "Asian Participation in Interreligious Dialogue." In *Religious Leadership: A Reference Handbook*, edited by Sharon Henderson Callahan, 2:427–33. 2 vols. Los Angeles: Sage, 2013.

"Interfaith Youth Core." *Wikipedia*. https://en.wikipedia.org/wiki/Interfaith_Youth_Core.

7

"A Small Intellectual Agora"
Richard Kearney's Anatheism and the Inner Space to Engage Otherness

HENK VAN DEN BOSCH

EXPERIENCES OF ALTERITY

"I am truly sorry, and please do not take it personally, but I cannot in good conscience celebrate holy communion with you." The final course in the curriculum of the three-year Master of Divinity program of the Protestant Theological University is meant to be a course on the threshold between university and church. Students have been preparing for ministry in the Protestant Church in the Netherlands. They have studied theology, done their internships, and worked hard to integrate the dimensions of ministerial, professional, and personal formation in their reflective theological practice. During this final course they take stock before crossing the threshold and entering the church.

It is standard practice to close the course with a celebration of holy communion. But not this time. This time the differences in theological outlook seem to prohibit the joint acceptance of the invitation of the Lord to the table of fellowship. A group of students takes offense at a fellow student who is in a homosexual relationship. They consider this to be a sinful lifestyle and invoke the warning of the apostle Paul in his first letter to the Corinthians, not to eat and drink judgment on yourself. Other students take offense at these students taking offense. Then there are a few students who have insurmountable objections against women in ministry, citing the same apostle that women should remain silent in the congregation. It goes without saying that the female students and most of their male colleagues take offense against this position. And gradually it becomes clear that it is not possible for us to celebrate holy communion together.

For all participants this experience is an extremely painful reminder of the divisions within the church, the discord within the body of Christ. The inability to recognize one another as sisters and brothers in Christ, the encounter with strangeness, estrangement, and exclusion is agonizing. It is also a valuable experience, since this is the reality of the church they are about to join as ministers. It is an important and formative experience of otherness, of pluriformity, of the fragmentation of truth both within the church and outside, in short: a painful but edifying encounter with pluralism.

The category of alterity, of otherness or strangeness, permeates the pluralistic age, an age characterized by postmodernism as a dominant hermeneutical paradigm. According to Charles Taylor, "we are now living in a spiritual super-nova, a kind of galloping pluralism on the spiritual plane."[1] This means that we need to be constantly aware of the relativity of our thinking, that we need to be suspicious of words like "truth" and "objectivity." And the fragmentation, pluralization, and fragilization of shared concepts of truth doesn't necessarily feel good or comfortable. On the contrary: Taylor speaks of the malaise of immanence and the loss of transcendence,[2] a malaise the aforementioned group of future ministers can testify to.

The Protestant Theological University uses a set of sixteen competencies a student has to master by the end of the study. Relevant to the experience of alterity is the second part of the so-called "personal competence" that aims at the ability: (1) to deal reflectively with one's own biography, faith identity and praxis, and the resultant behavior, and (2) to create the inner space to engage otherness. Impressive as this may seem, it is not immediately clear what this means. How does one create such an inner space, what does it look like?

---

1. Taylor, *Secular Age*, 300.
2. Taylor, *Secular Age*, 303.

PART III | OTHERNESS, COMMUNITY, AND THE COMMON GOOD

REFLECTION ON ALTERITY

This is not my first attempt to explore the issue of engaging with radical otherness. In an earlier essay I took a personal experience of an encounter with otherness as point of exit.[3] From 2005 to 2010 I worked as lecturer at Justo Mwale University, a seminary in Lusaka, Zambia. Simultaneously I served as minister to the Madalitso Congregation of the Reformed Church of Zambia, a small rural congregation some hundred kilometers east of Lusaka. One Sunday, during the sermon, a deaconess left the church building in a hurry. After the sermon I was called out of the service to attend to her. The elder who came to fetch me told me that she was possessed by an evil spirit and that I needed to perform an exorcism in order to cleanse her. I did what I had seen others do: I got to my knees by her side and started praying. "In the powerful name of Jesus, I command you to go out." After repeating these words for some fifteen minutes the woman regained consciousness, sat up and burped a few times loudly. The elder proclaimed my act of exorcism a success and the three of us returned to the church building to continue the worship service.

This is what happened. But ever since it happened I'm haunted by the question of what exactly happened. The strangeness of the experience and the radical otherness of the world view it presupposes made it hard if not impossible for me to come to an understanding of what happened.

In the 2019 paper I looked at this engagement with radical otherness from a number of perspectives. One of those perspectives I derived from missiological studies with its attention to cross-cultural processes. The engagement with otherness I experienced in Madalitso is an example of a cross-cultural process that reveals borders between one's own identity and that of the other. These borders can be experienced and treated as barriers behind which to hide and protect one's identity, or as frontiers that invite curiosity, openness, and possible influence from other identities. British historian of mission Andrew Walls perceives these cross-cultural processes as necessary for the understanding of Christ. No historical and culturally determined expression of the Christian faith can claim to be its final expression. On the contrary: the various expressions of faith, that by historical necessity are always limited and fragmented, should be perceived

---

3. See Bosch, "In the Powerful Name."

as complementary expressions that only in their pluriform coherence can express the full understanding of Christ.[4]

Another possibly helpful perspective is the concept of liminality, a concept coined in anthropological studies. The engagement with radical otherness invites one into a kind of "middle" or open space where social identity is suspended in order that it might be reconfigured. Four phases can be distinguished in this kind of liminal experience. In the first phase the existing reality is breached, our existence as we know and trust it is disrupted by the confrontation with otherness. The second phase is the experience of a threshold: the engagement with otherness invites a response, either to engage or to withdraw. The third phase is reflection on the question of what happened, and the fourth phase is one of reintegration of the disruptive event into one's existence.[5] Theologian Mark Kline Taylor argues that Christian existence is always liminal existence because Christ as incarnation of self-sacrificing love is a liminal character:

> Christian liminal existence orients one toward affirmation of the other that is necessary (1) for dialectical questioning, (2) for processes of mutual construction in intercultural communication, (3) for a shared unity that accentuates differences, and (4) for living in the uncertainty and discomfort that often attend the disclaiming of any privileged, imposed common ground existing outside of dialogical encounter.[6]

A third perspective is offered by the philosophical insights of Emmanuel Levinas. Particularly valuable proved to be his view that Western thinking is characterized by its systematic attempt to understand otherness as sameness, to reduce radical alterity to mere difference, to interpret what is unknown within the framework of what is known, "the claim to know and to reach the Other."[7] It helped me to come to an understanding that my interpretation of the behavior of the deaconess as evidence of something like an epileptic seizure was indicative of just this kind of thinking. It prohibited me to do justice to the irreducible alterity of the other. A meaningful encounter with otherness as an interruption of my own framework in order to create inner space for an engagement with otherness became impossible.

4. Walls, "Ephesian Moment."
5. Trebilcock, "Theology in Context."
6. Taylor, "Shaky Ground," 46.
7. Levinas, *Totality and Infinity*, 69.

PART III | OTHERNESS, COMMUNITY, AND THE COMMON GOOD

The other side of the same coin is Levinas's emphasis on the ultimate unknowability of the other, the impossibility to grasp the otherness of the other. This emphasis results in the ethical imperative of asymmetrical responsibility to the other, meaning that I am always more responsible for the other than the other is for me. The other of Levinas is another individual that is largely unknowable to the interpreting self but demands responsibility.[8] Basically, it means there is nothing to be said about and thus nothing to be learned and no insight to be gained from encounters with otherness. In the end I am utterly isolated from the other I am engaging with. What good would the creation of an inner space to engage otherness possibly do when there is no otherness to really engage?

A MIDDLE WAY: RICHARD KEARNEY ON OTHERNESS

The interaction with the ethical categories of otherness that Levinas proposes left me caught between a rock and a hard place. The rock in this case is what could be termed a Schleiermacherian hermeneutical position that aims to unite the consciousness of a subject with that of another in a process of appropriation, a process that according to Levinas reduces otherness to a form of sameness. The hard place, on the other hand, is the Levinasian position that emphasizes irreducible difference and separation, which makes any kind of relation to or genuine engagement with otherness impossible. How to escape this uncomfortable position?

Fortunately, I learned that I was not alone in my skepticism regarding this "irreducible dissymmetry of self and other."[9] I found similar ideas in the work of the Irish philosopher Richard Kearney (bn. 1954). Kearney studied in Paris with the likes of Ricoeur, Levinas, Breton, and Derrida and wrote his doctoral dissertation under the supervision of Ricoeur. He is thoroughly schooled in Continental philosophy and is viewed as a leading global thinker in post-metaphysical philosophy of religion. He shares the ambition of continental philosophers to grasp reality in its totality and their resulting interest in religion, and can be viewed as representative of the turn to theology in philosophy. He is therefore a very relevant dialogue partner for theologians.

---

8. Levinas, *Totality and Infinity*, 46.
9. Kearney, *Strangers, Gods, and Monsters*, 9, 17.

"A Small Intellectual Agora"

My first attempts to familiarize myself with his work, the result of which you are now reading, proved to be a daunting task, since he is a prolific writer who has produced a massive body of work. Luckily, Kearney himself was kind enough to offer a helping hand: in a brief autobiographical sketch he refers to his exploration of a hermeneutical phenomenology of otherness in which he is looking for a middle way between what he calls the ontological and the ethical categories of otherness.[10] This exploration resulted in the publication of three books, namely, *The God Who May Be* (2001), *On Stories* (2002), and *Strangers, Gods, and Monsters* (2003), together conceived as a trilogy entitled Philosophy at the Limits.[11] The quest for a God after God, that is a central question in the trilogy, is continued in *Anatheism* (2010). Although I do not presume to be able to do full justice to works so elegantly written, imaginatively constructed, and intelligently conceived as these, I take my point of exit for my further deliberations on the creation of an inner space to engage otherness in these books.

Strangers is the final volume in the trilogy but it is the first one I read. I was originally drawn to it because of the strangers in its title. Kearney makes the claim that strangers, gods, and monsters (three colloquial names for the experience of alterity) are not only "experiences of extremity which bring us to the edge" of our self-understanding and are therefore often "set apart in fear and trembling," but that they are also "tokens of fracture within the human psyche" that "speak to us of how we are split between conscious and unconscious, familiar and unfamiliar, same and other."[12] Alterity is then used to project the strangeness in ourselves in order to keep it at a comfortable distance. However, in doing so we deny ourselves the possibility of coming to genuine self-knowledge. Understood like this, strangers offer us a choice between understanding and accommodating otherness or repudiating it. The choice for understanding and accommodating otherness is then also a choice for understanding and accommodating ourselves.

The question of the interaction with alterity ("the conundrum of the Other") is as old as western metaphysics. In twentieth-century continental philosophy this quest leads to two extreme positions, absolute versus relative otherness. Kearney proposes a middle way between these extremes, between romantic and radical hermeneutics by way of a diacritical

---

10. Kearney, "Where I Speak From," 48.

11. Benjamins's discussion of Kearney's trilogy was very helpful for coming to an understanding of these works. See Benjamins, *Boven is onder ons*, 201–12.

12. Kearney, *Strangers, Gods, and Monsters*, 3–4.

hermeneutics that explores the possibilities of intercommunion between distinct but not fundamentally incompatible selves. The application of his diacritical hermeneutics aims to make the foreign more familiar and the familiar more foreign, allowing us to welcome strangers, respect gods and acknowledge monsters.[13]

In a series of essays, he puts a face on otherness by exploring various cultural and philosophical representations of the other, from the *Alien* movies to Shakespeare's *Hamlet*. The middle way between a "romantic" hermeneutic of the autonomous self (at the expense of alterity) and a "radical" hermeneutic of emphatic alterity (at the expense of the self) works on the premise that "there is no otherness so exterior or so unconscious . . . that it cannot be at least minimally interpreted by a self."[14] In order to be able to interpret otherness we need a narrative, the construction of a narrative self that is able to tell us who we are and how we have become what we have become, a "narrative identity woven from its own histories and those of others."[15] This narrative identity is able to transform itself, to re-tell its own story, in order to find a proper relation to self and other.

The exploration of cultural and philosophical representations of otherness brings Kearney to a contemplation of the absolute Other. He considers the possibility of a God who is not completely beyond the hermeneutics of diacritical discernment and who is still relevant in possibility to the larger project of understanding Others, namely in the conviction that "the eschaton still-to-come already intersects, however enigmatically and epiphanically, with the ontological order of being as loving possible."[16]

This idea of a possible God is the subject of the first installment of the trilogy, *The God Who May Be*: "God neither is nor is not but may be."[17] This God is not the onto-theological God of Scholasticism, the God of pure essence; Kearney favors a more eschatological notion of God as possibility to come: *posse* (possibility of being) instead of *esse* (actuality of being). "God will be God at the eschaton. That is what is promised." But because God is a possibility of being, the promise remains powerless until and unless we respond to it. "Transfiguring the possible into the actual, and thereby enabling the coming kingdom to come into being, is not just something God

---

13. Kearney, *Strangers, Gods, and Monsters*, 11.
14. Kearney, *Strangers, Gods, and Monsters*, 81.
15. Kearney, *Strangers, Gods, and Monsters*, 188.
16. Kearney, *Strangers, Gods, and Monsters*, 228.
17. Kearney, *God Who May Be*, 1.

does for us but also something we do for God."[18] The God who may be is a source of possibility, enabling us to actualize the promise of the kingdom. This then is a reminder that what seems impossible to us is possible with God: "For once transfigured by God all things are made possible again, disclosing the eschatological potentials latently inscribed in the historically im-possible."[19] These words bring the wonderful story of the feeding of the five thousand (Mark 6:30–44) to mind: the disciples have only five loaves available, making the task at hand an impossibility, but under the blessing hands of the Lord these meager loaves are transfigured into the possibility of an actual feast for the multitude.

An important method or vehicle for the transfiguring encounter with otherness and the actualization of unimagined possibilities is the narrative, the topic of the final volume of the trilogy: *On Stories*. Stories "offer us a newly imagined way of being in the world . . . by inviting us to see the world otherwise."[20] In the complicated encounter with otherness, in which we experience the mystery, the unthinkable, and unexplainable of otherness, in other words: the otherness of otherness, stories offer coherence in a fragmented world, in the relations between me, other, and world. "Story is not confined to the mind of its author alone. . . . Nor is it confined to the mind of its reader. Nor indeed to the actions of its narrated actors. The story exists in the interplay between all these."[21] In this related interplay, stories offer us the possibility to reorder our world and to reposition ourselves in this world, and thus to open ourselves to new possibilities and a new future.

Take, for example, what happens to the disciples when they place their five meager loaves at the disposal of the Lord in the story of the feeding of the five thousand. This story encourages me to place my own limited resources at the disposal of the Lord and do my work in the service of the coming kingdom, trusting that under the blessing hands of the Lord the people will be fed. The transfiguring potency of stories can only be realized if we do not anxiously hold on to what is familiar and known, but if we open up ourselves to otherness. Then stories offer us a shareable world.

---

18. Kearney, *God Who May Be*, 4.
19. Kearney, *God Who May Be*, 5.
20. Kearney, *On Stories*, 12.
21. Kearney, *On Stories*, 156.

PART III | OTHERNESS, COMMUNITY, AND THE COMMON GOOD

ANATHEISM

The idea that otherness and the encounter with the other opens up possibility and creates a surplus of meaning is taken up in *Anatheism: Returning to God after God* (2010). The starting point of this book is again the search for a middle way, this time a third way beyond the extremes of dogmatic theism and militant atheism.

> This third option, this wager of faith beyond faith, I call anatheism. *Ana-theos*, God after God. Ana-theism: another word for another way of seeking and sounding the things we consider sacred but can never fully fathom or prove. Another idiom for receiving back what we've given up as if we were encountering it for the first time.[22]

Kearney coins this neologism to define a position that is not atheism (an-atheism) and that transcends theism (ana-theism):

> The *ana* signals a movement of return to what I call a primordial wager, to an inaugural instant of reckoning at the root of belief. . . . Anatheism, in short, is an invitation to revisit what might be termed a primary scene of religion: the encounter with a radical Stranger who we choose, or don't choose, to call God.[23]

Kearney returns to the God question because it is an urgent question in today's public debate, compelling philosophers and theologians to be clear about what they mean when they speak of God. Beyond dogmatic theism and militant atheism, Kearney argues for the possibility of God, for "a small intellectual agora"[24] where theists and atheists can participate in a conversation on God. In this anatheist space, the free decision to believe or not believe is not just tolerated but cherished. Of course, all depends on how we define God:

> If transcendence is indeed a *surplus* of meaning, it requires a process of endless interpretation. The more strange God is to our familiar ways, the more multiple our readings of this strangeness. If divinity is unknowable, humanity must imagine it in many ways. The absolute requires pluralism to avoid absolutism.[25]

22. Kearney, *Anatheism*, 3.
23. Kearney, *Anatheism*, 7.
24. Kearney, *Anatheism*, xiii.
25. Kearney, *Anatheism*, xiv.

From this tentative definition, a few things follow. Kearney is a hermeneutic philosopher in the sense that he is convinced that meaning, making sense of otherness, is possible, on the condition of a respectful opening up for otherness and for the surplus of meaning that is to be found in otherness. The stranger is the embodiment of this surplus: "The stranger is sacred in that she always embodies something *else*, something *more*, something *other* than what the self can grasp or contain."[26] God is the ultimate sacred stranger, the one who is not known, who is unknowable, to whom we must wager whether to open ourselves. This wager is not a choice once and for all, no, time and again (*ana*) we have to choose (and we can choose: it is a free decision, the subject is autonomous) whether to engage otherness, whether to choose hospitality or hostility, whether to believe or disbelieve. "The stranger before me both *is* God (as transcendent Guest) and *is not* God (as screen of my projections and presumptions). Out of this tension faith leaps."[27]

The anatheistic wager is both a philosophical wager and an existential wager, which are two facets of one and the same wager. "The philosophical wager regarding the interpretation of diverse voices, texts, and theories about the meaning of the sacred in our time" concerns the aforementioned stance in hermeneutic philosophy: "Interpretation goes all the way down. Nothing is exempt.... There is no God's-eye view of things available to us."[28] The existential wager involves each of us in our engagement with otherness:

> The moment of not-knowing that initiates the anatheistic turn is not just epistemological. Nor is it a prerogative of elite intellectuals. The anatheist moment is one available to anyone who experiences instants of deep disorientation, doubt, or dread, when we are no longer sure exactly who we are or where we are going.... Anatheist moments are experienced in our bones—moods, affects, senses, emotions—before they are theoretically interrogated by our minds. And they are, I would insist, as familiar to believers as to nonbelievers. No human can be absolutely sure about absolutes.[29]

The words Kearney uses here to describe the existential wager take me back to my encounter with otherness in the exorcism of the deaconess, that

26. Kearney, *Anatheism*, 152.
27. Kearney, *Anatheism*, 15.
28. Kearney, *Anatheism*, xv, xvii.
29. Kearney, *Anatheism*, 5.

which Kearney calls the primary scene of religion: the encounter with a radical Stranger who we choose, or don't choose, to call God.

The anatheistic wager is always a movement through doubt, through unbelief, leading the subject "into possibilities of non-belief or second belief. No longer a given, faith becomes a choice, a matter of interpretation."[30] In the encounter with otherness we become acutely aware of our own contingency and of that of our religious traditions: had I been born in Madalitso, I would have believed in spirit-possession. The choice to call what we encounter in otherness "God" is indeed a choice, and not an easy one.

> Every Christian has to make the transition from the child's "we believe still" to the adult's "I believe *again*." This cannot have been easy to make at any time and in our age it is rarely made, it would seem, without a hiatus of unbelief.[31]

The difference between this anatheistic wager and agnosticism is that, although both concede epistemic uncertainty regarding God-talk, agnosticism understands this uncertainty as a shortcoming while anatheism embraces it as a strength, an acknowledgment of the surplus of meaning that allows for the possibility of the impossible made possible.

As we have seen above, according to Kearney the primary scene of religion is the encounter with a radical stranger. He gives three examples of such inaugural meetings, taken from the three religions of the book, Judaism, Christianity, and Islam. Genesis 18 tells the story of how Abraham provides hospitality to three strangers and in doing so hosts God. In the story of the annunciation in Luke 1, Mary is visited by an angel in the guise of an intruder and decides to trust his promise. In his cave on the summit of Mount Hira, Muhammad is woken by a strange presence, and on deciding to rely on this presence becomes the voice of the angel Gabriel. These stories demonstrate the basic ambivalence in human responses to the divine stranger, an ambivalence already present in the common root of our terms, hostility and hospitality. Yet in hospitality, in the open encounter of otherness, lies the possibility of a return to a God beyond God, a God who may come back to us from the future, the God who may be.[32]

Five main components are involved in the anatheistic wager: imagination, humor, commitment, discernment, and hospitality. To be sure, these

---

30. Kearney, *Anatheism*, 11.
31. Kearney, *Anatheism*, 15.
32. Kearney, *Anatheism*, 17–39.

five components are not five separate and sequential events but form one hermeneutical movement. A wager presupposes freedom to choose, and choice depends on the ability to imagine different possibilities in the other, "to see the Other before us as a stranger to be welcomed or rejected."[33] The gap between the irreducible alterity of the other and my perception of the other asks for an imaginative response, not for a cognitive one, for we cannot grasp otherness.

The encounter thus calls for a humble recognition of "the earthly and earthy limits of human experience,"[34] and humor is the expression of that humility. Absolutists are incapable of laughing at the divine comedy of existence; those open to the possibilities of the impossible upside-down kingdom (where the last comes first and the master is the servant) will laugh with the barren Sarah in her tent.

Despite our limitedness, our response to the stranger is a commitment, either to hostility or to hospitality. A central part in this commitment befalls the human will. Our willingness to make the wager forms the basis of our commitment: "We do not *know* the truth but we *do* the truth," action precedes abstraction and reflection. Kearney makes a play with the archaic "troth," which means both "truth" and "commitment, loyalty": "Commitment, in this sense of betrothal, is the movement of the wager that makes truth primarily—though not exclusively—a matter of existential transformation (*metanoia*)."[35] This is the kind of commitment referred to by Ricoeur when he acknowledged that he was a Christian by chance, but that this chance was transformed into a destiny by continuous choice. Our commitment bears witness to the truth to which we are committed, not as an epistemological gamble but as an existential, lived wager.

This wager is not blind, not irrational: Kearney claims that it is possible to make a wise and considered wager. Not every stranger is divine, and what is called for here is discernment, to discern between the voice that brings confusion or death and the voice that brings compassion and life. Abraham heard two voices; he discerned and chose wisely, love over death (Gen 22). "The drama of discernment involves an intense act of attention starting at the most basic carnal level and accompanying the reflective

---

33. Kearney, *Anatheism*, 40.
34. Kearney, *Anatheism*, 42.
35. Kearney, *Anatheism*, 44.

movements of imagination, commitment, and humility (which includes the wisdom to learn from initial mistakes and misreadings)."[36]

Decisive in all this is, finally, love: to love God and to love your neighbor as yourself. Hospitality means that love rather than fear is the point of exit, inclusion rather than exclusion. Of course, we run the risk of being mistaken and letting the wrong one in. But such risk is not unwarranted:

> Love—as compassion and justice—is the watermark. There is a discernible difference between one who gives water to the thirsty and one who does not, between one who heals and one who maims, between one who hosts and one who shuts the door.[37]

The aforementioned imaginative response to otherness as possibility takes shape in the idea of sacramental imagination. Kearney distinguishes two voices within Christianity, the pilgrim vocation and the sacramental vocation. The first is an outgoing movement, a prophetic voice, a quest for a kingdom still to come. The second vocation seeks "to welcome the stranger in the here and now: the kingdom already come."[38] Anatheism seeks to combine the commitment to protest and prophecy with a sacramental retrieval of the extraordinary in the ordinary, "those special awakenings of the divine within the bread and wine of quotidian existence."[39] The use of the words already indicates the eucharistic character of this imagination: we host God in the shape of bread and wine, while simultaneously God is our host who invites us to the table.[40] This imagination not only applies to the Eucharist: our everyday existence is sanctified, becomes sacred, when touched (consecrated) by sacramental imagination. This imagination allows us to re-enchant a disenchanted world, an "opening toward a God whose descent into flesh depends on our response to the sacred summons of the moment."[41]

Sacramental imagination, the restoration of the hyphen between the sacred and the secular, is inseparably linked to a response, to a *vita activa*. What is involved in translating epiphanies of transcendence into the immanence of everyday action? Kearney first stipulates what is not to be

---

36. Kearney, *Anatheism*, 47.
37. Kearney, *Anatheism*, 47.
38. Kearney, *Anatheism*, 85.
39. Kearney, *Anatheism*, 86.
40. Kearney, *Anatheism*, 27–28.
41. Kearney, *Anatheism*, 87.

done, namely to allow religion to dominate politics. History is littered with examples of this "ruinous temptation,"[42] and not just distant history: one has only to think of Putin framing the war in Ukraine as a battle between the holy Russian empire and the satanic forces of the West to know better. A proper response hinges on a creative relationship between the secular and the sacred, in which secularization prevents the sacred from becoming life denying, while sacralization prevents the secular from becoming banal. At this point, the hermeneutics of suspicion (the necessary demasking of the focus on God as sovereign) gives way to the hermeneutics of reaffirmation (opening our eyes for the possibilities of God as Stranger), and at this same moment we turn

> from the realm of critical interpretation to the world of quotidian praxis and transformation. This ultimate transformation from word to flesh is witnessed daily wherever someone gives a cup of cold water to a thirsting stranger. For in such situations one's faith in God as stranger is not a matter of theories or ideas but of living witness to the word made flesh. There are countless examples of this at every border, street corner, or threshold where a native meets a foreigner and opens the door to the messiah in our midst.[43]

This act of kenotic hospitality, in which we open ourselves to the gracious possibility of receiving God back again as a gift from the other, is the risky wager of anatheism. "For in surrendering our own God to a stranger God no God may come back again. Or the God who comes back may come back in ways that surprise us."[44]

THE CREATION OF AN INNER SPACE TO ENGAGE OTHERNESS

It is time to return to the question we started with, the creation of an inner space to engage otherness. Is the middle way suggested by Richard Kearney helpful in this regard? In his work, Kearney time and again quotes the first question Paul Ricoeur asked everyone participating in his seminars: *d'où parlez-vous*, where do you speak from. In narrating the students' experience of alterity in the inability to celebrate holy communion together, I already

42. Kearney, *Anatheism*, 138.
43. Kearney, *Anatheism*, 153–54.
44. Kearney, *Anatheism*, 181.

shared some information about the place I speak from. As a lecturer in spiritual and professional formation at the Protestant Theological University I'm involved in a Master of Divinity program that prepares students for ministry in the Protestant Church in the Netherlands. A central aspect in this attempt at self-identification is that I speak as a representative of the Protestant faith tradition.

It is my impression that several central aspects of Kearney's approach and some of the main principles of the Protestant tradition go very well together. This tradition started out as and continues to be a movement back to the sources, and from these sources a movement forward in a continuous reformation (*semper reformanda*) of Christian faith and Christian living. This movement is inherently suspicious of absolutes. I hear an echo of this position in Kearney's claim that anatheism is a movement that acknowledges that the absolute can never be understood absolutely by any single person or religion. Maybe the most telling illustration of this Protestant suspicion of absolutes is its confessional tradition. The Protestant tradition has always been characterized by a plurality of confessions and by its preparedness to embrace new confessional moments emerging in new situations. Think for example of the *Barmen Declaration* as a response to the situation in Germany in the 1930s. These confessional statements are an important voice in the self-identification of the Protestant tradition and as such can count on deferential reception. For example, the Barmen Declaration is part of the confessional self-identification of the Protestant Church in the Netherlands. Nevertheless, these confessional statements are never regarded as absolute statements but as expressions of faith that are characterized by their relativity, historicity and finitude.

Of course, the Protestant tradition does not always practice what it preaches. Like other faith traditions, it tends to absolutize particular interpretations of Christian identity. The use of a single identity qualifier like "Protestant" runs the risk of reducing identity construction to a single essence. Such a single essence self-identification can easily function as a barrier behind which to hide and protect one's faith identity without being able to engage otherness. The dialogue of the deaf with which I opened this contribution is an illustration of this logic.

It is exactly at this point that Kearney's middle way is a very appropriate invitation to return to the sources and from there to move forward. The two vocations Kearney distinguishes within Christianity, the pilgrim vocation and the sacramental vocation, remind me of this possibility. The pilgrim vocation, the quest for a kingdom still to come, is a commitment to protest and prophecy. The commitment to protest embraces an atheist critique of absolute truth claims of dogmatic theism, thus clearing the way for the possibilities of non-belief or second belief. The commitment to prophecy embraces the impossible possibility of speaking again and anew, fed by the prophetic imagination provided by the return to the sources. The sacramental vocation is the moment we turn to the world of quotidian praxis and transformation, the moment where epiphanies of the transcendent translate in the immanence of everyday action, in a living witness to the word made flesh. The moment where we are invited to incarnate the impossible possibility in a *vita activa*.

In focusing our attention to the divine in the stranger who stands before us in the midst of the world, I consider Kearney's anatheism to be a constructive contribution to the creation of an inner space to engage otherness. His anatheist space is a convincing example of what the inner space I'm looking for could resemble. When I am able to let go of (or to suspend) my absolute certainties (whether they are religious certainties leading to fixed moral standpoints that exclude otherness or cultural certainties leading to feelings of superiority that disparage otherness), a space opens in which I am both host welcoming otherness as well as guest welcomed by otherness. In this space the possibility presents itself that I may find in otherness what is undreamed of in myself.

Kearney's anatheistic wager to turn hostility into hospitality is risky business: we take the risk of losing all by opening up to the possibilities of both non-belief and second belief. Yet the possibility of loss comes with the possibility of gain: the loss creates room for the gift. As Kearney expresses it in a beautiful translation of Genesis 22: "Abraham has to lose his son as a given in order to receive him back as a gift; he has to abandon Isaac as possession in order to welcome him back as promise."[45] The inner space of engagement with otherness opens the possibility of transformation from an acquisitive identity into a eucharistic identity.

The contours of this inner space, of what is required in the engagement with otherness, become visible in the five components involved in the anatheistic wager. An act of gracious imagining, instead of an act of absolute knowing, in the encounter with otherness allows for the appearance of the other as a sign of God in all its possibilities and promises. Imagination is being shaped and enriched by the treasure trove of narrative that is our

---

45. Kearney, "God after God," 8.

religious tradition. The necessary suspension of knowing, the tolerance of ambiguity and uncertainty, is made possible by humor, the ability to relativize not absolutize ourselves. The response to otherness is a commitment to truth, not in the sense of a declaration of absolute truth claims but in the sense of an existential transformation. The embodied prereflective response is not a blind gamble but a considered wager based on discernment between compassion and confusion. The anatheistic wager then allows for and creates the space of a generous hospitality for otherness, a fundamentally inclusive mindset, a deeply dialogical frame of mind.

The strangeness of the encounter with otherness in the exorcism of the deaconess in Madalitso made it impossible for me to come to terms with what happened, to come to a basic understanding. A different approach might have resulted in a different reception: open instead of closed, imaginative not literal, humble rather than triumphal, exploratory not parochial, engaged instead of passive. Such an approach might have created space for the impossible possibility of retrieving something of what is lost when living in a disenchanted universe.

The closedness of the discussions regarding the shared celebration of holy communion, the positing of nonnegotiable absolute truth claims, made it impossible for the students involved to be open to the surplus of meaning that is to be found in otherness. It closed for them the opportunity to form an inclusive community, embracing the given of womanhood as a gift instead of a barrier in the service of ministry. The same occasion approached differently might have afforded them a glimpse of an impossible possibility, of the prophetic vision of "the feast of rich food for all people, a banquet of aged wine" (Isa 25:6). What a different start to their ministry that would have been.

BIBLIOGRAPHY

Benjamins, H. S. *Boven is onder ons: denken over God na God*. Middelburg: Skandalon, 2022.

Bosch, Henk van den. "'In the Powerful Name of Jesus': Een interculturele ervaring tussen vervreemding en verrijking," *Kerk en theologie* 70.3 (2019) 257–67.

Kearney, Richard M. *Anatheism: Returning to God after God*. New York: Colombia University Press, 2010.

———. "God after God: An Anatheist Attempt to Reimagine God." In *Reimagining the Sacred: Richard Kearney Debates God*, edited by Richard Kearny and Jens Zimmerman, 6–18. New York: Colombia University Press, 2016.

———. *The God Who May Be: A Hermeneutics of Religion*. Indianapolis: Indiana University Press, 2001.

———. *On Stories*. Thinking in Action. London: Routledge, 2002.

———. *Strangers, Gods, and Monsters: Interpreting Otherness*. London: Routledge, 2003.

———. "Where I Speak From: A Short Intellectual Autobiography." In *Debating Otherness with Richard Kearney: Perspectives from South Africa*, edited by Daniel P. Veldsman and Yolande Steenkamp, 31–62. Cape Town: Aosis, 2018.

Levinas, Emmanuel. *Totality and Infinity: An Essay on Exteriority*. Translated by Alphonso Lingis. Duquesne Studies: Philosophical Series 24. Pittsburgh: Duquesne University Press, 1969.

Taylor, Charles. *A Secular Age*. Cambridge: Belknap, 2007.

Taylor, Mark Kline. "In Praise of Shaky Ground: The Liminal Christ and Cultural Pluralism." *Theology Today* 43 (1986) 36–51.

Trebilcock, Michelle. "Theology in Context: Liminality." *Colloquium* 48 (2016) 74–86.

Walls, Andrew F. "The Ephesian Moment: At a Crossroads in Christian History." In *The Cross-Cultural Process in Christian History: Studies in the Transmission and Appropriation of Faith*, by Andrew F. Walls, 72–81. Maryknoll, NY: Orbis, 2002.

8

Neo-Levinas, Contra Milbank
Moral Realism Theory

William Greenway

Levinas in fact produces a bizarre inverted egoism . . . although it is now the other I and not I myself which is the foundation for understanding, a gulf is fixed upon its basis between the *il y a* of empty meaningless existence that cannot be redeemed, and which always engenders horror . . . on the one hand, and the ethical cosmos which establishes "the right" of the subject in the face of this horror, on the other. On the ethical plane, the result is a reactive ethics which falsely identifies self-obliteration with the final good and requires the good to be predatory upon pre-existing suffering.[1]

—John Milbank

Milbank's searing criticism misreads Levinas, misfiring on all counts . . . at least, so I thought when I began writing this essay.[2] As I reread Levinas in conversation with Milbank, I realized I had been executing what Richard Rorty called a "strong reading" of Levinas, interpreting him to be

---

1. Milbank, "Soul of Reciprocity," 342.
2. I owe thanks to David Jensen and the other members of the Frierson Conference, especially Martha Moore-Keish and John J. Thatamanil, for comments on an earlier draft of this essay.

saying what I thought he should say. It is doubtless significant that I studied Levinas backward, beginning with *Entre Nous* (1991) and *Of God Who Comes to Mind* (1982) and only then moving on to what are commonly considered his seminal works, *Otherwise Than Being or Beyond Essence* (1974) and *Totality and Infinity* (1961).[3] I think my reading of Levinas is faithful to the overall trajectory of his thought, but it is clearly outside the mainstream of Levinas scholarship.[4] And while I think my approach offers the most promising interpretation of Levinas, it stretches beyond the limits of even his most mature work, most definitively because I thematize with "agape" that "other," "beyond," "otherwise" to which Levinas will only gesture. While Milbank's reading is plausible, I will argue my neo-Levinasian philosophy, which I develop as "Moral Realism Theory," expands upon an equally plausible reading of Levinas.

* * * *

Moral Realism Theory builds upon a single revision to Levinas's philosophy. In a word, fearing reduction of "other" to "same," Levinas refuses to thematize an "otherwise than being" that he nonetheless meaningfully invokes. Moral Realism Theory (MRT) thematizes Levinas's Other as "agape" without compromising its pertinent otherness. For instance, where Levinas speaks of being "taken hostage"[5] or being placed in the "accusative"[6] by the face, MRT speaks of having been seized *by agape for* every Face. A cascade of structural revisions follows—revisions that retain Levinas's core witness while subverting common, justifiable criticisms. MRT jettisons Levinas's "asymmetry" and affirms "symmetry" (without reciprocity/economy). It replaces Levinas's "third" with the "second" as the point where one must "compare incomparables." It sets aside Levinas's "substitution" and highlights his "ethical proximity." It rejects Levinas's "hateful self" and affirms selves (including oneself) seized by agape. It sheds Levinas's sexism, heterosexism, and anthropocentrism, and acknowledges having

---

3. This in marked contrast to standard accounts of his work, which tend to see *Otherwise than Being or Beyond Essence* (1998) as his final major work and fail even to mention *Of God Who Comes to Mind* (1986) and *Entre Nous* (1998). In *The Problem with Levinas* (2015), Simon Critchley radically privileges early works, rooting his interpretation upon pre-Shoah essays, such as, "Reflections on the Philosophy of Hitlerism" (1934) and *On Escape* (1935).

4. E.g., see essays collected in Morgan, *Oxford Handbook of Levinas*.

5. Levinas, *Of God Who Comes to Mind*, 170.

6. Levinas, *Entre Nous*, 58–59.

been seized by agape for all creatures. Finally, MRT abandons Levinas's infamous attempts to gesture wholesale beyond being and hypothesizes that our most reasonable, good, and complete understanding requires post-representational (Rorty) utilization of three incommensurable families of vocabularies, those which constitute the three linguistic Spheres of Nature (vocabularies of modern causation), of Poetic I's (vocabularies of free will), and of Agape (vocabularies of agape).

Elsewhere I develop and defend at length this revisionist reading of Levinas and the three spheres of Moral Realism Theory. Here I unfold my neo-Levinasian reading in an existential modality in conversation with Milbank's influential critique.[7] I owe Milbank thanks for helping me read Levinas with more precision. Moreover, this is a defense of a neo-Levinasian philosophy, not a broadside against Milbank, whose attack I take as fair provocation and whose theology may benefit from integration of neo-Levinasian insights.

* * * *

Milbank objects to those like Levinas who contend that "the vulnerability of another" places "an ethical demand upon us greater than ourselves" such that "the demand of the other with a small 'o' passes mistily over into the claim of the other with a big 'O,' the demand of transcendence, of deity."[8] I agree about "passes mistily over" analyses, but whereas Milbank sees irremediable confusion, I think Levinas can be revised so as to dissipate the mists and articulate a rigorous account of agape. Milbank disagrees and, let me repeat, has considerable textual evidence.

"For Levinas," Milbank says, "the address of the other to self first arouses self, ensuring that ethics, not theory, is the fundamental horizon for all subjectivity."[9] Milbank contends Levinas's distinctive move is his prioritizing of the other self. The root of the ethical in Levinas, says Milbank, is a "surplus *in* the other (and by implication *in* me for another 'I' to whom I am in turn an other) which is *self-constituted*."[10] All this leads to the stunning indictment cited above: "Levinas in fact produces a bizarre, inverted egoism . . . a reactive ethics which falsely identifies self-obliteration with the final good and requires the good to be predatory upon pre-existing

---

7. In addition to the essay cited above, see Milbank, "Shares of Being or Gift."
8. Milbank, "Ethics of Self-Sacrifice," 33.
9. Milbank, "Soul of Reciprocity," 341.
10. Milbank, "Soul of Reciprocity," 342 (my emphasis).

suffering."[11] Again, Milbank's reading is justifiable, especially in Levinas's writings through the mid-1970s, including *Otherwise Than Being*, which is built around the self-negating dissymmetry of "substitution." And Milbank is not alone in thinking that Levinas's position is dependent upon suffering. For instance, Bernhard Waldenfels objects to Levinas's claim that, "'Thou shalt not murder' is the 'first word,'" because, "Reckoning with the worst when speaking of human affairs is one thing, relying on it is something else."[12] But Waldenfels and Milbank's readings misfire vis-à-vis the most promising trajectory in Levinas.

First, recall the concrete context. Levinas defends awakening to the priority of the ethical from the fiery bowels of the Shoah, where he was taken "hostage" by the faces of Jews being tortured and murdered, by faces crying out "do not kill me." More precisely—and signifying, I believe, the reality Levinas invokes—Moral Realism Theory says he is seized by agape for the Faces of those tortured, murdered faces. Levinas specifies all his work was "dominated by the presentiment and the memory of the Nazi horror," so it should be read in this context.[13]

Remembering being reduced by horror during more than four years of captivity by the Nazis in the hell of the Shoah, Levinas describes the haunting murmurings of *conatus essendi* amidst *il y a*, "a nothing that is not a nothing, for this nothing is full of murmuring," a "horrifying experience of naughting."[14] Levinas specifies his *il y a* is "not the Heideggerian *es*

11. Milbank, "Soul of Reciprocity," 342. Later in the same essay, Milbank concludes: "Again, if generosity means not the giving of a specific gift, and the opening of a specific path and goal to the other but is rather the allowing to the other of his own will and freedom, then this means that, before gift and sacrifice, we esteem the instance of self-possession in others. And this is because we know of such self-possession in ourselves and esteem it first of all in our own egos. If the gift, therefore, is primarily one-way sacrifice, then this is only because it is more originally a gift that one gives to oneself . . . where the gift does not include from the outset reciprocity, then it is self-regarding and self-rewarding before it is sacrificial. And this remorseless logic unmasks the 'call of the other' in both Levinas and Marion" (365).

12. Waldenfels, "Levinas and the Face of the Other," 72.

13. Levinas, *Difficult Freedom*, 291.

14. The "it" of the *il y a* marks "a nothing that is not a nothing, for this nothing is full of murmuring. . . . In that horrifying experience of naughting, the thematics of the 'there is' grounds the construction of a subject that, from the neuter, will affirm itself, posit itself. . . . This love of self is an egotism that founds being and constitutes the first ontological experience. This experience foreshadows the opening and true exiting from self . . . the fissure that opens up in the same toward the other . . . proximity of the other" (Levinas, *Alterity and Transcendence*, 99).

gibt. . . . On the contrary, the *there is* is unbearable in its indifference. Not anguish but horror, the horror of the unceasing, of a monotony deprived of meaning."[15] Falling through the abyss of the *il y a*, however, Levinas is caught by definitive contour. Amidst horror so extreme all capacity for intentional affirmation or self-assertion is decimated, all structures of meaning are rent asunder: precisely there Levinas is awakened with unprecedented clarity to the Face of the other, elected to the Face by the Other, awakened by agape to every Face, awakened by agape shining through the theory/history/concept-obliterating depths of the formless void, awakened to a call "more ancient" than any intention or willing, awakened to a call from beyond what can be deconstructed or rent through horror.[16]

* * * *

I must digress momentarily. Heidegger's *Being and Time* is widely misinterpreted among anglophone philosophers, for they read him within the parameters of materialism/metaphysical naturalism. The "being" and "time" of *Being and Time* are not the "being" and "time" of materialism, but the opening of lived be-ing amidst physical being, the opening which *is* temporality/spatiality/*dasein*, which is the transcendental condition (in the Kantian sense; not "transcendent condition") for "time" in the scientific sense (in a word, if no *dasein*, then no "time" in any sense).[17] That is, Heidegger breaks modern materialism/naturalism's grip by demonstrating it cannot account for the reality of time in physics' time *t* sense, unveiling the "clearing" or "opening" amidst modern material being, the *be*-ing of beings amidst being, *dasein* amidst *es gibt*, which Heidegger unveils as individuated, consciously mortal *sorge* (concern-full-ness). Thus, the Heidegger of *Being and Time* legitimizes the existentialists and their celebration of free will, poetic self-creation, and authenticity.

Two basic types of modern rationality are predominant among intellectual and cultural elites. First, *naturalistic* rationalities think reality is Cartesian "extension," brute causal flux, perhaps speckled with indeterminacy.

---

15. Levinas, *Is It Righteous to Be?*, 45.

16. "In the place of ontology—of the Heideggerian comprehension of the Being of being—is substituted as primordial the relation of a being to a being, which is none the less not equivalent to a rapport between subject and object, but rather a proximity, to a relation with the Other" (Levinas, *Difficult Freedom*, 293).

17. All this is the sense in which Husserl's *erlebnis*, "*living* present," a remainder/surd Husserl ever looked to integrate into his system, becomes the starting point for Heidegger's philosophy.

Neo-Levinas, Contra Milbank

Accordingly, the majority of philosophers think the idea of free will is incoherent (though many also argue that "free will" names an essential human meme; the idea, though false, may be vital).[18] Second, *secular* rationalities agree reality is brute causal flux, but—and here the work of Heidegger and Sartre is vital—they also affirm actual free will (not just the idea), and typically celebrate poetic self-creation and prize authenticity. Metaphysical affirmation of brute flux and free will cannot fund moral realism, hence modernity's centuries-old crisis of foundations in ethics, legitimization crisis in politics and interminable debates over sovereignty. Ethical and existential concerns among metaphysical naturalists have stimulated work on "emergence," "materialism 2.0," and "expansive" or "liberal" naturalism. These efforts remain marginal among intellectual elites. Moral Realism Theory should be numbered among them, distinguished theoretically by its neo-Rortian postrepesentationalism, most definitively by its neo-Levinasian affirmation of the vocabularies of agape, and by its frank embrace of pluralism/incommensurability among families of vocabularies. Definitions of naturalistic and secular rationalities in hand, I return to my argument.

* * * *

Levinas, an adoring student of Heidegger, first known for introducing phenomenology to the French—Sartre said Levinas's dissertation and 1931 translation of Husserl's *Cartesian Meditations* introduced him to phenomenology[19]—working on a book on Heidegger in the early 1930s, before Heidegger's Nazi sympathies were apparent, is a modern secular philosopher when he is caught up in the "Nazi horror." Amidst the unspeakable horrors of the Shoah and captivity he is taken hostage by the Faces[20] of faces tortured and murdered, and even—contrary to the natural ways of our world—by the Faces of their killers. In short, Levinas enters the camps a secular philosopher but amidst the horror he is seized by a reality undergone (not an idea thought) which is "Other" or "Beyond" the metaphysical parameters of naturalistic or secular rationalities; amidst the horror he is seized by the extra-historical force I signify with "agape."

Levinas's thought is definitely shaped by the presentiment and memory of the "Nazi horror," but it is not dependent upon this context. Levinas does not make "the good predatory upon pre-existing suffering," for we

---

18. For instance, Smilanksy, *Free Will and Illusion*.
19. Bakewell, *At the Existentialist Café*, 4.
20. See below on faces/Faces (this is my convention, not Levinas's).

are seized by precisely the same passion in joyful contexts, where agape provokes happiness and affirmation. Levinas presumes a context of suffering because biographically he is awakened to the reality of transcending love literally from the bowels of the Shoah. For Levinas, insofar as you are caught and saved by agape as you plunge through the rending depths of the *il y a*, you are existentially/spiritually saved from nihilism to the ultimacy of love—even as you suffer in the camps, even if you are murdered, and even if there is no resurrection.

There is stark, real-world realism here, but no "self-obliteration," let alone "self-obliteration" as the "final good." As will become clear, it is a strength of Levinas's philosophy that it is rooted in an actual hell of captivity, horror, and the killing of his brothers and parents among the millions of innocents slaughtered by the Nazis. It is a strength that that hell on earth is the originating context for Levinas's clarion testimony to the perduring, saving (from nihilism) reality of agape, for any "problem of evil" objections are disarmed *ab initio*.

Contra Milbank, this need not be read as "bizarre, inverted egoism," for, despite Levinas's problematic refusal to thematize agape and the resulting dissymmetry (which goes to Milbank's point), we need not propose any "surplus *in* the other." Some face is always the occasion for the manifestation of a Face in the event of the having been seized. In that sense some face always marks the occasion of the manifestation of a surplus, but the surplus, agape, is not literally *in* the other but is *what has one for* the Face of the other. The "gulf" that opens up is not between oneself and another but beneath oneself and all others, the gulf is the uncaring procession of being, the meaningless murmuring amidst the *il y a*, the formless void.

Existentialist and secular rationality generally finds refuge from the meaningless of the modern cosmos via appeal to the exertion of the autonomous, self-creating I. But, again, naturalistic and secular rationalities are unable to justify affirmation of any moral reality. So, for instance, a secular theorist like Richard Rorty can affirm the ideals of liberty, fraternity, and equality and condemn Nazism, but Rorty infamously refused to offer any realist justification for his ethical preferences, for Rorty frankly acknowledged the consequences of acknowledging that reality primordially, ultimately, and in and of itself has no moral contour. For naturalistic and secular rationality, the energy of salvation must stem from within I, perhaps supported, collectively, by communities and by ideal guides (Micah, Jesus, Gandhi, the Prophet).

Neo-Levinas, Contra Milbank

In stark contrast, Levinas emphasizes our passivity *ab initio* in the event of having been seized by agape. Again, for Levinas what arrests our plummeting through the horrors of the void, what awakens and saves us from nihilism is not existential courage in the face of the sheer murmuring of the *il y a*, but a force by which I am seized, agape, a passion that endures and shines through the otherwise all-rending oblivion of the void, a passion that breaks open the ontological order of the thing, that breaks open the *conatus essendi* (sheer desire for being to persevere in its be-ing), a passion which makes manifest the Face of every face, including our own (though Levinas, with his dissymmetry and "substitution," is lacking the "including our own").

* * * *

Levinas was powerfully awakened to agape by horrific injustice and suffering. People generally are most powerfully awakened to agape in precisely such contexts. Often such awakening to horror and injustice is confusedly taken as an obstacle to faith and fuels passionate rejection of God. To be sure, the supernatural gods of what Schleiermacher calls magical thinking rightly die in gulags and concentration camps. The god of Eli Wiesel's adolescence famously and rightly died with a boy on a gallows in Auschwitz.[21] But, Levinas says sharply of those who conclude that to reject the God "absent from Auschwitz," the God who might have intervened and changed the course of history, those who think that to reject *that* God is to reject God, they confusedly "finish the job of National Socialism."[22]

What Levinas makes clear with insight refined to crystalline clarity by the fires of the Shoah is that precisely the passion engendering his screamed "no" to the horror and injustice, the passion by which he finds himself seized as he plummets through the depths of hell on earth, that passion has contour, the contour of profound concern for the flourishing of every Face. On my thematization that passion *is* agape, is the divine, is God which *is* love, the God which *comes* to mind, is the blazing "glory" saving us from the all-rending abyss of the *il y a*.

In the immediate face of the horror of torture, captivity, and genocide, Levinas is not ultimately overcome by the formless void, for before and

---

21. Wiesel, *Night Trilogy*, 81–83.

22. "To renounce after Auschwitz this God absent from Auschwitz... would amount to finishing the criminal enterprise of National Socialism, which aimed at the annihilation of Israel and the forgetting of the message of the Bible" (Levinas, *Entre Nous*, 99).

Part III | Otherness, Community, and the Common Good

beyond his own intention, courage, or affirmation, he is seized by agape for the Face of every face. The passion manifest in the context of the Shoah as horror is not rooted in him or in others. Our passionate "No!" is engendered by the reality of agape. Contrary to ubiquitous modern confusion, which pits the reality of evil over against the reality of agape, it is *precisely in the face of the most horrifying evil that we are seized all the more powerfully by the burning reality of agape*. Agape is not negated by our horror over evil. Our horror is itself a manifestation of the passion of agape. It is by virtue of agape that we see evil as evil. This obliterates religious studies "problem of evil" and theodicies before and after Leibniz's—some as old and confused as "a certain reading of the Bible."[23] As Levinas says, if elliptically, "A last reversal of the analysis: evil strikes me in my horror as evil and thus reveals—or is already—my association with the good."[24]

* * * *

The theoretical closure that leads Milbank to misread Levinas is starkly visible in Milbank's attacks upon Levinas and others for affirming "disinterest." An "extreme 'disinterest' in one's activity, though it can only be exercised by a subject," says Milbank, "tends also to a suicidally sacrificial will against oneself"[25] and, he continues in the same vein a few pages on, toward a "*kenosis* . . . almost indistinguishable from demonic self-enclosure."[26] Vis-à-vis Levinas, Milbank is fundamentally confused, for Levinas never affirms disinterest. Levinas is careful to affirm not indifference or disinterest, but *non-indifference and dis-inter-estedness*—neologisms designed to refer beyond the bounds of the interested/disinterested binary and to open conceptual space for agape.[27]

---

23. Levinas, *Entre Nous*, 96–97.
24. Levinas, *Of God Who Comes to Mind*, 131.
25. Milbank, "Can a Gift Be Given?," 132.
26. Milbank, "Can a Gift Be Given?," 137. See further, Milbank, "Soul of Reciprocity," 365, 369–84. Milbank focuses his criticisms upon Marion, but only because "in the case of Levinas things are not so clear. . . . Marion is the more rigorous thinker, and so more clearly reveals the problems" (Milbank, "Soul of Reciprocity," 351). On my reading, the Levinasian ambiguity is due to Levinas's superior rigor and is a saving ambiguity because it retains an opening to an affirmation of the reality of agape—a possibility I first caught sight of in Marion's "Phenomenological Sketch of the Concept of Gift." See further, Milbank, "Shares of Being or Gift," 4, 30.
27. For example: "My responsibility for the other is precisely the non-indifference of this difference: the proximity of the other" (Levinas, *Of God Who Comes to Mind*, 71); "Proximity . . . signifies as a difference which is, outside of all knowing, non-indifference"

Neo-Levinas, Contra Milbank

Far from being rooted in disinterest, Levinas's distinction is grounded in lived undergoing of having been seized by agape for every Face, including his own.[28] Like free will, agape cannot (by definition) be captured by vocabularies rooted in the modern idea of causation (i.e., materialist, or naturalistic vocabularies), but agape is not epiphenomenal, not primordially an idea, not something deduced or concluded, not part of any interpersonal or socio-historical economy of exchange. Nor does agape originate in me or any other I. Agape is different in kind from gravity or magnetic forces, but it too names a constant force we directly undergo. Of course, potential for lived undergoing of gravity, magnetism, agape, or exercise of free will can be derailed by material conditions (e.g., neuropathology, brain trauma), but the inability of psychopaths, for instance, to undergo agape does not negate its reality.

Agape is not an irresistible force. We are free to "harden our hearts." As Levinas says, "If no one is good voluntarily [i.e., good does not originate in I's free will], no one is enslaved to the Good."[29] Still, agape is a constant force, undergone variably. Just as gravity is not consciously undergone when standing and looking through a clear sky down at the stars but is overwhelmingly manifest if you are grasping futilely after green tufts while sliding over the edge of the cliff, the felt undergoing of agape may be slight while making a spinach salad but overwhelmingly manifest in the bowels of the Shoah. For Levinas, this is when God directly and forcefully came to mind.

Let me pause to note that we should avoid anthropocentrism and affirm potentials in line with our best scientific knowledge. There is reason to affirm humans' lived undergoing of gravity and agape (not magnetic fields) and exercise of free will. Given similar brain structure and activity, there is also reason to affirm orcas' lived undergoing of magnetic fields, gravity, agape, and their exercise of a modicum of free will. If comparative

---

(97); "Proximity, difference which is non-indifference, is responsibility" (139); or "Dialogue is the non-indifference of the *you* to the *I*, a dis-inter-ested sentiment . . . a chance for what we must—perhaps with prudence—call love and resemblance in love" (147). To give Milbank a nod, the English title of chapter 1 in *Otherwise than Being* is, unfortunately, not "Essence and Non-Disinterest," but "Essence and Disinterest." Notably, Levinas uses the term "indifference" to characterize the disposition of the "shrewd" who have aligned themselves with "conquerors," as seen from Auschwitz to "Sarajevo to Cambodia" (Levinas, *Entre Nous*, 99–100).

28. On "lived," see Levinas, *Of God Who Comes to Mind*, 23.
29. Levinas, *Otherwise than Being*, 11.

ratios of brain mass are pertinent, orcas may be *more* sensitive to agape than humans.

Milbank, in concert with modern naturalistic and secular rationalities, rejects the idea that we directly experience agape. "If in fact one can *neither* first receive love from the other *nor* instigate it oneself," Milbank says, "then the prior love from the other must indeed concern the intervention of a *Deus ex machina*. Here ... it would be the case that the other was merely the occasion for a divine intervention that would miraculously override his autonomy."[30]

Milbank's named target here is Marion, but Milbank also implicates Levinas, and on that count he is confused, for on a Levinasian understanding there is no sense in which any other's autonomy is violated in one's surrender to having been seized by agape for their Face.[31] Nor, insofar as I can harden my heart, is my own autonomy negated. Vis-à-vis Christian theology, appeal to the direct influence of the divine (agape) explains how faith can authentically be mine and simultaneously not be my work—where "faith" names living surrender to having been seized by agape for every Face, including our own (*note bene*, "faith" here names not propositional assent but existential orientation: living surrender to agape). For insofar as I love with a love which I do not create or instigate, but to which I surrender, faith is not my work. At the same time, insofar as I am free to harden my heart, it is authentically my faith.

Milbank, however, contends that "love is actually unthinkable outside the series of hierarchical transmissions and therefore outside of our biological and cultural insertions."[32] He holds that "purified gift-exchange—and not pure 'gift' is what Christian agape claims to be," and that, "purified gift-exchange, unlike the pure gift, remains within the bounds of the ontological, which is to say the metaphysical."[33] This means Milbank self-consciously remains within the realm of Levinas's Totality/Same/Being/Essence and within my Spheres of Nature and of Poetic I's (i.e., Milbank remains within the bounds of naturalistic and secular rationalities!).

---

30. Milbank, "Gift and the Mirror," 301.

31. Again, my own thought was profoundly shaped by Marion's "Phenomenological Sketch of the Concept of Gift," which was a response to Derrida's *Given Time*, read in turn as a response to Marcel Mauss's *The Gift*. I appropriate Marion's insights in conversation with Levinas (see part 2 of Greenway, *Reasonable Belief*). Marion, however, develops his ideas in a very different direction, one quite susceptible to Milbank's critique.

32. Milbank, "Gift and the Mirror," 311.

33. Milbank, "Can a Gift Be Given?," 131.

Milbank argues the dynamics of the Christian love command are the same as the "command" associated with generosity, which is taken "as a virtue, and therefore in some sense an obligation," and so is "secretly pervaded by hidden contract and obligation."[34] For Milbank, the generosity commanded and elicited from us is secretly the manifestation of an *inference* that "we *should* be generous . . . because we *owe* something." What "commands" is a logic related to a sense of general indebtedness, and what is commanded is generosity.[35] For Moral Realism Theory, what "commands" is not a logic but agape.

For Milbank, then, a general sense of indebtedness lies behind the societal affirmation of generosity as a virtue and amounts to an open-ended command to be generous, to give, say, to the poor or to future generations. Milbank identifies this dynamic of the gift, of agape, as the "soul of reciprocity"—so for him "agape" names an economy—and locates it in the socio-historical dynamics of gift exchange such as those unfolded in anthropologist Marcel Mauss's seminal work, *The Gift: Forms and Functions of Exchange in Archaic Societies*.[36] Writ large, "the gift" names an "unending spiral" of "asymmetrical reciprocity," a hierarchy of indebtedness wherein a sense of general indebtedness stimulates giving, which perpetuates a new, forward-facing sense of indebtedness, which stimulates new giving, and

---

34. "It is the same case here [i.e., with generosity, where 'giving is secretly pervaded by hidden contract and obligation'] as with the Christian command to love: love is something spontaneous, elicited from us rather than willed by us, and yet for all that, the subject of a strange commandment. An obligation to give appears puzzling: if we *should* be generous, then this is because we *owe* something, perhaps an infinite something, to others—the poor, maybe, our neighbors, or else future generations" (Milbank, "Can a Gift Be Given?," 123).

35. Notably, Milbank's "generosity" softens "love," since "generosity" typically signals safe giving from excess (so, for example, we do *not* say, "there is no greater *generosity* than to give one's life for a friend"). In the final two sentences of one essay, "Can a Gift Be Given?," seeming to sense the inadequacy of "owe," "obligation," and "indebtedness," language, Milbank abruptly shifts back to "love" talk, saying: "The one given condition of the gift" is that "we love because God first loved us," it "being given that God is love" (Milbank, "Can a Gift Be Given?," 154). My neo-Levinasian unveiling of the reality of agape can fund these latter claims far more precisely and powerfully than Milbank.

36. Mauss—even more poignantly than Milbank, for Mauss writes in the 1920s (*Essai sur le don* [1925]) with a clear sense of the horrors on the horizon—is caught within the parameters of secular rationality as he repeatedly but unsuccessfully attempts to gesture, beyond all economies of exchange, to the reality of agape.

PART III | OTHERNESS, COMMUNITY, AND THE COMMON GOOD

so new indebtedness, and so more giving, and so on across and down the generations.[37]

The dynamics of reciprocity could be used to manipulate others, so Milbank cautions we should never give *in order to* create indebtedness.[38] Milbank also specifies that when we give and receive in this way our mutual participation binds us into an increasingly large community. Here too Milbank echoes Mauss, who documents the ways economies of exchange create bonds among diverse individuals and communities, bonds that can span generations. True generosity, Milbank stresses, is also elicited by our desire for this greater mutuality, a mutuality which, as it grows over generations, he sees as a reversal of creation's fractured fall from divine unity. We give, Milbank claims, "for the sake of interest in a greater return of mutuality that is forever forthcoming only as the immediate increase of the original loan and its positive debt."[39] "Our love," he declares, "may trade in nothing else."[40]

Mauss and many other anthropologists who have affirmed and developed Mauss's work in parallel ways are metaphysical naturalists, affirming only the vocabularies of the sphere of nature. Milbank does not accuse them of being irrational. When Milbank speaks of our general sense of being indebted, for instance, he insists that we "must assume [there is] this debt because spirit as conscious knowledge, or the capacity to give, is in no way derivable from material existence without recourse to a reductive genealogy that would reduce spirit to epiphenomenal illusion."[41] Again, Milbank does not deny the reasonableness of the reductive genealogy of naturalism or secularism. He rejects it because of its nihilistic consequences; because it "would reduce spirit to epiphenomenal illusion."[42]

Elsewhere Milbank acknowledges that one can indeed see all the dynamics of the gift as epiphenomenal, evolutionary potentials blindly working themselves out within a philosophy which accepts the "supreme axiom

---

37. Milbank, "Gift and the Mirror," 310.
38. Milbank, "Can a Gift Be Given?," 129.
39. Milbank, "Gift and the Mirror," 313.
40. Milbank, "Gift and the Mirror," 313. In an earlier essay, harkening to the Middle Ages, Milbank depicts "charity" as "a reciprocal state of being that persons had to enter with *familiar* others ... with friends with whom they were conjoined in a common purpose" ("Ethics of Self-Sacrifice," 38).
41. Milbank, "Gift and the Mirror," 267.
42. Milbank, "Gift and the Mirror," 267.

that reality as such is nothing."[43] Milbank rightly delineates the nihilist implications of this axiom, making clear that it subjects us to "continuous fractal vanishing" by turning us into fleeting consolidations of ever-changing awareness soon to dissolve back into the raw flux of sub-atomic processes.[44] Significantly, Milbank objects to the nihilism of the reductive genealogy and of this supreme axiom not because they are unreasonable, but because the nihilist understanding of the world is "massively counter-intuitive."[45] By contrast, his speculative vision preserves "the unreflexive reception of the world by the yeoman."[46]

In order to salvage the yeoman's understanding of the world and our intuitive, realist affirmation of the gift, Milbank argues, we must see the gift as "a sign of a reserved being, *whose existence we speculatively affirm*. . . . This is the thesis that the world is created. . . . Under this thesis one begins to consider the gift . . . *within our speculative experience of all reality*."[47] Milbank speculatively experiences creation as an emanation from a God who "is intrinsically a free-giving love," such that "the Creation did not have to be."[48] In Milbank's speculative experience, creation has fallen away from God, fallen away from true, loving mutuality, a fall which can be reversed through the intergenerational increase of mutuality as we collectively rehabilitate and expand the bonds of mutuality through the generations via Milbank's dynamics of the gift.

Critically, for Milbank's thesis, God guarantees the ultimate justice of history's unending spiral of asymmetrical reciprocity. In this regard, Milbank rejects Levinas in part because in Levinas's God is "no longer seen as the source of compensating heavenly rewards."[49] For Milbank, this undercuts ethics, for it cuts off any possible return when our very lives are at stake, and thereby undercuts the reasonableness of giving, potentially even

---

43. Milbank, "Gift and the Mirror," 298.
44. Milbank, "Gift and the Mirror," 277.
45. Milbank, "Gift and the Mirror," 277.
46. Milbank, "Gift and the Mirror," 277.
47. Milbank, "Gift and the Mirror," 277–78.
48. Milbank, "Gift and the Mirror," 298. Despite his disavowals, do we not glimpse in Milbank's affirmation of God's "intrinsically free-giving love" an affirmation of pure agape? Milbank says this explains how we should interpret the contention that we "love as we are loved" ("Gift and the Mirror," 312). But on his account, the initiating love of God does not stem from indebtedness, obligation, or need, so it is different in kind from the love subsequently elicited from us.
49. Milbank, "Ethics of Self-Sacrifice," 33–34.

PART III | OTHERNESS, COMMUNITY, AND THE COMMON GOOD

unto death, in response to a sense of indebtedness and a hope for mutuality, since the power of that ethical compulsion is legitimate and compelling only in the context of a system which is ultimately just. Milbank says that most especially when the failures of some requires sacrifice of others, even unto death,

> faith in resurrection doubly sustains the project of charitable society, founded on the widest extension of reciprocity. First of all, because of this faith, one can have hope for the victims of the failures of others; and secondly, in the case of necessary self-sacrifice, one need not surrender oneself to the consuming totality.[50]

Accordingly, Milbank contends that "only with faith in the resurrection is an ethical life possible."[51]

Milbank's justification for his speculative affirmation of God is not grounded in an argument from indubitable first premises, nor in an argument against the reasonableness of nihilism, nor in any undergoing of the divine, but in the superior way his wholesale speculative affirmation meets our best and dearest desires and hopes, especially in contrast to nihilism. On this count, Milbank's affirmation of the character of Socrates's understanding of philosophical commitment is revealing. Socrates, says Milbank, thinks "the philosopher is a person who begins with absolute confidence, with a vision of eternal truth, goodness, and beauty, and with his own psychic kinship to these abiding forms. For this reason, the philosopher can act positively, truly without fear even unto death."[52]

For Milbank, similarly, a person of faith is one who begins with a speculative affirmation of a vision of eternal truth that includes a God of free-giving love and that love revealed incarnate in time, a vision that includes ever-expanding bonds of mutuality and ultimately resurrection, a vision with which the faithful find such profound confirmation in their speculative experience of reality that they can live joyfully and act positively without fear even unto death.[53] Milbank strives to give "speculative

---

50. Milbank, "Ethics of Self-Sacrifice," 38.
51. Milbank, "Ethics of Self-Sacrifice," 34.
52. Milbank, "Ethics of Self-Sacrifice," 36.

53. Milbank also contends we can understand love only in light of incarnation and trinitarian reflection ("Gift and the Mirror," 299, 312). Moral Realism Theory would contend we can only understand incarnation and the trinity in light of our lived undergoing of agape and would not privilege Christian thematization of agape over Jewish, Islamic, Hindu, Buddhist, or any other thematization of the same reality.

experience" experiential content, claiming that, while the conceiving of the thesis and initiative for speculative affirmation lies within the individual, this is not solely a conceptual event:

> Nor does the human spirit seek to represent God to itself by positing a concept of the first principle that it has already presupposed. Rather, the human spirit seeks to enter into the divine gift that provides unilaterally a created response by enacting within itself and its ritual performances in the world the imitative descriptive approximation to the divine source that follows ineluctably upon its "axiomatic" imagining of the divine nature. God is not something we represent, but something we receive, such that to enact the effect is to know, by perpetuating the cause.[54]

In the course of acting in accord with our ideal speculative affirmation, then, we find ourselves taken up through our performance into a confirming, speculative experience of reality as the creation of a loving God.

* * * *

Is Milbank's talk of obligation, of indebtedness, and of giving out of an interest in a greater return of mutuality, accurate to the love which we undergo and which the Torah and the gospels on Levinas's reading command? While Milbank's descriptions surely have their place vis-à-vis some economies of exchange, they are utterly unsatisfactory in a host of profound contexts. Say I am giving aid, comfort, and safety to a young boy victim of pedophilia, or say I am applauding and affirming a young girl's delight and excellence in playing soccer. To say my response to the boy or girl is rooted in a general sense of debt and/or out of an interest in securing a greater return of mutuality does not come close to capturing the phenomenological dynamics of the occasions, especially in comparison to saying that, without a thought for my own interests and benefits, I find myself directly seized by agape for the boy and the girl, such that in one case, horrified, I move to protect and aid, and in the other, joyful, I smile and applaud in celebration.

To bring the contrast with Levinas into focus, I cannot imagine telling those brutalized, tortured, and murdered in concentration camps, or in slavery, or held captive in a host of other hells on earth, that they should feel a need to give to others out of a general sense of obligation or indebtedness. I cannot imagine urging broken soldiers or desperate refugees to enact within themselves and in their ritual performance effects consistent with

---

54. Milbank, "Gift and the Mirror," 298.

the speculative affirmation of a theological axiom in order to receive confirmation of a theological vision. It would be wholly reasonable for those suffering, tortured, without hope and soon to die at the hands of brutal oppressors—if, *in extremis*, they even retain the wherewithal for response—it would be wholly reasonable for them to reject Milbank's speculative affirmation as naïve, wishful thinking, utterly contrary to the appearances, and to affirm, perhaps with Nietzschean resolve, the nihilistic axiom (for understandable reasons, some may opt for wishful thinking).

Levinas is literally saved from nihilism by agape in just such a hell on earth. Milbank scorns this as an appeal to a *Deus ex machina*. Moral Realism Theory says "no" to scorn, "yes" to "Deus." Justifiably. At the heart of Levinas's salvation is undergoing of agape, not confident affirmation and enacting performance in accord with a speculative affirmation. Milbank's affirmation presumes an I with existential strength, an I reflecting, positing and acting, all beginning from "absolute confidence." Captives and survivors of such hells on earth may find Milbank's breezy confidence more naïve than courageous. Not only beyond all naivete but amidst the depths of hells on earth, Levinasian undergoing of the force of agape can save an I broken to the utter passivity of murmuring existing.[55]

The passive voice is pivotal, for it distinguishes a dynamic which is not rooted in material causation and not initiated/intended by an I, a dynamic in which the I *ab initio* finds itself seized by agape. Naturalistic and secular rationalities, circumscribed by the bounds of the Spheres of Nature and of Poetic I's, must scorn this appeal beyond their parameters as an appeal to some *Deus ex machina*. But for Moral Realism Theory, this appeal grounds an awakened rationality, a rationality which affirms the vocabularies of the modern sciences, of free will, and of agape. Precisely because of its passivity, the passive voice necessarily appeals to undergoing of agape, which roots our action in a passion beyond the bounds of natural and secular explanation and yields "ethics as a first philosophy" (Sphere of Agape), just as modern "causation" yields "materialism/naturalism as a first philosophy" (Sphere of Nature), and free will yields "existentialism as a first philosophy" (Sphere of Poetic I's).

Levinas's witness is compelling and his descriptions felicitous both when we are seized by agape for the dogs playing happily in the field, and

---

55. Of course, Levinasian awakening also applies to those with existential strength in ordinary circumstances who nonetheless recognize and surrender to having been seized by agape for all Faces.

also amidst horror *in extremis*, precisely where Milbank is least convincing.[56] Levinas is awakened to agape in the grip of heinous evil. In contexts so extreme that the injustice, violence, and horror obliterate human constructions of meaning and decimate the I, casting it into a stupor of absolute passivity: amidst such living hell and existential brokenness, Levinas was awakened. Levinas testifies to having been directly seized by a reality that establishes even as it transcends the ethical opposition between good and evil, finds himself seized not by an idea, theory or indubitable first principle, but by passionate love for every Face. Remarkably, he even finds himself seized by love for the Faces of his Nazi tormentors (though this does not entail pacifism towards their faces).[57]

Levinas's "ethics as first philosophy" names the realization that God *qua* agape is as fundamentally given, as properly basic as modern causation (the Sphere of Nature) and free will (the Sphere of Poetic I's). Whether moved to joy in wondrous contexts or moved to sorrow in the face of suffering or oppression, insofar as we are awakened and seized by love for the Faces of all the creatures surrounding us, we immediately and directly undergo and know the truth of the passion to which Levinas testifies.

Recall that for Milbank, God, unlike us, does not "love" in response to any indebtedness but initiates the series. So, for Milbank God's love is different in kind from human love (which is within the series). On my reading of Levinas, agape does not beget a different kind of love but, insofar as we surrender to agape, empowers incarnation of that very love in our lives and world.

---

56. These theoretical differences are acute, but I think it is also vital to bear in mind the strong possibility that Milbank and Levinas are both attempting to narrate the same reality, and I would expect almost no difference between them with regard to a vast preponderance of significant and concrete ethical imperatives.

57. "If an SS man has what I mean by a face. A very disturbing question that calls, in my opinion, for an affirmative answer" (Levinas, *Entre Nous*, 231). Note, contrary to a widespread confusion, that when Levinas, like Jesus, calls upon us to love our enemies, he identifies them as enemies and does not (*contra* Freud) confuse them with friends. Moreover, here again like Jesus, Levinas's position only entails we might give our lives for friends. Insofar as for Jesus and Levinas this is an *ethical* call, not about personal preferences and affiliations, "friends" and "enemies" should be read in terms of "friends of agape" and "enemies of agape." One does not give one's life on behalf of an enemy of agape, which would be to abet evil. But one may in this unjust, conflicted-ridden world find oneself giving one's life for a "friend of agape" (who may or may not also be a personal friend), resisting evil in accord with one's having been seized by agape for their Face.

PART III | OTHERNESS, COMMUNITY, AND THE COMMON GOOD

Vis-à-vis my own tradition, Christianity, the Jesus of history evidently incarnated agape profoundly to the death. "God incarnate, Jesus Christ" signifies perfect incarnation of surrender to agape. "Spirit" signifies lived undergoing of agape. "Father" signifies agapes' origin outside of history, not necessarily outside of being. Agape begets agape. Not in the sense that *my* agape begets agape *in* others, but in the sense that my active loving or testimony to agape awakens others directly to their own lived undergoing of the reality of agape. I take this Levinasian understanding, wherein I am always directly seized by agape insofar as I do not harden my heart, to be wholly consistent with the spiritual testimony of "yeomen" from every faith tradition.

* * * *

In Levinas the relation of ethics and faith is tight: "Moral consciousness is not an experience of values, but an access to external being: external being is, *par excellence*, the Other,"[58] and, "Ethics is not the corollary of the vision of God, it is that very vision."[59] Moral Realism Theory overtly thematizes "agape" wherever Levinas says "Other" or "God." But within the conceptual parameters of Moral Realism Theory, "God" signifies a moral force, the primordial phenomenological ground of both monistic and monotheistic faith traditions, not necessarily a person, let alone a trinity, though these and diverse other possibilities are nowise precluded.

Where I reference "the divine" or "God," then, I mean "God" insofar as "God *is* agape" and "agape *is* God." For Fiona Ellis, who notes this was Feuerbach's formulation, that would make me an atheist.[60] On the other hand, Michael Morgan describes those who would indict me for offering "nothing more than modified theology" wherein Levinas's "face-to-face is a camouflage for a divine command theory of moral normativity," for what "is presented as interpersonal is in fact a relation to a heteronomous ground, and such a figure is theological through and through."[61] I concur with Morgan's contention that in Levinas we should "avoid the belief that God is a being who authorizes through command,"[62] while distancing myself from his unqualified contention—unwarranted and, on my reading,

58. Levinas, *Difficult Freedom*, 293.
59. Levinas, *Difficult Freedom*, 17.
60. Ellis, *God, Value, and Nature*, 156.
61. Morgan, "Levinas on God," 321.
62. Morgan, *Cambridge Introduction to Levinas*, 147.

Neo-Levinas, Contra Milbank

a betrayal of Levinas—that "the term 'God' does not pick out or describe any reality or fact,"[63] for thereby Morgan appears to deny that what we signify with "agape" is as real and as constructed as what we signify with "gravity."[64] Moreover, there is no possibility of moral realism without *some* heteronomous ground, so I unapologetically affirm agape as a heteronomous ground.

Morgan's later essay, "Levinas on God," offers an analysis of Levinas's God talk more in line with Moral Realism Theory—though it remains essentially secular, problematically reliant on intentional action ("accept," "take," "orient"), and never signifies the force Moral Realism Theory signifies with "agape." For instance:

> Levinas's point is clear enough: the idea of "becoming like God" or being created in the divine image is not about drawing close to God in some ecstatic experience; nor is it to be rational or to model oneself after divine actions. Rather, it is to accept and assist other persons, to take one's responsibilities seriously, and to orient life around interpersonal responsibility.[65]

I am not concerned about labels of "theist" or "atheist." I am happy to number Feuerbach and a multitude of Arapaho, Buddhists, Christians, Hindus, Humanists, Jains, Jews, Muslims, Navaho, Wiccans, and adherents of many more traditions as fellow travelers insofar as their spiritualities are grounded in agape.

While the force signified by "agape" serves as a heteronomous ethical ground, Moral Realism Theory does not magically resolve ethical quandary cases, but it does situate them within a morally realist context, so it provides a ground for public global ethics vis-à-vis a vast array of ethical contentions common to diverse faith and philosophical traditions, resolving modernity's "crisis of foundations" in ethics and its "legitimization crisis" in political theory and making clear the basic ethical obligations of any sovereign. Furthermore, since agape is a force we undergo as a passion, it resolves modern ethics' "dualism of practical reason" and vexed attempts to appeal beyond varieties of self-interest (e.g., enlightened self-interest) and describe truly moral motivation.

Moral Realism Theory does not need the signifier "God," but it rejects modern Western intellectual elites' disdain for "God" and faiths and

---

63. Morgan, *Cambridge Introduction to Levinas*, 144.
64. See further, Levinas, *Of God Who Comes to Mind*, 56–57, 61–63.
65. Morgan, "Levinas on God," 333.

PART III | OTHERNESS, COMMUNITY, AND THE COMMON GOOD

suspects the primordial source of the most profound invocations of "God" or "the divine" across faith and philosophical traditions is the force of agape. So comprehensive historical understanding of agape requires understanding of faith and philosophical traditions across the globe. At this primordial level we operate beneath the distinctions that separate monistic and monotheistic faith traditions, let alone species of monistic and monotheistic belief systems.

Moral Realism Theory's affirmation of agape, then, signifies a force at the heart of historic faith traditions, though just as Aristotle, Newton, and Einstein signified and thematized differently the force most of us still think of in terms of "gravity," different faith traditions differently signify and unfold the implications of the force I signify with "agape." Accordingly, Moral Realism Theory can celebrate the rich plurality of faith traditions while not falling into relativism, for the plurality are true faiths only insofar as they remain faithful to the force contingently signified by "agape."

* * * *

Finally, the reality of agape stands even if there is no happy ending, even if existence is ultimately tragic.[66] However, while resurrection/nirvana/the Pure Land is not required, the character and perduring power of agape gives some basis for hope in some sort of heaven, most especially on behalf of myriad Faces whom we grieve because their lives have been brutal and short. This is realistic and loving hope grounded in agape. Still, in no sense is agape dependent upon resurrection so, *contra* Milbank, faith in resurrection is not "necessary for an ethical life to be possible."[67] Indeed,

---

66. "I have no optimistic philosophy for the end of history" (Levinas, *Entre-Nous*, 114, see also 187). *Contra* Levinas (and, no doubt, *contra* many Christians), I think Christians—and, in analogous ways, many Buddhists, Jews, Hindus, Muslims, and others—are right to hope in a "happy end," but that no "happy end" (let me limit myself to speaking for my own tradition here) is essential to Christianity (Levinas, *Is It Righteous to Be?*, 267). Also, in accord with my identification of agape/the divine/God with the passionate concern and care *received* for others and self in the event of the having been seized, when Levinas says, "I mean that you [i.e., Christians] begin with 'God is love.' The Jew begins with obligation," he names a distinction without a difference (Levinas, *Is It Righteous to Be?*, 267). On Judaism, Christianity, and "Christian *charité*," see also Levinas, *Is It Righteous to Be?*, 137.

67. Methodologically, note well, my neo-Levinasian philosophical spirituality is founded upon this very delimited and so very general point of maximum surety. That is, it is *de facto* affirmed (self-consciously or not) by people who are ethically moved from every faith tradition. In Milbank, by contrast, one begins with a complex and

we should never speak of "faith in resurrection" (or use any other formulation that confuses faith and belief) for at the most general and primordial level faith—wholly reasonable faith, faith kindling joy and celebration or, in contexts of horror, inciting anguish and resistance, faith which is not conceptual, not assent, affirmation, or belief, but existential orientation to a force—faith is living surrender to having been seized by agape for every Face, including our own.[68] No matter our journey, even in hells on earth, agape gifts us with love for our own beloved Faces, unites us with mutually awakened Faces in "love made complete" solidarity, and fuels concrete struggle for what is loving, just and good.[69]

BIBLIOGRAPHY

Brock, Bahler. "Emmanuel Levinas, Radical Orthodoxy, and an Ontology of Originary Peace." *Journal of Religious Ethics* 42.3 (2014) 516–39.
Bakewell, Sarah. *At the Existentialist Café: Freedom, Being, and Apricot Cocktails*. New York: Other, 2017.
Critchley, Simon. *The Problem with Levinas*. Edited by Alexis Dianda. Oxford: Oxford University Press, 2015.
Derrida, Jacques. *Given Time: 1. Counterfeit Money*. Translated by Peggy Kamuf. Chicago: University of Chicago Press, 1992.
Ellis, Fiona. *God, Value, and Nature*. Oxford: Oxford University Press, 2014.
Greenway, William. *A Reasonable Belief: Why God and Faith Make Sense*. Louisville: Westminster John Knox, 2015.
———. *Reasonable Faith for a Post-Secular Age: Open Christian Spirituality and Ethics*. Eugene, OR: Cascade, 2021.
Levinas, Emmanuel. *Alterity and Transcendence*. Translated by Michael B. Smith. New York: Columbia University Press, 1999.
———. *Difficult Freedom: Essays on Judaism*. Translated by Seán Hand. Baltimore: Johns Hopkins University Press, 1997.
———. *Entre-Nous: Thinking-of-the-Other*. Translated by Michael Smith and Barbara Harshav. New York: Columbia University Press, 1998.

---

expansive—and so very specific—theological vision (i.e., not general but significantly delimited and exclusive).

68. See especially, Greenway, *A Reasonable Belief* and Greenway, *Reasonable Faith for a Post-Secular Age*.

69. Despite Milbank's harsh rejection of Levinas, we should remember his rejection pivots upon misinterpretation. While there would be systemic implications for Milbank, his theology may be significantly strengthened if he were to integrate Levinas, properly interpreted, into his reflections. While I differ in some particulars of interpretation, see in this regard Brock Bahler, "Emmanuel Levinas, Radical Orthodoxy, and an Ontology of Originary Peace."

Part III | Otherness, Community, and the Common Good

———. *Is It Righteous to Be? Interviews with Emmanuel Levinas*. Edited by Jill Robbins. Stanford: Stanford University Press, 2001.
———. *Of God Who Comes to Mind*. Translated by Bettina Bergo. Stanford: Stanford University Press, 1986.
———. *On Escape: De l'évasion*. Translated by Bettina Bergo. Stanford: Stanford University Press, 2003.
———. *Otherwise than Being or Beyond Essence*. Translated by Alphonso Lingis. Pittsburgh: Duquesne University Press, 1998.
———. "Reflections on the Philosophy of Hitlerism." Translated by Seán Hand. *Critical Inquiry* 17.1 (1990) 63–71.
———. *Totality and Infinity: An Essay on Exteriority*. Translated by Alphonso Lingis. Pittsburgh: Duquesne University Press, 1969.
Marion, Jean-Luc. "Phenomenological Sketch of the Concept of Gift." In *Postmodern Philosophy and Christian Thought*, edited by Merold Westphal, 122–43. Bloomington: Indiana University Press, 1999.
Mauss, Marcel. *The Gift: The Form and Essence of Exchange in Archaic Societies*. Translated by W. D. Halls. New York: Norton, 1990.
Milbank, John. "Can a Gift Be Given?: Prolegomena to a Future Trinitarian Metaphysic." *Modern Theology* 11.1 (1995) 119–61.
———. "The Ethics of Self-Sacrifice." *First Things* 91 (1999) 33–38. https://www.firstthings.com/article/1999/03/004-the-ethics-of-self-sacrifice.
———. "The Gift and the Mirror." In *Counter-Experiences: Reading Jean-Luc Marion*, edited by Kevin Hart, 253–318. Notre Dame: University of Notre Dame Press, 2007.
———. "The Shares of Being or Gift, Relation and Participation: An Essay on the Metaphysics of Emmanuel Levinas and Alain Badiou." Unpublished paper. http://theologyphilosophycentre.co.uk/papers/Milbank_Metaphysics-LevinasBadiou.pdf.
———. "The Soul of Reciprocity (Part One)." *Modern Theology* 17.3 (2001) 335–91.
Morgan, Michael L. *The Cambridge Introduction to Emmanuel Levinas*. Cambridge: Cambridge University Press, 2011.
———. "Levinas on God and the Trace of the Other." In *The Oxford Handbook of Levinas*, edited by Michael Morgan, 321–41. Oxford Handbooks. Oxford: Oxford University Press, 2019.
———, ed. *The Oxford Handbook of Levinas*. Oxford Handbooks. Oxford: Oxford University Press, 2019.
Smilanksy, Saul. *Free Will and Illusion*. Oxford: Clarendon, 2000.
Waldenfels, Bernhard. "Levinas and the Face of the Other." In *The Cambridge Companion to Levinas*, edited by Simon Critchley and Robert Bernasconi, 63–81. Cambridge Companions to Philosophy. Cambridge: Cambridge University Press, 2002.
Wiesel, Elie. *The Night Trilogy*. Translated by Marion Wiesel. New York: Hill & Wang, 2008.

9

Rendering the Secular Sacred
Protestant Military Chaplaincy in a Pluralistic Age

DEBORAH VAN DEN BOSCH-HEIJ

INTRODUCTION

With the Russian invasion in Ukraine in 2020, with shifting power situations and alliances globally, with the advancement of methods of (hybrid) warfare, there has been renewed attention and appreciation for the significance of a nation's armed defense forces. In the slipstream of this renewed attention for the military, there is growing awareness of the significance of military chaplaincy. Military chaplaincy refers to those services and roles that a religious expert typically offers in relation to a military organization and to the individuals serving in it.[1]

Military chaplains offer their services at the intersection of society, religious institutions and (inter)national concerns. They are commissioned and sent by their church or other (non)religious institution to serve people within the military system. They join these soldiers when they are on deployment for many months away from home, and they offer moral, faithful care in many different ways. Military chaplains represent something that transcends the often strict, efficient, disciplined, harsh, violence-shaped defense organization. Together with, but different from, other professional

---

1. Brekke and Tikhonov, *Military Chaplaincy*, 14.

caregivers, military chaplains continuously remind us of our sacred humanity and our vulnerable unicity even when we wear the uniform, appearing all the same, and are trained to use weapons on behalf of the society.

One of the features of military chaplaincy is its ambiguous position. A military chaplain belongs to a particular denominational entity, but is "transferred" to the secular organization of the military. In the Dutch context, for example, it means that the confessional military chaplain is fully embedded in the secular armed defense forces—a position that perpetually raises interesting questions touching all sides of the military chaplain's work. It is about the relation between being ordained clergy and being a professional caregiver simultaneously. It is about embodying peace in a military context. It is about being with the combatants without being one of them. It is about how to be a helpful, trustworthy chaplain for people who are not familiar with religious language or tradition. It is about how to be a Protestant chaplain in a multi-denominational chaplaincy body that itself is fully entrenched in the military body. These are just a few aspects, but they reveal military chaplaincy's inherent ambiguity.

In this contribution I would like to enter this field of ambiguity from a Dutch perspective. Being a Protestant military chaplain myself, I have come to appreciate and embrace this ambiguous identity because it celebrates the interplay of the secular and the sacred. It has been said that if you want to know what ministry will look like in twenty years, then look at military chaplaincy today. This applies to the Netherlands as well. The Dutch context is a setting of diversity, of plural perspectives and traditions. Dutch military chaplaincy is thus heavily influenced by plurality, characterized by lengthy processes of individuality and secularization. For a military chaplain, what is at stake at the intersection of the secular and the sacred, is the need for ongoing theological reflection on this ambiguous relation. Paying attention to this particular need may help the confessional military chaplain who is expected to serve any combatant who comes along, regardless his/her way of life.

How does one render the secular sacred—what language to use when people do not have religious language, how to be faithfully present when people are continuously on tour in war zones, how to represent grace and patience when people are under (group) pressure, not allowing themselves to be personal or vulnerable, how to address moral injury, how to honor plurality and offer the treasures of Christian faith simultaneously? These are but a few questions that have their place in the discourse of military chaplaincy.

Embracing the interplay of the secular and the sacred asks for compatible perspectives at a theological level. Acknowledging that there are multiple venues corresponding with the question how to be present in the secular, I would like to explore one venue in particular, and that is the pneumatological perspective. As a Protestant theologian and military chaplain I have come to understand that the work of the Holy Spirit is essential in the relation between the secular and the sacred. I realized that if I were to be asked: *When is your ministry "going well"? What is then happening to the soldiers? What are they responding to, in spite of them being secular or with a different set of values than I?* that I would then refer to the reality of the Holy Spirit as the One who renders the secular sacred. In this essay, therefore, I will explore a *pneumatological* perspective on military chaplaincy.

As far as I know, this pneumatological-theological angle on military chaplaincy is a novel venue. I will introduce some pneumatological reflections developed by the Dutch Protestant theologian Arnold van Ruler. His creative approach to pneumatology may be helpful in exploring the interplay of the secular and the sacred.

MILITARY CHAPLAINCY'S AMBIGUITY

Military chaplaincy can be understood as spiritual care in the armed forces. This kind of chaplaincy is about care for combatants, including veterans and combatants' families, by chaplains who are, on the one hand, commissioned by a (non)religious institute to do their work within the armed forces and who are, on the other hand, embedded in the secular organization of the military. Thus, the role and the services of the military chaplain are always related to two institutions simultaneously. This binarity of being commissioned by Church and State[2] is coined as "chaplaincy in ambiguity,"[3] the bipolarity of chaplaincy,[4] chaplaincy's double or split identity.[5]

This ambiguous nature of military chaplaincy has various implications for military chaplains.[6] There is, for example, the obvious dilemma

---

2. Martin, *Reflections on Sociology and Theology*, 149.
3. Davie, "Military Chaplain." See also Smedema, "Vraag naar eigenheid."
4. Heitink, "Ambt en Ambacht," 161.
5. Zock, "Chaplaincy in the Netherlands," 14.
6. See Hansen, *Military Chaplains and Religious Diversity*.

of *divided loyalties*, since the military chaplain has to navigate between the concerns of being ordained clergy and the demands of the military. And there is the question of *legitimacy*, since the military chaplain may belong to the church but is (often) remunerated by the public military institution. This arrangement allows for the ongoing query into the relevance and validity of the presence of chaplains in the armed forces. Who is to decide on military chaplaincy's legitimacy, and on what basis? Another area of impact inherent to military chaplaincy's ambiguous nature is the focus on *diversity*. Diversity in the sense that military chaplains serve and collaborate with different groups of people: people who are familiar with the Christian tradition, people who are familiar with another faith tradition, and people who are agnostic or atheist. In addition to serving a diverse and plural group of combatants, military chaplains themselves inevitably represent "otherness" or dissimilarity within the uniformity of the military institution.

The discourse of military chaplaincy is satiated with the notion of ambiguity. Basically, all disciplines circle around the indissoluble relation between the secular and the sacred. In their multidisciplinary review, Liuski and Ubani provide an overview of prominent military chaplaincy leitmotifs in the past two decades.[7] They studied the way European military chaplaincy is portrayed in European scientific journal articles between 2000 and 2019, and the themes they identified correspond roughly with various disciplines of military chaplaincy: An extensive discipline is the historical description of military chaplaincy, studying the situation of military chaplains in times of war (World War I, World War II, and post-World War II) in various geographical contexts.

Another discipline is the practical theological discipline, covering the category of the basic functions of the military chaplain. These basic functions concentrate mainly on pastoral care and on religious ceremonies, including field services, funerals, and bereavement procedures.

Another discipline addresses the field of ethical perspectives of military chaplaincy. This is an essential trait of military chaplaincy, revolving around the relationship between the autonomous or vocational position of the military chaplain on the one hand and the military structure or operation on the other hand, leading to ethical reflection. Stimulating moral reflection, among combatants as well as among military chaplains themselves, is an ongoing and vital process based on the conviction that chaplaincy presence in the military is always affected by military dynamics.

---

7. Liuski and Ubani, "Military Chaplaincy in Europe."

Thus the military chaplain cannot afford to withdraw from these dynamic forces in order to remain on morally neutral ground.[8] The growing body of research and literature on moral injury[9] and just war can also be seen as part of this discipline. Much has been written on the moral dimensions of war and peace from a theological point of view.[10] Also within the Dutch context, substantial theological-ethical perspectives are being offered in revisiting Just War Theory.[11]

Another discipline examines the changing nature of military chaplaincy, exploring the "postmodern military," how military forces adapted to the post-Cold War environment by incorporating more civilians, more women and minority groups, more involvement of reserve forces personnel, and by focusing on non-combat missions with peacekeeping and humanitarian aid. This approach explores how these developments altered the role of military chaplains.[12] The concept of postmodern military is closely connected to contextual, cultural processes of pluralization, religious diversification, secularization, etc. The discourse of military chaplaincy is broad and diverse, but in all various disciplines the core issue of ambiguity cannot be overlooked.

A clear illustration of the desire (or need) to embrace this ambiguity, this interaction of "church identity" and "professional care giver within a secular institute," is the development of military chaplaincy in the Netherlands. In the following section I will describe the situation of Dutch military chaplaincy, alluding to the idea that the interplay of the secular and the sacred asks for compatible perspectives at a theological level.

DUTCH MILITARY CHAPLAINCY

To understand the current situation of Dutch military chaplaincy, one should consider the genesis of Dutch chaplaincy in general: Dutch societal

---

8. Vos, "Rechtvaardige Oorlog," 376.

9. See, e.g., Brock and Lettini, *Soul Repair*; Graham, *Moral Injury*; Ramsay and Doehring, *Military Moral Injury*; Powers, *Full Darkness*.

10. For significant representatives of Just War Theory, see, e.g., Ramsey, *Just War*; O'Donovan, *Just War Revisited*; Cook, *Moral Warrior*; Biggar, *Defence of War*.

11. See, e.g., Bruggen, "Moral Responsibility"; Vos, "Peace after the Mission"; "Rechtvaardige Oorlog"; Iersel, *Future of Just War Theory*; Oosterhuis, "Het verhaal achter de moraal."

12. Rennick, "Towards an Interfaith Ministry," 78–79. See also Moskos, *Postmodern Military*.

Part III | Otherness, Community, and the Common Good

structure used to be organized along denominational lines or so-called "pillars" based on religion or world-view (Catholic, Protestant, socialist). Within these pillars, there were Protestant ministers and Catholic priests who provided spiritual care for those who belonged to their pillar.

During the 1960s, when this societal pillarized structure began to collapse under processes of individualization and secularization, spiritual care was no longer made available exclusively by the churches, but was considered a public service provided by the welfare state.[13] The disintegration of Dutch pillarization entailed a move from religious practices towards professionalization of the chaplain's role and position within state institutions such as hospitals, the judiciary, and the military. The chaplain became someone whose position was embedded within the organization rather than someone who is an "outsider" or a confessional representative. Since this turning point, "chaplaincy" transformed into "spiritual care profession," shifting from a religious context to a more neutral setting, with chaplaincy's services available for anyone who is in need of spiritual care, regardless his/her preference of (non)religion.

This development towards professionalization led to renewed questions about the identity and distinctiveness of chaplaincy. Why should the state finance the provision of chaplaincy? What is the role of the churches pertaining to chaplaincy in state institutions? In due course it was stated that the chaplain as spiritual caregiver is an embedded professional and a religious representative simultaneously, an insider and an outsider at the same time. Since then, the organization of chaplaincy services has been marked by this ambiguous position and split identity.

The implication of this development is at least twofold. The first implication is that in its organizational structure Dutch military chaplaincy intrinsically offers space for a plurality of religious and other worldview perspectives. One could say that this innate openness to plurality is tied with its own legitimacy in the public domain, as its genesis reveals: chaplaincy services within the Dutch armed forces have developed into its current status quo in response to cultural, societal, political developments, with plurality and diversity as one of its main characteristics. This plurality predisposition is still evident in the remnants of the pillarization structure of Dutch military chaplaincy: all (non)religious denominations are to be represented, and the distinctive identity of the various denominations should be nurtured. This approach, i.e., that all (non)religious denominations are

---

13. Zock, "Chaplaincy in the Netherlands," 13.

to be represented, is about the legitimation of military chaplaincy. It is a consequence of: (1) the principle of the church/state separation, and of (2) the principle of the state's neutrality concerning religion/worldview. Since the state cannot interfere with matters of religion/worldview, it validates the presence of chaplains who are responsible for the content and the supply of spiritual care.

Where other chaplaincy bodies may be formed by only a few denominations (for example Catholic, Protestant, Jewish and/or Muslim), Dutch military chaplaincy consists of as many as seven distinctive denominations. This chaplaincy body evolved slowly yet steadily. The first military chaplains were Protestant ministers and Catholic clerics who provided pastoral services during World War I, the interbellum, and World War II. The number of military chaplains was extended with the arrival of Humanist chaplains, soon followed by Jewish chaplains. Since the organization of military chaplaincy reflected the position of religion in society, on the basis of the church/state separation and the state's neutrality principle, chaplaincy organization was broadened with Muslim chaplains and Hindu chaplains. Since 2021, with the appearance of Buddhist chaplains, the chaplaincy body has grown into a full-fledged seven pillar chaplaincy unity embedded in the armed forces. These chaplains are endorsed or commissioned by their own (non)religious institution, yet they operate together interreligiously,[14] serving anyone who is in need of spiritual care.

Another implication of the ambiguous identity of Dutch military chaplaincy is that its openness to plurality paradoxically shows a lack of shared theological or philosophical reflection on the professional identity of the chaplain. Ironically, the situation of the pluralistic, multidenominational make-up of Dutch military chaplaincy creates so much space for other perspectives and worldviews that there seems to be a reluctance to articulate one's own distinctiveness within the chaplaincy body. The state (more specifically the Ministry of Defense) is the authority deciding whether the military chaplaincy body can or should be expanded with new representatives of a religion or worldview, so the validation of one's proper identity and in relation to other denominations may have lost its urgency.

In addition, this reluctance may also partly account for the lack of a shared theological or philosophical substructure of the profession of the chaplain. For instance, Zock argues that this absence of a joint theological underpinning of the profession is the consequence of the pillarized religious

---

14. See Pleizier and Schuhmann, "Military Context," 5.

organization of spiritual care (or chaplaincy) since each worldview sector or pillar has its own particular theological and/or philosophical inspiration for the work.[15]

The same point has been made by various Dutch (practical-)theologians, identifying the essential, necessary relation between chaplaincy praxis and theological frame of reflection: Heitink, reflecting on the bipolarity of the chaplain, asserts that both poles of the chaplain's function (confessional/particular and professional/general) should be embraced in a constructive tension.[16] Over against polarizing the two poles, Heitink proposes an integrative approach. In doing so, he draws attention to the dialectical relation between *identity* and *plurality*. Chaplains as office holders from different traditions/world views are challenged to develop their proper identity, in order to offer meaningful spiritual care.

In their valuable contribution, Ganzevoort and Visser offer a thorough reflection on chaplaincy and pastoral care.[17] The "pastoral care" nomenclature may raise the impression that chaplaincy is directed to the domain of the church, but that is a misinterpretation. According to Ganzevoort and Visser, chaplaincy's proprium is found in the *combination* of: (a) its relation to other forms of ecclesial presence, (b) its relation to other forms of professional care and counseling, and (c) its relation to other forms of compassion. It is in the combination of these three trajectories where chaplaincy's distinctive character comes to light. In a response to a colleague's critical feedback on this broad approach, Ganzevoort continues to stress the importance of the plurality-identity relation as a core issue of chaplaincy.[18] He argues that plurality in worldviews is not to be considered an optional extra; it is a given fact. Needless to say, we live in a diverse and plural world, with many different worldviews and traditions, which means that the chaplain must not assume that the other person shares the same frame of reference. Precisely this reality propels the need for addressing, strengthening, and deepening of the theological dimension of chaplaincy. By "theological dimension," Ganzevoort means theological professionality rather than specific (Christian) theological content. He says that chaplains should be capable of identifying, analyzing, interpreting, evaluating, and, if necessary, re-routing our approach to the sacred in our reality.

15. Zock, "Chaplaincy in the Netherlands," 14.
16. Heitink, "Ambt en Ambacht," 166–69.
17. Ganzevoort and Visser, *Zorg voor het verhaal*.
18. Ganzevoort, "Geestelijke verzorging," 25.

Borgman responds to the same plurality-identity dialectics in chaplaincy when he argues that the development of the chaplain's professional identity led to a certain imbalance within chaplaincy: by focusing on professionality, chaplaincy moved away from "care for the soul" towards (psychological) counseling.[19] The chaplain transformed into a professional perceiving the other as a client with needs that have to be addressed rather than as a person with a soul. Understanding the other as a person with a soul, as someone longing for "living a good life" is the core of chaplaincy. "Soul" and "longing for living a good life" are theological concepts, says Borgman, hence the need for theological reflection on chaplaincy.[20] Acknowledging the inherent fact of plural worldviews, Borgman concludes that we need a kind of chaplaincy that redefines the ways in which society understands the value of human life. This is about human life in all its plurality, yet this redefinition is to be considered a theological task of chaplaincy. Theological too in the sense that chaplaincy cannot be embedded safely in public institutions but, with a reference to Mark 10:45 about the Son of Man who came to serve instead of being served, chaplaincy has to dare putting itself at stake.

Smedema addresses the same core issue when it comes to military chaplaincy of the Protestant denomination.[21] Mostly in the same line as Heitink, Ganzevoort and Borgman, he draws attention to the crucial link between plurality, (Protestant) identity, and theology. Protestant military chaplaincy, as part of the plural chaplaincy body, continues to search for its distinctive identity and its proper role in the relation between church and society. What makes a Protestant chaplain a *Protestant* chaplain in the obvious plurality and (non)religious diversity of Dutch society? Therefore, theological reflection is essential.[22]

RENDERING THE SECULAR SACRED

What makes a Protestant chaplain a *Protestant* chaplain in the military context? This stimulating question is carefully and excellently attended to with the mission statement of the Dutch Protestant military chaplaincy body.

19. Borgman, "Pleidooi."
20. Borgman, "Pleidooi," 9.
21. Smedema, "Vraag naar eigenheid."
22. Smedema, "Vraag naar eigenheid," 355. See also Mæland and Lunde, "From Confessional to Concessional," 182.

Part III | Otherness, Community, and the Common Good

It states: "The narrative of Jesus Christ is leading for us. Our core values are (1) belief that people are valuable and vulnerable, (2) hopefulness that peace and justice will prevail, (3) confidence that love's power is stronger than weapons."[23] This mission statement reveals a focus on Jesus Christ. This is both an inspiring and logical perspective for Christian military chaplaincy, especially when considering the fact that Protestant military chaplaincy is heavily influenced by Karl Barth's theology with its focus on the absolute "otherness" of God in Jesus Christ.

The beauty of this Christocentric frame of reference is its leading perspective on God's everlasting and gracious love for humankind, implying careful attention for those who are in need of help in the midst of violence, in war and in all other situations of injustice. The narrative of Jesus Christ is a normative account for Protestant chaplains, meaning that they want to represent a spiritual, Christological reality that transcends this broken world. In our daily praxis this Christian countercultural narrative can offer hope in disheartening situations, it can deliver peace and grace in places of hate and misunderstanding.

There is, however, also a complexity when it comes to Protestant military chaplaincy's normative Christocentric perspective in a military setting. For example, as a military chaplain I'm supposed to offer so-called "moments of reflection and encouragement" on Sundays when we are away from home, on tour abroad, or on military training. The infantry battalion that I serve is a very diverse group of combatants. They differ in age, life experience, rank, and spiritual orientation. Some of them are vaguely familiar with the Christian tradition, and only a handful will call themselves Christian or will identify with another faith tradition. Most of the battalion can be described as agnostic or atheist. Considering this plurality and diversity, it is unthinkable to offer a traditional church service. Instead, I prepare a "moment of reflection and encouragement" that goes by the name "*Soultime*—time for the soul, time for yourself." *Soultime* is open to anyone who feels the need to take a break from deployment life. The main purpose of *Soultime* is to offer a bit of rest and reflection in a world of action and vigilance. The main elements of a *Soultime* resemble Protestant liturgy, e.g., there is a (Bible) story, a message, a prayer (by lighting candles), (rock or pop) music, and a blessing, but there is plenty space for other forms of philosophy of life. *Soultime* is a way of rendering the secular sacred without a Christocentric approach that is fixed, closed or exclusive: a kerygmatic

---

23. PCN, *Jaarschrift 2024*, 5.

inclination, a universal claim, the conviction that salvation requires pulling humanity towards God through Christ is to be absent, because it will fend off those who long for mercy but who are anxious about being molded by Christian church and faith.

Soultime exemplifies the complexity of our normative Christocentric perspective in a military setting. But it also reveals new perspectives on rendering the secular sacred: as a Protestant military chaplain I have always experienced those *Soultime* moments as a domain where the Holy Spirit is hovering and brooding. These specific Soultime moments, as well as many other encounters in my military chaplaincy praxis, made me wonder about vital theological notions that generate processes of rendering the secular sacred in the military context.

In the following section, I will explore two theological notions that I understand *and* experience to be essential in rendering the secular sacred. These are: relationality and appreciation of earthly existence. In exploring these notions, I will include the voice of Arnold van Ruler, a Dutch theologian who passionately and creatively developed his theology against the background of increasing plurality and secularization in society.

Arnold van Ruler

Arnold van Ruler (1908–1970) was a theologian whose contributions had a major influence on church and theology in the Netherlands. Ruler radicalized sixteenth-century Reformed motifs and turned them into relevant notions for twentieth-century church and theology. Ruler developed a relatively independent pneumatological approach—though not a comprehensive one, but rather intriguing suggestions and theological ideas—that became a clear and distinct voice in protestant theology. In developing his theology, Ruler slowly distanced himself from Karl Barth without failing to remain appreciative of Barth's theology. Ruler deliberately opted for a full-scale trinitarian perspective instead of Barth's christocentric line. In doing so, Ruler was one of the first twentieth-century Reformed theologians choosing another distinctive path.[24] According to Ruler, trinitarian theology entails the labor of multi-perspectivity: one has to look at subjects from different perspectives. Doing theology from an exclusive, singular perspective—either christological or pneumatological—will lead to narrowness, which should be avoided, because that is like looking at the outside

24. See Keulen, "Theologie van A. A. van Ruler."

world always through one and the same window. A trinitarian approach will inherently create tension: sometimes it is difficult to harmonize different perspectives. Ruler claimed that we must learn to accept tension and inconsistencies in theologizing. This inspiring attitude may be helpful in our exploration of underlying theological notions of rendering the secular sacred.

One of the most significant ideas is Ruler's lecture on "structure differences" between Christology and pneumatology.[25] He extensively explains that the work of the Spirit is to be distinguished from the work of Christ, whereby it must be understood that in the relation God-creation the work of the Spirit is of the same quality as the work of Christ, and that pneumatology has a relatively self-sufficient status: one cannot copy and paste the structure of the christological dogma onto the structure of the pneumatological dogma. This means that one, thinking about the relation God-creation from a pneumatological viewpoint adheres to completely different rules than when one reflects on this relation from a christological viewpoint.[26]

One example of these structural differences is the first difference mentioned by Ruler. It is fundamental for the rest of the differences. The first one is about the absence of enhypostasis in pneumatology. Enhypostasis means that the assumed human nature of Christ does not have its own individuality. There has never been a "Mister Jesus" but always only God-the-Son-in-the-human-flesh.[27] Enhypostasis can be seen as the core of the incarnation, but it has to be rejected in pneumatology. The work of the Spirit aims at restoration of creaturely existence, but this does not entail the return of creation to God ontologically. Because creation, in being created, is already good. The sending, outpouring, and inhabitation of God's Spirit is not focused on leading human life into God, but rather the other way around: God is moving towards creation.[28] The work of the Spirit emphasizes the importance of creaturely existence, which is a way of being distinct from God. Different from Christology, pneumatology is thus not about human life becoming part of God, but about the distinctiveness of creation through the presence of the Spirit.

---

25. Ruler, *Theologisch Werk*, 1:175–90.
26. Ruler, *Theologisch Werk*, 1:176.
27. Ruler, *Theologisch Werk*, 1:178.
28. Ruler, *Theologisch Werk*, 6:9–40.

Appreciation of Earthly Existence

Ruler has been identified as a "theologian of the good creation."[29] In his theology, he emphasized that the Trinitarian God is deeply committed to creation, and that every aspect of God's (salvific) involvement is focused on the restoration of creation. His ideas about creation must be seen as fundamental part of his vision of God's kingdom and thus of the eschaton. According to Ruler, God is involved in the present *from the future*. God doesn't act from the beginning or the middle, but shares trinitarian life from the eschaton in the present time: this world receives its full meaning in the light of the kingdom, and thus cannot be separated from it. With this trinitarian theocratic kingdom perspective Ruler revisits the God-creation relationship after Karl Barth: the ultimate purpose of creation is re-creation, the work of Christ is the *means* and the work of the Spirit is the (preliminary) *purpose*.[30] So, God's kingdom is God's dynamic involvement in this world in such a way that the eschaton sheds its light on reality, so that creation cannot but be identified as *good*. Ruler's doctrine of creation does not allow a separation between creation and God's reign, so there also cannot be dualism between heaven and earth, between material and spiritual, and between trinitarian life and human existence. This is where, in Ruler's perspective, the Spirit is crucial: "This relation of the Spirit with the reign and with the world is more important than the Spirit's relation with Christ and his work, in whom God's reign was shaped into this world and in whom this reality was restored."[31] The Spirit continues to share trinitarian life with humanity, with earthly existence. So there will not be a new creation, but a re-creation. With his doctrine of creation, Ruler provides contemporary theologians with a firm foundation for their endeavors to offer contours of an eco-theology.[32]

In the same line, Ruler's pneumatological focus on creation may also be helpful for Protestant military chaplaincy in a pluralistic context: "The world, in its plurality and its contrasts would offer a better entrance to pneumatology."[33] A pneumatological perspective helps to gain *a positive understanding of the public domain in relation to Christian faith and*

---

29. Beek, "Theologie van van Ruler," 14.
30. Ruler, *Theologisch Werk*, 6:22.
31. Ruler, *Theologisch Werk*, 6:25.
32. See, e.g., Conradie, *Earth in God's Economy*.
33. Ruler, *Theologisch Werk*, 6:25.

tradition. The world, in itself, is good: its very existence is willed by God and therefore imprinted with quality, but the world itself is not divine. The world, our daily physical reality, is an entity on its own, and has to be valued as such. This deep and serious appreciation implies society in its secularity and its plurality as well. It stands on its own, and there is no urge to draw the world into God's presence. It is the other way around: God moves towards and into the world and public life because that is the realm where trinitarian life (love, equality, dignity, justice, peace) can be of service.

Relationality

Protestant theology has a history of accentuating the unity of the Trinity, but since the 1950s there has been a shift. The attention has shifted to the *three-ness* as being fundamental to God's unity.[34] Ruler's approach is one example of this shift. Moltmann's pneumatology, with its starting point in the three-ness of the Trinity, is another leading example. This emphasis on the plural identity of God leads to the perspective that the Spirit is a distinct, relatively independent person of the Trinity.

Articulations about the relative independence of the person and the work of the Spirit are rooted in the idea that the Spirit is the One who creates relationships and life-giving bonds. These relationships concern both the inner-Trinitarian communion as well as communion *ad extra*. As Shults indicates, relationality was in the early Protestant tradition already an important concept in understanding of the whole person as the image of God: the understanding of personhood as *being in relation* rather than as absolute entity with various faculties influencing material reality.[35] Under the influence of the turn to relationality in modern philosophy and science, the notion of relationality has now also been brought to Protestant pneumatological discourse[36]—the Spirit as a distinct person of the Trinity, communicating Trinitarian life and providing human existence with notions of love, equality, dignity, justice, liberation, and the affirmation of life. The personal and equal relationality of the Triune God is "a metaphor of not what we have but what we do and *who we are in the intricate web of connections* with God, self, others, and the planet."[37]

34. See Webster, "Identity of the Holy Spirit," 4–7.
35. Shults, "Philosophical Turn," 333.
36. Shults, "Spirit and Spirituality," 271–87.
37. Medley, *Imago Trinitatis*, 4 (my emphasis).

Who we are in the intricate web of connections, is the key question for Protestant military chaplaincy. The intricate web of connections is made of the plurality of perspectives, worldviews, understandings, ways of being—and this web encompasses society, military organization, interdenominational body of chaplaincy, church-and-state relation, and the individual or pastoral relationship chaplain-soldier. If one could say that relationality and being in a plurality of relationships form the very matter of military chaplaincy, then this perspective might intersect with the theological understanding that the Spirit's presence is found in relationality. This perspective brings to the fore that relationality can be perceived as the realm where Trinitarian life can be represented: "In looking at the Spirit's connecting with the world we see that the nature of God as 'ecstatic' or, 'standing out of Godself' is especially visible when God engages with what is 'other' than God."[38] This can be a helpful perspective for Protestant military chaplaincy: that its inherent ambiguity and incorporated dialectics is always part of engaging with "otherness," and this engaging in otherness can be seen as being part of Trinitarian life.

GATHERING FRAGMENTS

How does one render the secular sacred in a military setting? This is an essential question for military chaplains, for they offer their chaplaincy services at the intersection of church, state, military, and international politics. The military chaplain always has a "split identity" as being part of and belonging to two institutions simultaneously. The confessional institute and the secular institute require the military chaplain to navigate between the concerns of being ordained clergy and the demands of the military. The model of Dutch military chaplaincy illustrates the complexity of the ambiguous nature, because the Dutch context is heavily shaped by extensive processes of secularization, pluralization, and diversification. There are seven denominations (religious and non-religious) of military chaplains, collectively serving all military personnel and their families, regardless their preferred way of life or spirituality.

For Dutch *Protestant* military chaplains, embracing the plural and secular perspective moves the question about rendering the secular sacred to a theological level. Theologizing the interplay of secular and sacred draws our attention to the field of pneumatology, since pneumatology is

38. Bergin, "Holy Spirit," 271.

Part III | Otherness, Community, and the Common Good

about the distinctiveness of creation through the presence of the Spirit. The distinctive voice of Dutch theologian Arnold van Ruler, who developed his trinitarian-pneumatological thinking against the background of early secularization and pluralization, suggests two crucial aspects in rendering the secular sacred. The first aspect is "deep appreciation of earthly existence," every inch of creation, which implies society in its secularity and its plurality as well. The perspective is that earthly existence stands on its own, and there is no urge to draw the world into God's presence. It is the other way around: God moves towards and into the world and public life because that is the realm where trinitarian life (love, justice, forgiveness) can be of service to mankind. The second aspect is "relationality," because from a trinitarian-pneumatological perspective relationality can be perceived as the realm where trinitarian life can be represented: the nature of God as being ecstatic and moving away from Godself, is especially perceptible when God engages with what is "other" than God. These two notions, underscoring the significance of the Holy Spirit in relation to Protestant military chaplaincy, are fundamental in exploring how to render the secular sacred in a military context, an exploration that invites further theological reflection.

BIBLIOGRAPHY

Beek, Abraham van de. "De Theologie van van Ruler." In *Men moet telkens opnieuw de reuzenzwaai aan de rekstok maken: Verder met van Ruler*, edited by Dirk van Keulen et al., 13–22. Zoetermeer: Uitgeverij Boekencentrum, 2009.

Bergin, H. F. "The Holy Spirit as the 'Ecstatic' God." *Pacifica* 17 (2004) 268–82.

Biggar, Nigel. *In Defence of War: Christian Realism and Just Force.* Oxford: Oxford University Press, 2013.

Borgman, Erik. "Pleidooi voor een theologische visie op geestelijke verzorging." *Handelingen: Tijdschrift voor Praktische Theologie en Religiewetenschap* 48.4 (2021) 5–13.

Brekke, Torkel, and Vladimir Tikhonov, eds. *Military Chaplaincy in an Era of Religious Pluralism: Military-Religious Nexus in Asia, Europe, and USA.* Delhi: Oxford University Press, 2016.

Brock, Rita Nakashima, and Gabriella Lettini. *Soul Repair: Recovering from Moral Injury after War.* Boston: Beacon, 2013.

Bruggen, Jan Peter van. "The Moral Responsibility of the Dutch Soldier and Just War Theory." In *The Present Just Peace/Just War Debate: Two Discussions or One?*, edited by Ad de Bruijne and Gerard den Hertog, 153–69. Beihefte zur Ökumenischen Rundschau 121. Leipzig: Evangelische Verlagsanhalt, 2018.

Conradie, Ernst M. *The Earth in God's Economy: Creation, Salvation, and Consummation in Ecological Perspective.* Studies in Religion and the Environment/Studien zur Religion und Umwelt. Vienna: LIT, 2015.

Cook, Martin L. *The Moral Warrior: Ethics and Service in the US Military.* Albany: SUNY Press, 2004.

Davie, Grace. "The Military Chaplain: A Study in Ambiguity." *International Journal for the Study of the Christian Church* 15.1 (2015) 39–53.

Earl, Murray D. "Christian Military Chaplaincy: 'Being There.'" *Expository Times* 124.2 (2012) 53–63.

Ganzevoort, R. R. "Geestelijke verzorging kan niet zonder theologie: Een reactie op Pitstra & Zock." *Handelingen* 36.2 (2009) 21–26.

Ganzevoort, R. R., and J. Visser. *Zorg voor het verhaal: Achtergrond, methode en inhoud van pastorale begeleiding.* Zoetermeer: Meinema, 2007.

Graham, Larry Kent. *Moral Injury: Healing Wounded Souls.* Nashville: Abingdon, 2017.

Hansen, Kim Philip. *Military Chaplains and Religious Diversity.* Basingstoke, UK: Palgrave Macmillan, 2012.

Heitink, G. "Geestelijk verzorger: een ambt en een ambacht." In *Nieuw Handboek Geestelijke Verzorging*, edited by J. Doolaard, 161–69. Kampen: Kok, 2006.

Iersel, F. van. *The Future of Just War Theory.* Zurich: LIT Verlag, 2019.

Keulen, Dirk van. "De Theologie van A. A. van Ruler." *Kontekstueel: Tijdschrift voor gereformeerd belijden* 26.2 (2011). https://www.kontekstueel.nl/archief-kontekstueel?view=article&id=794:nr2-2011-de-theologie-van-aavr&catid=35:algemene-artikelen.

Krainz, Ulrich. "'Newcomer Religions' as an Organisational Challenge: Recognition of Islam in the Austrian Armed Forces." *Religion, State & Society* 43.1 (2015) 1–14.

Liuski, Tiia, and Martin Ubani. "How Is Military Chaplaincy in Europe Portrayed in European Scientific Journal Articles between 2000 and 2019? A Multidisciplinary Review." *Religions* 11.10 (2020) 540. https://doi.org/10.3390/rel11100540.

Part III | Otherness, Community, and the Common Good

Mæland, Bård, and Nils Terje Lunde. "From Confessional to Concessional: The Adaptation to Religious Pluralism by the Chaplaincy of the Norwegian Armed Forces." In *Military Chaplaincy in an Era of Religious Pluralism: Military-Religious Nexus in Asia, Europe, and USA*, edited by Torkel Brekke and Vladimir Tikhonov, 163–84. Dehli: Oxford University Press, 2016.

Martin, David. *Reflections on Sociology and Theology*. Oxford: Clarendon, 1997.

Medley, Mark S. *Imago Trinitatis: Toward a Relational Understanding of Becoming Human*. Lanham, MD: University Press of America, 2002.

Moskos, Charles C., et al., eds. *The Postmodern Military: Armed Forces after the Cold War*. New York: Oxford University Press, 1999.

Netherlands Ministry of Defense. *Professionele Standaard voor Geestelik Verzorgers in de Krijgsmacht*. Amsterdam: Netherlands Ministry of Defense, 2023.

O'Donovan, Oliver. *The Just War Revisited*. Current Issues in Theology. Cambridge: Cambridge University Press, 2003.

Oosterhuis, Thijs. "Het verhaal achter de moraal. Protestantse theologie en de morele vorming van militairen." *Kerk en Theologie* 73.4 (2022) 393–411.

Pleizier, Theo, and Carmen Schuhmann. "How the Military Context Shapes Spiritual Care Interventions by Military Chaplains." *The Journal of Pastoral Care & Counseling* 76.1 (2022) 4–14.

Powers, Brian S. *Full Darkness: Original Sin, Moral Injury, and Wartime Violence*. Grand Rapids: Eerdmans, 2019.

Protestant Church in the Netherlands (PCN). *Jaarschrift 2024: Mensen Helpen Mens te Blijven: Diversiteit*. Amsterdam: Protestant Church in the Netherlands, 2024.

Ramsay, Nancy J., and Carrie Doehring, eds. *Military Moral Injury and Spiritual Care: A Resource for Professional Caregivers and Religious Leaders*. St. Louis: Chalice, 2019.

Ramsey, Paul. *The Just War: Force and Political Responsibility*. Lanham, MD: Rowman & Littlefield, 2002.

Rennick, J. B. "Towards an Interfaith Ministry: Religious Adaptation and Accommodation in the Canadian Forces Chaplaincy." *Studies in Religion* 39.1 (2010) 77–91.

Ruler, A. A. van. *Theologisch Werk*. Vol. 1. Nijkerk: Uitgeverij Callenbach, 1969.

———. *Theologisch Werk*. Vol. 6. Nijkerk: Uitgeverij Callenbach, 1973.

Shults, F. LeRon. "The Philosophical Turn to Relationality and the Responsibility of Practical Theology." In *Redemptive Transformation in Practical Theology: Essays in Honor of James E. Loder Jr.*, edited by Dana R. Wright and John D. Kuentzel, 325–46. Grand Rapids: Eerdmans, 2004.

———. "Spirit and Spirituality: Philosophical Trends in Late Modern Pneumatology." *Pneuma* 30 (2008) 271–87.

Smedema, Ids. "De vraag naar eigenheid: Protestantse geestelijke verzorging in de krijgsmacht in de ruimte tussen kerk en staat." *Kerk en Theologie* 73.4 (2022) 341–56.

Vos, Pieter. "Peace after the Mission: Spiritual Care and Ethical Assistance to Veterans Experiencing Moral Guilt." In *The Present Just Peace/Just War Debate: Two Discussions or One?*, edited by Ad de Bruijne and Gerard den Hertog, 170–86. Beihefte zur Ökumenischen Rundschau 121. Leipzig: Evangelische Verlagsanhalt, 2018.

———. "Van rechtvaardige oorlog tot vredesethiek: Theologisch-ethische bronnen voor protestantse geestelijke verzorging bij de krijgsmacht." *Kerk en Theologie* 73.4 (2022) 375–92.

Webster, John B. "The Identity of the Holy Spirit: A Problem in Trinitarian Theology." *Themelios* 9.1 (1983) 4–7.

Zock, Hetty. "Chaplaincy in the Netherlands: The Search for a Professional and a Religious Identity." *Tidsskrift for Praktisk Teologi: Nordic Journal of Practical Theology* 2 (2019) 11–21.

www.ingramcontent.com/pod-product-compliance
Lightning Source LLC
Chambersburg PA
CBHW052058230426
43662CB00036B/1657